THE ESSENTIAL TEACHINGS OF THE BUDDHA

Dharma is a rich term with many connotations, commonly referred to as one's duty, principle or truth. Yet it represents not this doctrine or that teaching but a great current of spiritual life in which we can participate, and help others to share. This book puts together the very essence of Buddhist teachings and practices to help us towards Enlightenment.

The Essential Teachings of The Buddha

SANGHARAKSHITA

New Age Books

ISBN: 978-81-7822-270-7

First Indian Edition: Delhi, 2007

This edition is published by arrangement with Windhorse Publications.

The Publishers acknowledge with gratitude permission to quote extracts from the following:

p.207 and p.209 *Perfection of Wisdom* in 8,000 Lines © 1973 by Edward Conze. Reprinted by permission of Four Seasons Foundation. pp. 24-5 Bhikkhu Nanamoli, *The Life of the Buddha*, Buddhist Publication Society, Kandy 1984.

Text illustrations Varaprabha

Publisher's Note:
Since this work is intended for a general readership, Pali and Sanskrit words have been transliterated without the diacritical marks that would have been appropriate in a work of a more scholarly nature.

Published by
NEW AGE BOOKS
A-44 Naraina Phase-I
New Delhi-110 028 (INDIA)
Email: nab@vsnl.in
Website: www.newagebooksindia.com

For Sale in Indian Subcontinent

Printed in India
at Shri Jainendra Press
A-45 Naraina Phase-I, New Delhi-110 028

CONTENTS

EDITORS' PREFACE

In 1946, the Singapore Lodge of the Theosophical Society 'discovered a lecturer. What made the members think that a soldier of twenty-one would be a good speaker I do not know. To my own astonishment, if not to theirs, my first lecture was a success. Ideas, I found, wove themselves Persian carpet-wise into intricate patterns, and these patterns dipped themselves in colourful words, without the slightest difficulty. Nervousness I experienced only before rising to speak.'

Thus began a long career of public speaking, and the beginning of a public avowal of Buddhism, to which the young man had already been wholeheartedly committed since he discovered it in wartime London at the age of sixteen. A few years later, in India, he was ordained as a Buddhist monk and given the name Sangharakshita.

Almost fifty years after his lecturing debut in Singapore, Sangharakshita was invited to speak as a 'senior teacher' at a conference of Western Buddhists in Tucson, Arizona. At the start of his talk he teased the organizers of the conference a little about this designation – 'I concluded it simply meant I was an old teacher'. He also suggested that it wasn't quite accurate to describe him as a Mahayana Buddhist: 'I do not identify myself exclusively with the Mahayana tradition. I have no less appreciation for the Theravada, for Zen or Ch'an, and for the Vajrayana in its various forms. They are all in their so many different ways among the glories of Buddhism. But I don't identify myself with any of them exclusively. I've had teachers belonging to many different traditions. So I prefer to think of myself as being simply a Buddhist.'

This approach to Buddhism is reflected in this book, which focuses, if anything, on the teachings of the Pali Canon, but includes ideas and teachings taken from many different strands of the Buddhist tradition. The book is based on material taken from several periods of Sangharakshita's speaking career: from his addresses to the Theosophists in Singapore in the 1940s; from talks given in the sixties to Londoners getting their first taste of Buddhism as a practical proposition; from the eighties in India, where he addressed thousands of new Buddhists; from talks given under the auspices of the Friends of the Western Buddhist Order, the Western Buddhist movement which he founded in 1967; and from lectures given in America in the nineties.

These talks were addressed to diverse audiences at different points in the early development of Buddhism in the West, but it has been quite simple to edit them together; throughout the fifty years there has been a strong continuity in both style and content. It's true that Sangharakshita's speaking style has changed a little over the years. The transcripts give the impression that in his youth he tended to speak with the formality and gravitas of a much older man, while in later years he has become more relaxed and playful in his style. But he has always had a sense of humour, together with a rigorous clarity; we have tried to make sure that both clarity and humour have been preserved in this translation of the spoken word into writing.

As for the content of the teaching, that has changed very little over the years. We have chosen to bring together a series of variations on a single fundamental theme, to which Sangharakshita has returned again and again: what is the Dharma? Drawing on a very broad range of Buddhist texts and traditions, his concern has always been to find ways of making the Dharma accessible and practicable for the people of the modern world. In this, as in other books based on his talks and seminars, we have tried to convey the direct personal appeal of these teachings; this results in a very different 'writing style' from that of the literary works – *A Survey of Buddhism* and *The Three Jewels*, for example – for which Sangharakshita is perhaps better known.

In preparing this book for publication, we are grateful for the help of Silabhadra, who provided many of the lecture transcripts, and of Vijayanandi, who also helped with transcription. We also wish to express our appreciation of the help we've received from the team at Windhorse Publications, especially Shantavira, whose editorial work has greatly enhanced the text. We have added quite a few endnotes to the text to facilitate the tracing of teachings and stories back to their canonical sources; and help with this from various people has been much appreciated. And it has been a great pleasure, as ever, to work with Sangharakshita, who has been very generous in his response to our work.

Vidyadevi and Jinananda
Spoken Word Project
Autumn 1997

INTRODUCTION

WHAT IS THE DHARMA?

I ONCE VISITED Delphi, the place in Greece to which, in ancient times, people flocked to consult the oracle of the god Apollo. As I walked up the hill through the olive trees I came across a spring, bubbling vigorously from rock to rock in a little cascade. At first I didn't pay much attention to it; but the same little cascade reappeared higher up – it was falling down from level to level – and then higher up still. As I eventually discovered, this was none other than the famous Castalian Spring – famous because the drinking of its clear waters was said to make one a poet on the spot. Continuing my ascent, I at last came to the source, the point at which the water welled out from between two enormous rocks in a rather mysterious way, so that you couldn't quite see where it came from or how it came.

In the same way we can trace Buddhism back to its own deep and mysterious source. If we trace that great river, with its many tributaries, back to its point of origin, we find that it all springs from the Buddha's spiritual experience: the experience of Enlightenment. Everything springs from *that*. The connection may not always be obvious. Sometimes the living waters of Buddhism get lost among the stones and the sand. But if you follow them upstream you come, sooner or later, to this ever-living source and fount, the Buddha's experience of supreme perfect

Enlightenment, by virtue of which he became the being we call the Buddha ('the Enlightened', or 'the Awake').

What we call Buddhism, but for which the more traditional, Sanskrit term is the Dharma, is essentially the sum total of the different ways in which the Buddha and his disciples after him tried to communicate some hint, some suggestion, of the experience of Enlightenment to others, so that they too might eventually come to have that experience. If we put to one side the complexities of Buddhism – the schools and the systems, the philosophical theories and the doctrinal analyses – it is really very simple. Buddhism or the Dharma is nothing other than the means to this experience. It is *the way to Enlightenment*.

But what is Enlightenment? What was it that transformed the man called Siddhartha Gautama into 'the Buddha'? It's difficult to express it in words – the Buddha himself at first despaired of being able to do so, as we shall see – but one way of putting it is to say that the Buddha saw the true nature of existence. Not that he simply had an idea; not that he worked out the true nature of existence in his head, intellectually. He saw 'the way things really are' *directly*, and this direct seeing transformed his whole being, in its depths and in its heights.

THE MEANING OF THE WORD 'DHARMA'

The word *Dharma* is used to refer to both the reality the Buddha experienced and also to his conceptual and verbal expression of that experience, his teaching. These two usages are closely connected; indeed, what they refer to are two aspects of the same 'thing'. The first – Dharma as truth or law or principle or reality – refers to the objective content of the Buddha's experience of Enlightenment. And the second – Dharma as doctrine or teaching – refers to the Buddha's expression of his experience for the benefit of others. The experience, we could say, corresponds to the wisdom aspect of Enlightenment, and the expression to the compassion aspect – wisdom and compassion being, as D.T. Suzuki says, 'the twin pillars of the whole edifice of Buddhism'. From our point of view we can distinguish between experience and expression, wisdom and compassion, but in reality – from the point of view of a Buddha – they are indistinguishable.

These are not the only meanings of the word 'Dharma' in Buddhism, although they are the principal ones. It is a rich term, with many connotations. In India it is commonly used to refer to one's duty as a member of a particular hereditary class, and thus is associated with the caste system. It is not used in this way in Buddhism, which repudiates the idea of caste, but there are many other definitions of the term.

To deal first with the two I have already mentioned, we find an example of 'Dharma' used to mean 'law, principle, or truth' in the classic Buddhist text called the *Dhammapada*, where it says, 'Not by hatred is hatred ever pacified here [in the world]. It is pacified by love. This is the eternal law.'[1] The word for 'law' here is Dharma. It's in the very nature of things that hatred does not cease by hatred, but only by love. This is the principle, this is the law, this is the truth. Here *Dharma* is a psychological and spiritual law – a spiritual principle, one might say. Then there's Dharma as doctrine or teaching – at least, these English words approximate to what is meant. It's not quite 'doctrine' in the theological, 'I believe in', sense; and it's not quite 'teaching' – it's more like an exposition, a making clear, a presentation. The Sanskrit expression is *Dharma deshana*, which means 'exposition of the Dharma' or *Dharma katha*, 'talking about the Dharma'.

And – just to touch upon other definitions – *dharma* (here with a small d) can also mean simply thing (or 'phenomenon', to be more technical and philosophical). Used in this way, the word can refer to any kind of thing, whether physical, mental, spiritual, or transcendental. Again in the *Dhammapada*, there's a well known verse which says 'All things [whatsoever] are devoid of unchanging selfhood.'[2] What 'devoid of unchanging selfhood' might mean we shall see later. The point here is that the word used for 'things' in the original is *dharma* (the Sanskrit form of the word) or *dhamma* (the same word in Pali, the ancient Indian language in which many early Buddhist texts have come down to us).

Dharma can also mean 'mental object'. In the West we usually speak of five senses, but the Indian tradition, including the Buddhist tradition, counts six: as well as the five sense organs – eye, ear, nose, tongue, and body (skin) – there's a sixth, mind. Just as the eye has material form as its object, and the ear has sound, so the mind has ideas or mental objects – and the word used for 'idea' in this context is *dharma*.

Lastly, dharma can mean a state or condition of existence, as in what are known as the eight *loka dharmas*. *Loka* means 'world', so these *loka dharmas* are the 'eight worldly conditions': gain and loss, fame and infamy, praise and blame, and pleasure and pain. And we're advised, of course, not to allow ourselves to be blown around by them. (They are also sometimes called the 'eight worldly winds'.) The *Mangala Sutta*[3] says that the greatest of all blessings is to have a mind which cannot be disturbed by any of these eight *loka dharmas*. It is a great blessing to be –

or rather to learn to be – unmoved whether we win or lose, whether we're famous or infamous, whether people blame us or praise us, and whether we experience pleasure or pain. Of course, one can think of many other such pairs – for example, whether we're young or old, resting or working, well or sick. All these states or conditions are dharmas.

Thus the term 'Dharma' is very rich in meaning, and one has to be very careful in studying the original texts to sort out the appropriate meaning of the word if one is to make sense of what is being said. In this book we are going to be focusing on the Dharma as principle or truth and the Dharma as teaching or path. One could say, perhaps, that we will be looking at the theory and the practice – except that really the whole of Buddhism is about practice.

THE NATURE OF THE DHARMA

We get a strong sense of the practical nature of the Dharma from the way it is described in one of the traditional Buddhist formulas. The 'Ti Ratana Vandana', or 'Salutation to the Three Jewels',[4] is chanted and recited by many thousands of Buddhists throughout the world. As often happens with things that are done regularly, even habitually, its meaning is sometimes forgotten; but this is a shame, because in just a few words it tells us a great deal about the nature of Buddhism. The section on the Dharma, in a few adjectives, gives us a clear idea, not so much of the content of the Buddha's teaching, as of its character, its nature.

First of all it describes the Dharma as *svakkhato*. This literally means 'well-taught', or 'well-communicated', and it suggests that the Buddha is in touch with other human beings. He knows their needs, he knows their mental states, he knows how to help them, he knows how to put things to them in a way they can understand. The Buddha was neither an ordinary man nor a god or a son of a god, but an Enlightened human being. Being Enlightened, he had many sublime qualities: supreme purity, great wisdom, and absolute compassion. And it was out of that compassion that he communicated with other human beings, to help them grow and develop. The Dharma is the communication of the Enlightened individual to the non-Enlightened individual, the encouragement of the spiritually free individual to the individual who is not yet spiritually free. Or, more simply, it is one human being talking to another, encouraging another, trying to help another.

An early record of the Buddha's teaching to his disciples is found in the *Ti Pitaka* or 'Three Baskets' of the Pali Canon, which comprises about forty-five printed volumes and contains accounts of teachings given to people in all sorts of ways.[5] Sometimes we find the Buddha giving a short and simple explanation, in just a few words. Sometimes he doesn't say anything – he just sits in silence – but nevertheless meaning is communicated. On the other hand, sometimes we find him giving a long discourse, spending an hour, two hours, or even a whole night explaining things in detail. Sometimes he gives teachings of an ethical nature, sometimes psychological teachings, sometimes teachings about spiritual life, and sometimes, even, teachings about politics in the sense of the principles of communal existence.

Sometimes we find him explaining matters in abstract general terms, but sometimes he makes use of beautiful illustrations, speaking of the trees and the flowers, the sun and the moon, animals and ordinary human life. Often we find him telling stories, because sometimes people understand things more easily in the form of a story. The Buddha taught in all these different ways, in order that his message should be understood by everybody.

For the same reason he insisted that his teaching should be made available to people in their own language. One day two disciples of his who were of brahmin birth and 'of fine cultivated language and fine eloquent speech' came to the Buddha and requested permission to put his words into Vedic, the exclusively brahminical language out of which Sanskrit later developed. But the Buddha refused to allow this. People were to learn the Dharma in their own language or dialect. This principle has been followed throughout Buddhist history. There is no one sacred language. When the Buddha's teaching went to Tibet, the scriptures were all translated into Tibetan. When it went to China, they were translated into Chinese. In fact, wherever Buddhism went it gave a stimulus to the local language and literature. The basic idea is that the Dharma is to be shared with everybody in a way that they can understand. Some religions have a priestly class with a sacred language and in this way knowledge of the scriptures is confined to a small circle of people, but the Buddha insisted that his teaching should be spread as widely as possible, in as many ways as possible. This is what is meant by that teaching being *svakkhato* – 'well-communicated'.

Next, the Dharma is described as *sanditthiko*, which can be translated as 'immediately apparent'. In other words, you will see the results of your practice of the Dharma yourself, in this lifetime. Some religions teach that you will taste the fruits of your spiritual practice only after death – your reward will be in heaven – but according to Buddhism we needn't wait that long. Sometimes, indeed, we can see the results in five minutes. Enlightenment, the ultimate goal of Buddhist practice, may be a long way off; but spiritual change, a move in the direction of Enlightenment, can happen almost straight away. Indeed, if one is practising Buddhism and not experiencing any result, one needs to ask oneself whether what one is practising is really Buddhism.

The next description of the Dharma is that it is *akaliko*, which means 'not connected with time'. The Dharma was practised for the first time two thousand five hundred years ago, and it changed, even transformed, people's lives. It has the same effect today; and in ten thousand years' time, if people do the same practices, they will experience the same results. The Dharma is not limited by time. It is also universal, in that you don't have to live in a particular country or culture to practise it. I have noticed in visiting Buddhist centres in different parts of the world that they all have the same kind of atmosphere. The culture may be different, manners and customs may be different, but the Dharma is the same, because the minds and hearts of men and women are the same everywhere.

One might think that this is true of all religions, but in fact some religions are very much tied to a particular place or culture. For example, the river Ganges in India is sacred to Hindus, so that if you're a Hindu who happens to live in England, you will have to rely on the international postal service if you have to perform a ritual involving holy Ganges water, and this may be inconvenient, or impossible. But you can practise Buddhism anywhere. Even if you happened to go to the North Pole you could practise Buddhism there. The Dharma is limited neither by time nor by space.

Then, the Dharma is *ehipassiko*. *Ehi* means 'come' and *passiko* derives from a word meaning 'see', so *ehipassiko* means 'come and see'. The implication is that we need not take on the Dharma in blind faith, or believe it because somebody tells us to believe it, or because it is written in some holy book. Also, you don't have to believe it because some great guru tells you that you should.

Perhaps the vogue for gurus of the sixties and seventies has worn off a bit now, but there are still a few around, and most of them say the same kind of thing. They say that they are God, or, if they're a bit more modest, they say they have been sent by God. And they say they know everything. 'Ask me any question, and I will know the answer. All you have to do is believe in me, follow my teaching, do whatever I say, and you'll be all right. Don't think for yourself, just come to me, I'll save you.' This is the typical line of the average great guru. And some of them have a lot of followers, because people are very confused and frightened, and they want to be saved.

But there is nothing like this in Buddhism. Even the Buddha didn't speak in this way. He just said, 'I'm a human being, and I've had a certain experience. Listen to what I have to say, by all means, but listen to it critically, test it in your own experience.' He even went as far as to say, 'Just as the goldsmith tests the gold in the fire, so you should test my words.' No other religious teacher, perhaps, has dared to say this.

Next, the Dharma is *opanayiko*, which means 'leading forward' or 'progressive' – not progressive in the modern, scientific sense, but in the cultural and spiritual sense, in that it leads the individual human being to higher and higher levels of human development. This is quite simply what the Buddha's teaching is for: to lead us forward, to lead us up, to make us happier, kinder, wiser, more full of energy and joy, more able to help others.

Finally, the 'Ti Ratana Vandana' describes the Dharma as *paccatam veditabbo vinnuhi* – a phrase which can be translated 'to be understood individually, by the wise'. This means that the Buddha's teaching is to be experienced by each person for himself or herself. You can't practise the Dharma at second hand. You have to do it yourself: it's *your* life. You can't ask a priest to do it for you. You can't pay anybody to do it for you. Even a great guru can't do it for you. The Buddha himself can't do it for you. He shows the way, but it is you who must tread that way.

THE BUDDHA WAS NOT A PHILOSOPHER

All in all, the 'Ti Ratana Vandana' gives the impression of the Dharma as being eminently practical. But, one might think, isn't Buddhism all about theory and abstract thought? What about all those volumes of Buddhist philosophy and doctrine? Well, it's true that some schools of Buddhism have developed, and refined, elaborate philosophical systems, but these systems were developed in the context of spiritual practice by people for whom the Buddha's words were not just of academic interest but of vital spiritual concern. And the Buddha himself – let us be very clear about this – was not a philosopher. In the scriptures he at one point says emphatically, 'I have no views' – that is, no views on 'metaphysical' subjects such as the eternity or non-eternity of the cosmos.[6]

Hence the Buddha has nothing to teach – this is what he is saying here, and that is why he is sometimes said to have remained silent from the night of his Enlightenment to the night of his death. Of course, this is not to be taken literally; as the scriptures make clear, he spent those forty-five years talking to people and teaching the Dharma – but at the same time he had nothing to teach. One could say that, in a way, there's no such thing as Buddhism. There's a language, but there's nothing to communicate – because what you're trying to communicate is beyond communication. The only purpose of attempting to communicate is to help the other person realize that what you're trying to communicate is beyond communication. When they see that, then you really have communicated!

This isn't easy for us to grasp. We like to think that we've got Buddhism *here*, in a book, or a list of important teachings or principles, or a certain tradition of practice. And when we think we've got it, of course we hang on to it. But the Buddha's hands are empty; he isn't holding anything, not even Buddhism. In other words, Buddhism is only a means to an end. In Mahayana Buddhism there are what appear to be philosophical systems, what appear to be metaphysics, but they are not quite philosophy in the Western sense – though there are exceptions even in Western philosophy. In his 'Seventh Epistle' Plato solemnly declares that no treatise by him on the higher subjects exists or ever will exist, for 'It is not something that can be put into words like other branches of learning; only after long partnership in a common life devoted to this very thing does truth flash upon the soul, like a flame kindled by a leaping spark, and once it is born there it nourishes itself thereafter.'[7] Students of Plato's dialogues tend to be rather disconcerted by this. They have the idea that Plato ought to be teaching a definite, consistent system that can be given definitive written form; but Plato says plainly that he has no such system. He is only trying to strike a spark, so that the disciple will be able to see things for himself.

It's the same with Buddhism. It's no use thinking that when one has acquired the teaching about karma and rebirth, the teaching about the three characteristics of conditioned existence, the teaching about *shunyata*, and a handful of concentration techniques, then one has 'got' Buddhism – not at all. One has learned the language of Buddhism, but one hasn't started speaking it. And some people never get round to speaking it at all. Of course, one should not confuse this silence of ignorance with the Buddha's silence of wisdom.

THE PARABLE OF THE RAFT

This is all by way of a warning as we embark on a study of these very teachings and practices – a warning that the Buddha himself was very concerned to give. On one occasion he gave it in the form of a parable: the parable of the raft.[8] 'Suppose', he said, 'a man were to come to a great stretch of water, a great river. If he wanted to get to the other shore, the opposite bank, but there was no ferry to take him across, what would he do? He'd chop down a few saplings, lash them together, and make a raft. Then, sitting on the raft and plying a pole, or using his hands to paddle with, he'd get across to the other side. Having arrived there, what would he do with the raft? He'd abandon it. He wouldn't, thinking how useful it had been, out of gratitude load it on to his shoulders and continue his journey with it. He'd just leave it where it was.'

'In the same way,' the Buddha said, 'the Dharma, my teaching, is a means to an end. It's a raft to take you to the other shore of nirvana. It's not an end in itself; it's the means to Enlightenment.'

This is one of the most striking and important of all the Buddha's teachings: that Buddhism itself, the Dharma itself, is just a raft. Religion is just a raft. It's for getting across the water, not for carrying with one when one has reached the further shore. That's one extreme one may go to. But of course there's another extreme to be avoided – one that is much more common – and that is not actually using the raft to cross the river at all.

Some people board the raft but don't ply the pole. In fact, they tend to forget that they ever intended to cross the river. Their main concern is to make the raft a bit more comfortable. They start building walls on it, and maybe a roof; then they install furniture and cooking utensils; and then they bring on board their family and friends. In short, they turn the raft into a house, and they moor it securely to this shore. And they don't like any talk about releasing the mooring or weighing anchor.

There are other people who stand on the bank and take a good look at that raft. 'It's a fine raft,' they say. 'It's a magnificent raft – so big, so solid, so well constructed, so impressive.' And they take out their measuring rod or their tape, and they measure it. They can tell you its exact dimensions, the sort of wood it's made of, and where and when that wood was felled. They may even produce a beautiful monograph on rafts which sells like hot cakes. But for all that, they've never set foot on the raft, let alone thought about crossing the river.

Others, again, stand around on the bank, saying, 'No, the raft isn't very well made. Twelve saplings should have gone into its construction, not ten, and they ought to be lashed together more securely. And I don't like the way the raft floats on the water. I'd build it bigger and better.' So they remain on the bank – speculating, discussing, disputing, but going nowhere. There are yet other people who think the old raft's a bit plain and unattractive, a bit rough and ready. After all, it's just a lot of logs lashed together. So they paint it and decorate it and cover it with flowers and make it look quite pretty. But they don't ever get on board – don't ever start using that pole and ferrying themselves across to the other shore. There are also people who claim they've inherited the raft: it's their ancestral property; it belongs to them. Consequently they don't have actually to make use of it. It's enough that it's theirs.

The shore we are standing on represents our present, ego-bound existence, with its suffering and its disharmony. The other shore represents what we aspire to be, or what we ideally are; it represents our goal – Enlightenment, nirvana, or whatever else one cares to call it. Buddhism is simply the raft that carries one over the intervening waters. That's its only function. 'The raft,' the Buddha declared, 'I teach as something to be left behind.'

Later in the history of Buddhism, in the Japanese Buddhist tradition, we find the beautiful image of the finger pointing to the moon. You use the finger to indicate the moon, but once you have seen the moon that becomes the focus of your attention. So don't mistake the finger for the moon. In the same way, you pass from a religious teaching to a spiritual experience. You don't remain stuck with that teaching or doctrine, that practice or method, hanging on to it, hugging it. No, you look beyond the finger to see the moon shining in the heavens.

One might say that the Buddha perhaps took greater precautions against the possibility of his followers mistaking the finger for the moon than the founder of any other religion. So far as I know, Christ never warned his disciples not to take his words too literally. Nor did Muhammad ever explain that when he spoke about the delights of heaven it was only as a skilful means. But in Buddhism the point is insisted upon again and again, because human nature is such that, especially in matters of religion, we always tend to cling to the means and treat it as though it was the end itself.

WHAT IS THE DHARMA?

The parable of the raft makes the function of the Dharma clear. But of what should the raft be made? These days there are so many spiritual teachings around that it can be hard to know what is really going to help us. This is not a new problem. In the Buddha's day one could be quite confused about what Buddhism really was. There were so many apparently contradictory versions, one disciple saying this, another that. Even someone as close to the Buddha as his aunt and foster-mother Mahaprajapati Gautami, who had followed in his footsteps and had become a homeless wanderer, and was dwelling in the forest – even she could become confused.

The story is well known. One day she came to the Buddha rather upset and disturbed. She didn't know what to think, she said. His disciples were giving out different versions of the Dharma. Some said that he taught this, others that he taught that, and so she had become confused. How was she to know what the Buddha really taught, what was really the Dharma?[9]

This was Mahaprajapati Gautami's question, and the Pali scriptures record the Buddha's reply. He said, in effect, 'Don't worry. Take it like this. Whatever you find in practice conduces to peace of mind, conduces to purity, conduces to seclusion, conduces to fewness of desires, conduces to contentment, conduces to insight and wisdom and detachment from the world, conduces to an understanding of the transcendental, whatever you find in your own experience conduces to these ends, take that as my Dharma, take that as my teaching.'

This is the guideline the Buddha himself gives. In other words, the criterion is not logical or philosophical, but pragmatic and empirical – though the pragmatism is spiritual and the empiricism is a transcendental empiricism.

If we can only remember this, it can save us a lot of trouble. There are many forms of Buddhism in the world. It's a very old religion, having now been going for two thousand five hundred years. In the East it has spread from the snowy tablelands of Tibet to the sweltering jungles of South-east Asia, from the beautiful islands of Japan to the deserts of Central Asia and the tropical plains of India. Everywhere it has changed in accordance with local conditions, so that there are many different forms of Buddhism, many different presentations. In the West we have been deluged in recent decades by presentations that are actually in conflict. One school of Buddhism tells us 'Rely on your own efforts. You are the one who has to do it; no one can do it for you – no God, no Buddha.' Another school says 'You can do nothing. Only the Buddha Amitabha can do it for you, in fact has already done it. Rely on him, trust in him.'[10]

Bombarded by conflicting interpretations such as these, we are very much in the position of Mahaprajapati Gautami. We don't know what to think, sometimes. In these circumstances we need to remember what the Buddha said to his aunt, 'If it works, if it helps you spiritually, it's my teaching.' If you find in your own experience that it helps you become more concentrated, more sensitive, more intelligent, wiser, kinder, more understanding – well, it is the Dharma, it is the true teaching, it is what the Buddha really taught and really meant.

The great emperor Ashoka, who lived a century or two after the Buddha, inscribed in his Rock Edicts this memorable saying: 'Whatever the Buddha said was well said.'[11] But the Mahayana sutras, which were written down a little later than Ashoka's time, reversed this to say, 'Whatever is well said, that is the word of the Buddha.'[12] In other words, whatever helps you, take it as the word of the Buddha, because in principle that's all that the word of the Buddha is: that which helps you across, that which helps you on your journey.

Sometimes people say, 'Well, such and such' – it might be t'ai chi ch'uan, perhaps, or drawing classes, or one of any number of things – 'helps me in my spiritual life. I feel much better for it; it helps me to concentrate – though of course it isn't anything to do with Buddhism, it isn't part of the Dharma.' But in fact if it helps you spiritually it is essentially, by definition, part of the Dharma.

Of course, we need to keep asking the same question – 'Is this helping me to grow spiritually?' – of Buddhism itself, or of whatever is presented to us as being Buddhism. If we want to be sure whether any form of Buddhism – whether it's Theravada or Tibetan Buddhism, Tendai, Shin, or Zen – is authentic, we have to ask ourselves whether it really helps people towards Enlightenment. Or is it a venerable museum piece – ancient, beautiful, admirable, but for the museum, not for real life? It's only the Dharma if it's alive, if it works, if it still helps people to follow the spiritual path.

We must resist the temptation to think that the Dharma is this teaching or that teaching. Provisionally that may be true but not in the long run. We're probably familiar with the credal statements of Christianity: 'I believe in God the father almighty, maker of heaven and earth …' and so on. But we find no such statements in Buddhism. There are formulations, there are presentations, but they're all provisional; they're fingers pointing to the moon.

As Buddhism develops in the West, it is unlikely to follow any existing Buddhist pattern, because our needs, our approach, and our background, are different from those of any Eastern country. We need to draw upon the essence, the inner spirit, of the Buddha's teaching as preserved in all schools. We need to take the best – not just in an eclectic way, or just intellectually, but drawing upon the teachings deeply, blending them all into one great stream of spiritual tradition adapted to our needs. This is really the task before us. It won't be easy; it will demand a great deal of effort and spiritual experience on our part. And to do it we will need to bear in mind that the Dharma represents not this doctrine or that teaching, but a great current of spiritual life, in which we can participate, in which we can help others to share, and which bears us on in the direction of Enlightenment.

In this book are gathered not an exhaustive collection, but a basic starter kit, if you like, of Buddhist teachings and practices – enough, certainly, to help one make a start. They are, on the whole, of the very essence of Buddhism, not specific to any one school or culture. And they all have the same intention: to help us towards Enlightenment.

PART 1: THE TRUTH

1

THE ESSENTIAL TRUTH

IN THE BUDDHA'S TIME, in a village near Nalanda – which later became the site of a great Buddhist university – there lived two young men called Shariputra and Maudgalyayana. They had been close friends since child hood; and now they made a pact. They decided to leave home in search of the truth, in search of a great Enlightened teacher – not an unusual thing to do at that time in India. The pact between the two friends was that they would start their search by going in opposite directions. Whoever found an Enlightened teacher first would go and tell the other, and they'd become his disciples together. So Shariputra went in one direction and Maudgalyayana went in the other.

Shariputra was the lucky one. He hadn't gone far, or wandered for many weeks, before he saw someone coming in the distance who seemed – well, he hardly dared hope that this was true – but there was something about this man that seemed special. Could he be Enlightened? As the stranger drew nearer, Shariputra was still more impressed by his appearance, his bearing – so much so that he didn't hesitate to put to him a question which is *the* question in India, even today. People don't tend to remark on the weather or anything like that. They don't even necessarily enquire about your health. As Shariputra did on this occasion, they come straight to the point and ask, 'Who is your teacher?'

In the East, especially in India and Tibet, it has been the tradition for thousands of years that everybody has a spiritual teacher from whom he or she has received some kind of religious practice. It is not so much the case these days, perhaps, but people still often have the attitude that if you don't have a spiritual teacher, you hardly exist as a human being. You might just as well be a dog or a cat as be a human being and not have a spiritual teacher. Hence the first thing you want to know about anybody is what lineage of spiritual practice they belong to.

So Shariputra asked the stranger, 'Who is your teacher?' Now the stranger, as it happened, was one of the Buddha's five original disciples, a man called Ashvajit. After his Enlightenment, the Buddha had decided to seek out five former companions of his and share with them his experience of the truth. He had caught up with them at a place called Sarnath and – after some initial resistance on their part – he had managed to communicate his experience to them. Indeed, in a short while these five men too became Enlightened. Other people came to hear the Buddha teach, and they also became Enlightened. Before long there were sixty Enlightened beings in the world. And the Buddha said to them, 'I am free from all bonds, human and divine. You also are free from all bonds, human and divine. Go now and teach all beings for the benefit and the happiness of the whole world, out of compassion, out of love for all living beings.'[13] So they scattered in all directions, and they traversed the length and breadth of northern India, everywhere trying to communicate the teaching of the Buddha.

So Ashvajit said at once, 'My teacher is Gautama who has gone forth from the clan of the Shakyas, the Enlightened One who is now the Buddha.' Shariputra was of course overjoyed to hear this, but he still wasn't quite satisfied. His next question – predictably enough – was, 'What does the Buddha teach?' This is obviously the second thing you are going to want to know.

Ashvajit had himself gained Enlightenment, but he was a modest man. He said, 'I am newly converted. I don't know much of the teaching. But what little I do know I shall tell you.' And so saying, he recited a verse which has since become famous all over the Buddhist world. 'The Buddha has explained the origin of those things which proceed from a cause or a condition. Their cessation too he has explained. This is the doctrine of the great shramana.'

That was all he said. But when Shariputra heard this verse, his whole being rose up in a sort of flash of insight and he knew that this was the truth. Whatever arises does so in dependence on conditions; when those conditions are no longer there, it ceases. Seeing this, Shariputra at once became what is called in Buddhism a 'Stream-entrant' – that is, he entered the stream leading ultimately to the liberation of Enlightenment. And, of course, he immediately went to find his friend Maudgalyayana, to tell him that they had found their teacher. The two friends subsequently became the Buddha's two chief disciples.[14]

The verse which Ashvajit recited, and which had such a tremendous effect on the young Shariputra, is to be found all over the Buddhist world. You find it in India, stamped on the base of images. You find it on clay seals in the ruins of monasteries: thousands and thousands of little clay seals just stamped with this verse. You find it in China, you find it in Tibet. In Tibet, when they consecrate a Buddha image, very often they print hundreds of thousands of tiny copies of this verse and stuff them all inside the image, as part of the consecration.

This verse is really the essence of Buddhism; on the doctrinal level there's nothing more basic. It is common ground to all the Buddhist schools, whether Theravada or Mahayana, Zen or Tibetan. They all have their origin in the great law of conditionality, *pratitya-samutpada* in Sanskrit, sometimes translated as dependent arising, or conditioned co-production. This is the single source to which all Buddhist teachings can be traced back, the most basic conceptual expression of the Buddha's spiritual experience.

THE DECISION TO TEACH

We find an early reference to this great teaching in the *Ariyapariyesana Sutta* (the 'Discourse on the Noble Quest') of the *Majjhima-Nikaya*. This is a sort of autobiographical discourse, one of several in the Pali Canon, in which the Buddha, as an old man, relates some of the experiences of his younger days, describing how he practised asceticism, how he gained Enlightenment, his thoughts and doubts, the way he began to teach, and so on. Thus the Buddha here relates the story of how after his Enlightenment he wasn't sure whether or not to try to make known the truth he had discovered.

The text represents him as saying to himself, 'This Law [Dharma] that I have attained to is profound and hard to see, hard to discover; it is the most peaceful and superior goal of all, not attainable by mere ratiocination, subtle, for the wise to experience.' And then he goes on to reflect: 'But this generation relies on attachment, relishes attachment, delights in attachment. It is hard for such a generation to see this truth, that is to say, Specific Conditionality, Dependent Arising [*pratitya-samutpada*]."[15]

When the Buddha said to himself, 'It's going to be difficult for humanity to understand what I have discovered,' the way he described his discovery was in terms of universal conditionality, conditioned co-production. This is the first presentation of the Buddha's insight. It's as if, when the Enlightened mind looks out at all existence, at the whole of the phenomenal universe, the first thing that strikes it, the most obvious thing about the universe, is that it is conditioned. It arises in dependence on conditions, and when those conditions cease it disappears. This is the basic insight, as it were, about the world, from the standpoint of Enlightenment.

The story goes on to explain how it happened that the Buddha did decide to teach after all. Here is the account given in the sutta[16] itself. It involves, I should warn you, the sudden appearance of 'Brahma Sahampati', who, in traditional Buddhist mythology, is 'the ruler of a thousand worlds'.

> *Then it occurred to Brahma Sahampati, who became aware in his mind of the thought in the Blessed One's mind, 'The world will be lost, the world will be utterly lost; for the mind of the Perfect One, accomplished and fully Enlightened, favours inaction and not teaching the Law.' Then, as soon as a strong man might extend his flexed arm, or flex his extended arm, Brahma Sahampati vanished in the Brahma world and appeared before the Blessed One. He arranged his robe on one shoulder, and putting his right knee on the ground and raising his hands palms together towards the Blessed One, he said, 'Lord, let the Blessed One teach the Law. Let the Sublime One teach the Law. There are creatures with little dust on their eyes who are wasting through not hearing the Law. Some of them will gain final knowledge of the Law.'*
>
> *When Brahma Sahampati had said this, he said further:*
>
> *'In Magadha there has appeared till now*
> *Impure law, thought out by men still stained:*
> *Open the Deathless Gateway: let them hear*
> *The Law the Immaculate has found.*
> *Ascend, O Sage, the tower of the Law.*
> *And just as one sees all the folk around*
> *Who stand upon a pile of solid rock,*
> *Survey, O Sorrowless All-seeing Sage,*
> *This human breed engulfed in sorrowing*

That Birth has at its mercy and Old Age.
Arise, O Hero, Victor, Knowledge-bringer,
Free from all debt, and wander in the world.
Proclaim the Law; for some,
O Blessed One, will understand.'

The Blessed One listened to Brahma Sahampati's pleading. Out of compassion for creatures he surveyed the world with the eye of an Enlightened One. Just as in a pond of blue, red, or white lotuses some lotuses that are born and grow in the water, thrive immersed in the water without coming up out of it, and some other lotuses that are born and grow in the water rest on the water's surface, and some other lotuses that are born and grow in the water come right up out of the water and stand clear, unwetted by it, so too he saw creatures with little dust on their eyes and with much dust on their eyes, with keen faculties and dull faculties, with good qualities and bad qualities, easy to teach and hard to teach, and some who dwelt seeing fear in the other world, and blame as well.

When he had seen, he replied:

'Wide open are the portals of the Deathless.
Let those who hear show faith. If I was minded
To tell not the sublime Law that I know,
'Twas that I saw vexation in the telling.'

Then Brahma Sahampati thought, 'I have made it possible for the Law to be taught by the Blessed One.' And after he had paid homage to him, keeping him on his right, he vanished at once.[17]

That's the episode – and it represents a crucial point in the Buddha's life. To communicate or not to communicate, that was the question. It was a crucial question not only for him, but for the whole world. Without it, what we know as Buddhism would not exist. A lot could be said about this episode, the episode of Brahma's request, as it's generally called. It contains a lot that one can reflect and meditate upon. There is, to begin with, the question of who Brahma is, what he represents. And then, why did the Buddha have to be requested to teach? What does that mean?

THE RAIN OF THE DHARMA

In this context I want to draw attention to just one feature of the episode. The simplest way to put it is that the story represents the surging up of compassion in the Buddha's heart, as if to say that the wisdom of Enlightenment is inseparable from compassion. Then, the image of the pool of lotuses shows that, however difficult it may be to communicate the experience of Enlightenment, it can be done. Human beings are capable of growth, of development, of transformation; and each of us is at our own stage of the process.

We find the same kind of simile in the *White Lotus Sutra*, which is one of the great Mahayana sutras – Mahayana sutras being canonical texts that purport to record the words of the historical Buddha Shakyamuni. I say 'purport' because according to modern scholarship many of the sutras do not so much record the actual words of the Buddha as try to recast in contemporary format something of the essence, the spirit, of the Buddha's teaching as it had come down through the centuries. The *White Lotus Sutra* was committed to writing in about the first century CE, and it is full of beautiful parables, myths, and symbols which are of absolutely epochal importance for Buddhist spiritual life throughout the Far East. And of its parables perhaps one of the most important is the parable of the rain cloud, also known as the parable of the plants.

The parable describes how, just as a rain cloud pours refreshing rain on all the plants of the earth without discrimination, so the Buddha teaches the Dharma to all living beings. The rain of the Dharma falls on all equally – not more to some and less to others.[18] In other words, the Buddha does not discriminate. We know that the historical Buddha taught his Dharma to all alike: to princes, to peasants, to men, to women, to merchants, to outcasts, to murderers, to robbers.

And those on whom the rain of the Dharma falls, the living beings – in other words ourselves – grow. But we each grow in accordance with our own individual nature. When the rain falls on a palm tree, the palm tree grows into a bigger palm tree. When the rain falls on a flower, the flower grows into a more luxuriant flower. But the flower doesn't become a palm tree, and the palm tree doesn't become a flower. Each grows nourished by the same rain, but it grows in accordance with its own nature. In the same way we all learn and practise the same Dharma, but we develop spiritually each in our own way; though at the same time we all grow towards Enlightenment.

This is illustrated by another passage in the Pali Canon in which the Buddha is talking to and about his disciples, enumerating their distinctive qualities. Sometimes people think that a teacher's disciples must all be alike, just copies of the teacher. And sometimes Buddhist art reinforces this impression. You see a picture of the Buddha with yellow robe, shoulder-bag, bowl, and *ushnisha* (that's the bump on his head, the 'bodhic protuberance'), and then you see a whole row of little disciples, and they all look exactly like the Buddha, except for the *ushnisha* – same shaven head, same yellow robe, same shoulder-bag, same begging-bowl, same meek expression. But this idea that disciples are more or less clones of their teacher is a big mistake, as we see in this passage in the Pali Canon where the Buddha is praising his disciples.

We might think that the usual thing is for the disciples to praise the teacher; and sometimes they do. But on this occasion the Buddha praised his disciples. He said 'Look, there's Shariputra. Shariputra is the greatest of you for wisdom and for ability to expound the Dharma. And Ananda? – well, he's the greatest for popularity and friendliness.' (It was Ananda, by the way, who made it possible for women to join the Sangha, the spiritual community of the Buddha's followers, so women in the Sangha thereafter regarded him almost as a sort of patron saint.) Then the Buddha singled out another disciple as the greatest for austerities; another as the greatest preacher. And, because some disciples naturally had greater qualities than others, in the end the Buddha had to scrape the barrel a bit, and he mentioned one disciple as the disciple who always managed to collect the greatest quantity of alms when he went on his alms round. Even he was the best at something.[19]

In this way the Buddha praised his disciples for their distinctive qualities. And this distinctiveness is borne out throughout the Pali scriptures. If you read them simply as documents of the lives of human beings, you come across so many of the Buddha's disciples, and they're all so different; their characters are so different, their qualities so different. Shariputra and Maudgalyayana, though great friends, are completely different from each another. Ananda is amiable and popular, while Kashyapa's a bit grumpy – or at least that's the impression one gets. Some disciples are shy and retiring, while others are rather forward and active.

It's always the same. If you're a true follower of the Dharma you'll grow in accordance with your own nature. And this is what the parable of the rain cloud and the plants brings out very well. When the rain falls the tree grows and becomes a bigger and better tree. But an oak tree will never grow into an apple tree, however much you water it; and an apple tree will never become an oak.

In the same way, someone of a more devotional temperament will not usually become predominantly intellectual; and someone of an intellectual nature will not usually become predominantly devotional. Although both may develop the opposite quality to some extent, their temperaments will stay pretty much the same right up to the point where they both gain Enlightenment. One will be an Enlightened devotee, and the other will be an Enlightened intellectual – or even an Enlightened academic, though that's rather harder to imagine. One person may be an Enlightened monk; another may be an Enlightened householder – but they will both be Enlightened. It might sound like a paradox, but as people on the spiritual path grow towards Enlightenment, they don't grow more like one another; they grow more different – though at the same time communication between them improves.

The simile of the lotuses and the parable of the plants also remind us that human beings can change. They can change from worse to better, and even from better to best. To take a few examples from the scriptures and Buddhist history, Angulimala murdered nearly a hundred people, and then managed to become an arhant – in other words gained Enlightenment – all within the same lifetime.[20] That should give us a great deal of food for thought. Then in Tibet in the eleventh century there was a certain black magician who had been guilty of the death of about thirty people, but he became the greatest of the Kagyupa saints. That, of course, was Milarepa.[21] And from Indian history we can take the example of Ashoka, who wanted to unite the whole of India under his rule. He slaughtered hundreds of thousands of people; but then he experienced remorse, and started going against the grain, as it were. He changed. In the end he became known as Dharma-Ashoka, 'righteous Ashoka', one of the great benefactors of Buddhism.[22]

This change in these and so many other people was brought about not by the grace of God, but by a change in the direction of the human will, a change originating within the human psyche itself. We are responsible for our own spiritual destiny. We are free to develop or not to develop, just as we wish. Circumstances may hinder us, may even appear to crush us, but no circumstance can ever deprive us of our basic freedom of will. This is what the Buddha saw when in his mind's eye he saw that pond of blue and red and white lotuses; and this is what the parable of the rain cloud and the plants also tells us.

BRIDGING THE GAP

But although the Buddha had this vision, which gave him such confidence in the spiritual potential of human beings, we may not – on the strength of what I've said about it so far, at least – feel convinced that we are going to realize our own potential through the apprehension of the law of conditionality. As we've seen, the reality to which the Buddha attained was 'profound and hard to see'. It was 'the most peaceful and superior goal of all'. Not only that. It was 'not attainable by mere ratiocination'. It was 'subtle' – incredibly subtle. And it was 'for the wise to experience'.

But what are *we* to make of this great truth? For Shariputra – who must have been very receptive – the mere, bare statement of it was enough to give him insight into the truth, but it is hardly likely to have the same impact on us. Indeed, it may be hard for us to make any sense of it at all. Of course, as we have seen, the Buddha himself anticipated this difficulty. Buddhism may essentially be a communication – a communication from the Buddha to those who are not Buddhas, from the Enlightened mind to the unenlightened mind – but such a communication is not easy to make, even for a Buddha, because between the Buddha and the ordinary person there is a tremendous gap.

We can't really conceive how tremendous that gap is. It's all very well for us to say – as some Buddhists do say, rather glibly – that we're potentially Buddha, we're potentially Enlightened. But those are usually just words. We don't realize the vast extent of the gulf that separates us from the Buddha. Sometimes people talk about the Buddha in a very familiar way, almost as though he was their next-door neighbour and they knew him well – knew about his realization and his Enlightenment, and just what it consisted in. But this is really a sort of profanity. We don't really know the Buddha, we don't understand the Buddha. There's a vast gulf between his ultimate realization and our own unenlightened experience.

It's very difficult even for a Buddha to bridge that gap, to make real contact with the unenlightened mind. Mahayana Buddhism has powerful myths of Bodhisattvas like Avalokiteshvara and Kshitigarbha descending into the depths of hell to help the beings there.[23] But that hell isn't necessarily another world – it can be this world; and the myth of the descent represents the difficulty that the Bodhisattva or the Buddha has in establishing real contact with our unenlightened, mundane mentality. But – and the Buddha felt this as a burning compulsion – contact has to be made, the truth has to be communicated. A bridge, however frail, however slender, has to be flung across the abyss separating the Enlightened from the unenlightened mind. So how did the Buddha do this?

BUDDHISM IN A NUTSHELL

There are two principal modes of communication: through concepts and through images. In the Pali scriptures the Buddha tends to make greater use of concepts, though images – parables, myths, similes – are by no means lacking. In the Mahayana scriptures, on the other hand, he tends to make much greater use of images, though here again concepts are by no means absent, and a few of the Mahayana sutras are communicated almost entirely through them.

The story of the Buddha's decision to teach given in the Pali scriptures is communicated through a mixture of concepts and images, as we have seen. But when it comes to referring to the reality he had experienced, the Buddha chose to express it in terms of a concept: the concept of conditionality, as we've come to call it in English. This, as we have seen, is the basic concept of Buddhism. To the extent that Buddhism is reducible to a concept, it's reducible to the concept of conditionality, and the whole of Buddhism, both theoretical and practical – philosophy, meditation, the Buddhist life itself – is founded upon it.

Or, at least, Buddhism is founded upon the experience of which it is an expression. Conditionality isn't something that the Buddha merely thought out; it's an expression, a direct expression, of his Enlightenment experience. Though I've said that Buddhist philosophy is based on it, this is not philosophy in the Western sense. Buddhist 'philosophy', as we call it, is no more than an attempt at the further, more detailed elucidation of the Buddha's vision of reality.

The Buddha felt compelled to communicate his experience of reality somehow. He had to give expression to it in conceptual terms if he was to say anything at all. At the same time, he had to find a way of putting it that would be intelligible to ordinary unenlightened people, and that would provide a basis upon which the ordinary person could eventually gain insight into the true nature of reality. The concept he chose was universal conditionality – of which we can certainly gain at least an intellectual understanding, at least up to a point.

The formula usually given in the scriptures is as follows. It is, in fact, almost exactly what Ashvajit said to Shariputra. The language the Buddha uses is simple, abstract, almost mathematical. He simply says 'This being, that becomes; from the arising of this, that arises. This not being, that does not become; from the ceasing of this, that ceases.'[24] This is the formula in its highest degree of generality and abstraction; and it holds good for the whole of existence, whether material or mental or spiritual.

So if anyone ever asked you what Buddhism is in a nutshell – not in one word, because that word would be 'conditionality', but in one phrase – you could just tell them 'A being present, B arises. In the absence of A, B does not arise. That's the essence of Buddhism.' Then you could leave them to work out the implications for themselves. If one thought about it for long enough, one could work out the whole of Buddhism from this simple statement. Of course, they might think that you were being deliberately obscure. Perhaps most Buddhists, if asked to summarize the teaching of the Buddha so succinctly, would say 'All things are impermanent' or 'Actions have consequences.' But it doesn't take much reflection to see that both these statements spring from this same fundamental truth: conditionality.

THE IMPLICATIONS OF CONDITIONALITY

The Buddha, you may be glad to hear, chose to make a few concessions and explain conditionality in rather more detail. Probably the best known formulation of the principle is that of the Four Noble Truths: the truth of suffering or unsatisfactoriness; the truth of the cause of suffering, which is craving; the truth of the cessation of suffering, cessation being the equivalent of nirvana; and the truth of the way leading to the cessation of suffering, the way leading to nirvana – which is the Noble Eightfold Path.[25] In other words, in terms of this formulation, craving being present, suffering arises; craving not being present, suffering does not arise.

I should perhaps mention that here the 'suffering that does not arise' is mental suffering, not physical suffering. There's a passage in the Pali Canon to which one of my teachers, Bhikkhu Kashyap, with whom I studied Pali and Abhidhamma, was very fond of referring. In this passage, the Buddha is seated cross-legged teaching his disciples; and after he has been teaching for a long time, his back starts aching. Even a Buddha's back aches. Shariputra happened to be there and, well, the Buddha didn't just grin and bear it as some people might say we ought to. He said, 'Shariputra, my back is aching. Please take over the teaching. I'll just lie down.'[26] My teacher, Kashyapji, used to be fond of referring to this incident because, as he emphasized, it illustrated the humanity of the Buddha – not in the sense that the Buddha had human weaknesses in the mental or emotional sense, because he didn't, but he had physical weaknesses. He had an ordinary human body, and that body, as he grew older, caused him pain.

In Buddhism a distinction is made between physical pain and mental pain. When you gain Enlightenment you no longer experience any mental pain, or emotional turbulence, or anything of that sort, but you are still subject to physical pain – which you bear, as the Buddha did, with equanimity. Anyway, that's by the way. The basic point is that craving not being present, suffering – mental suffering, avoidable suffering – does not arise. Incidentally, this is *not* to say that all suffering is the result of craving; this would amount to karmic determinism. There are some sufferings – especially physical sufferings – that are *not* due to one's previous unskilful mental actions, whether in this life or in any previous life.

THE CIRCLE AND THE SPIRAL

Elaborating further on this concept of conditionality, the Buddha said that it had two principal trends: a cyclical trend and a spiral trend. The first, cyclical trend is an oscillation between pairs of opposites. In dependence upon pleasure there arises pain; in dependence upon pain, pleasure. In dependence upon loss there arises gain; in dependence upon gain, loss. In dependence upon winter, summer; in dependence upon summer, winter.

In traditional terms the whole process of cyclical action and reaction is called the round of existence, or the Wheel of Life – that is to say, the wheel of birth, death, and rebirth, best known in its Tibetan iconographic form.[27] If we look at a picture of the Tibetan Wheel of Life it gives us a detailed presentation of the whole cyclical mode of conditionality. It depicts all living beings, all sentient existence, as involved in the cyclical process, acting and reacting between pairs of opposites, going up and down, round and round, in accordance with the law of karma and rebirth.

With the second, spiral trend of conditionality, you get not oscillation between opposites but a movement between factors which progressively augment one another. In dependence upon happiness you get joy; in dependence upon joy, rapture; in dependence upon rapture, calm; in dependence upon calm, bliss. This is the progressive spiral series. And we can say that the spiral trend of conditionality constitutes, in principle, the spiritual path.

These are the two basic types or kinds of conditionality at work in the universe, at all levels: the cyclical and the spiral. It is the first which keeps us within the realm of the 'conditioned', circling round and round, as the Wheel of Life so graphically shows. And it is the second which gives us the possibility of growth and development, so that we can transcend conditionedness and ultimately enter the realm of the Unconditioned which is Enlightenment.[28] In a way, the rest of this book is simply an extended consideration of the workings of these two kinds of conditionality. In the first part, we shall explore the nature of the conditioned, in terms of the twelve links of conditioned co-production depicted by the Wheel of Life and in terms of what are called the three characteristics or marks of conditioned existence, before moving on to consider the nature of the Unconditioned, nirvana, and the concept of emptiness, popularly, though rather misleadingly, known as 'the void'.

In contemplating emptiness we shall come to see that ultimately no distinction can actually be made between the 'conditioned' and the 'Unconditioned'. But at our present level of spiritual development the distinction is very real, so that perforce we must think in terms of moving from one to the other, in other words in terms of a spiritual path. This is the main theme of the second part of the book.

After an introduction which sees the path in terms of escaping what I call the 'gravitational pull' of the conditioned and responding to the attraction of the Unconditioned, we shall explore various ways of seeing the spiritual path, starting with a consideration of the twelve links of the spiral path, the most explicit demonstration of the way spiral condition ality works. Then we shall consider a few of the many other ways of viewing the path: the Noble Eightfold Path, the seven factors of Enlightenment, the seven stages of purification, the five spiritual faculties, and then, lastly, three chapters each devoted to one of the stages of the Threefold Path: ethics, meditation, and wisdom. The intention is to show not only the doctrinal context of Buddhist practice but also how the teachings can be applied to everyday life. And, to remind us that there can be no wisdom without compassion, we will finish with a chapter on the Bodhisattva Ideal, that most sublime expression of the altruistic dimension of Buddhism.

And as we consider all these many and varied ways of answering the question 'What is the Dharma?' we should always bear in mind that all these concepts, all these teachings, all these practices, come back to one basic truth, one basic insight: conditionality.

2

THE DYNAMICS OF BEING

'BEING' IS NOT REALLY a very Buddhistic word. It is rather too static. The word we should be using is 'becoming'. In fact, the subject of this chapter is the underlying dynamics of our 'becoming' that make nonsense of the term 'being' which we commonly apply to this process. In more traditional terms we will be concerned with the 'links' of 'conditioned co-production' which chain us to a continuous cycle of rebirths, and with how the Buddha's analysis of this process offers us an ever-present opportunity to bring it to an end.

It must be admitted that the topic of karma and rebirth is not as fashionable in Buddhist circles as it used to be. In view of the central importance of this teaching to all schools of Buddhism it is probably worth examining how this has happened. If we find that one aspect of the Dharma appeals to us strongly it is usually because there is some imbalance in ourselves, a certain need in ourselves to which that aspect of the teaching corresponds. And if there are aspects of the Dharma that we leave on the side of our plate, so to speak, then it may be that those aspects correspond to aspects of ourselves and of our experience that we are not yet prepared to address. While it is certainly appropriate to follow our own personal bias to some extent, we need also to be aware that the bias is there and that an adjustment will need to be made at some point.

We can take a balanced view of the Dharma only if we ourselves become psychologically and spiritually balanced.

KARMA AND REBIRTH IN WESTERN BUDDHISM

In little more than a hundred years, the Dharma has come to appeal to people in the West in a wide variety of ways. And the different elements, aspects, and schools within the whole, sometimes bewilderingly complex, body of Buddhist teachings have not all found the same general favour at all times throughout this short epoch. Different teachings, different schools, have come to the fore at different times according to the different cultural conditions in force at any one time.

If we look at how Buddhism came to the West, we find first a period of purely scholarly interest, connected with the growth of 'orientalism'. This movement of fascination with all things oriental arose in the wake of the vast colonial interests exercised by various European states – particularly by Britain. The study of Buddhism was often initiated by civil servants who were simply concerned with gaining a deeper understanding of the local administration. For instance, T. W. Rhys Davids, the great Pali scholar, developed his interest in Buddhism when, as a judge in Ceylon in the 1870s, he had to delve into the Vinaya to clear up some rather complex questions of Buddhist law.

Then, from the close of the nineteenth century, a few Westerners began actually to call themselves Buddhists and to take up Buddhism as a way of life. Finally, Buddhism may be said to have definitely arrived in the West when, at about the beginning of the twentieth century, Western bhikkhus and bhikshus started to appear, when you got not only Western lay people but also Western monks.

Those aspects of Buddhism that appealed most strongly to the first Western Buddhists are nowadays often of more peripheral interest to people. Judging by the Buddhist literature being produced eighty or so years ago,[29] Westerners at that time – at least those of the English-speaking world – were attracted to Buddhism, if at all, mainly by three things: firstly by the personality of the Buddha – as a teacher, as a historical figure, as a wise and compassionate human being; secondly, by the ethics of Buddhism; and, thirdly, by the Buddhist teaching of karma and rebirth. And it seems – judging now from my own experience – that it is not these aspects that are decisive in bringing people to Buddhism today.

There are both negative and positive reasons for this change. To begin with, one cannot isolate the history of Buddhism in the West from

Western religious history in general. That Westerners should take up Buddhism at all may have seemed eccentric or even bizarre in the eyes of many at that time, but such an exotic development still partook of the Western religious zeitgeist.

During the second half of the nineteenth century this zeitgeist was deeply informed by scientific discoveries, particularly by Darwin's *The Origin of Species*, by the 'higher criticism' in biblical studies, and by the study of comparative religion. As a result, Christianity in its traditional dogmatic forms became less and less intellectually acceptable to a great many sincere and reflective and even spiritually sensitive people. At the same time, such people retained a strong emotional connection with Christianity. They could emancipate themselves intellectually from the dogmatic, doctrinal side of Christianity, but their heartstrings remained tied to the beliefs, practices, customs, and traditions of their childhood and youth.

For these people, Christianity had originally meant three things. This is especially true of the evangelicals who were prominent in English religious, and even social and political, life in those days. Christianity meant in the first place devotion to the person of Christ as the saviour, as the incarnate son of God. It meant an ethical code by which they could shape their actions: the Ten Commandments of the Old Testament, and the Sermon on the Mount of the New Testament. And finally, Christianity gave them the hope of life after death.

It is hard to appreciate nowadays how strong and pervasive this belief in life after death was in the nineteenth century. But I remember when I was a boy of fourteen I was sent down to the west country to stay with some elderly people in a rambling old house, decorated and furnished in the style of the 1860s and '70s. And what I came away with above all was a memory of the pictures hanging in the bedroom where I was put. They were huge, framed images of a single religious theme that exercised our Victorian forebears perhaps more than any other. One showed angels welcoming the departing soul into heaven; another was of a bevy of angels having what appeared to be a little gossip; and yet another depicted the heavens opening and a faithful soul aspiring upwards. They all inspired – or attempted to inspire – a hope of the life to come. Probably the best known literary illustration of this sort of thing is Dickens' pathetic description of the death of poor Little Nell in *The Old Curiosity Shop* – how the snow was falling, and as she passed away the voices of the angels could be heard calling her to her everlasting rest. It is all laid on with a trowel, which is how the Victorians liked their sentimentality.

So even after many people felt obliged to abandon Christianity as an intellectual proposition, they still hankered after something equivalent to those three elements in Christianity that had meant so much to them. And some people found them in Buddhism. In the person of the Buddha, they found a 'non-theological' Christ: a historical figure with all the virtues traditionally associated with Christ – even, perhaps, a few more – but without the encumbrance, not to say embarrassment, of Trinitarian theology. In the Buddhist precepts they found a code of ethics without any supernatural sanction; with, if anything, a purely humanistic sanction. They found the Sermon on the Mount without the Mount – that is, without the dogmatic, doctrinal background. Finally, they found in the teaching of karma and rebirth what appeared to them to be a more rational basis for their hope in a future life.

It is this final point which would come as something of a surprise to most traditional Buddhists. In the East the idea of having to come back again for another lifetime after the flames of your funeral pyre have died down is accepted implicitly. No one ever argues about it, no one ever discusses it; it's just accepted. It is taken for granted that you keep coming back to the world for lifetime after lifetime. But rebirth is also viewed as a terrible thing. Having to endure all the limitations of a human body, all its pains, all its sufferings, over and over again, is regarded as a miserable sort of process. The blessed release of nirvana represents, for most ethnic Buddhists, essentially freedom from rebirth.

In the West, by contrast, a century ago, it was the prospect that after death there would be no life, just annihilation, that was the most terrible thing. The teaching of karma and rebirth even taken in isolation represented some sort of salvation: the possibility of escape from this terrible, post-Christian, nihilistic predicament.

That Buddhism should thus have been effectively treated as a sort of Christianity-substitute is only to be expected at that intermediate stage in the development of Western Buddhism. It is hardly possible to jump all at once into something totally new, totally strange. You have to go down into it step by step, gradually assimilating it, accommodating it, harmonizing it. You have to go to the unknown from the known.

Today, however, the position is rather different. The majority of us who come into contact with Buddhism are not so heavily conditioned by Christianity that we are looking – whether consciously or unconsciously – for a Christianity-substitute. We are post-Christian. We are not so much reacting *against* Christianity as simply registering that it just doesn't mean much to us.

We no longer, for example, think of religion in terms of devotion to a person. This was an integral part of religious ideology in the nineteenth century and it is an integral part of the faith of many orthodox Christians even today. But as Western Buddhists we don't think of religion in those terms at all. We are not searching for someone to worship; we are not looking for a relationship with a person.

In a Buddhist this is not just a spirit of rebellion. There is a positive and clear principle involved. To those who were devoted too exclusively to his person, the Buddha used to say, 'He who sees the Dharma, sees me.'[30] It is only when we understand the Dharma, the principles and practices taught by the Buddha, that we can truly see and understand the living embodiment of those principles and practices, the Buddha himself. A further simple reason for the shift of interest from the person of the Buddha to his teaching is that we have far more of the Buddha's teachings translated into European languages than people had even fifty years ago.

If we are no longer looking for a Christ substitute, neither are we looking for an ethical code. We may need some guidance in the way we lead our day-to-day life, but not a list of dos and don'ts. We get so many conflicting moral messages from various quarters that most of us made the decision long ago to assess for ourselves what is right and wrong. We tend to sit loose to any systems or codes of ethical behaviour. Most of us work out our positions on moral issues and how to act on them simply by rule of thumb.

In the case of Buddhists, a more positive reason for the less central importance accorded to ethics is the greater attention paid to meditation. If one had been reading books and articles about Buddhism a hundred years ago one would have found plenty of discussion of ethics, and very little reference to meditation. Nowadays one would find the direct opposite. It's not that ethics are necessarily neglected, but it is understood that ethical behaviour is important not only for its own sake but because of its effect on the mind, effective meditation being possible only on the basis of a good conscience.

So too with the question of life after death. This is simply not the preoccupation for people that it used to be. In the nineteenth century it was a burning issue, but nowadays many people seem to be able to contemplate with some degree of equanimity the possibility that after death they might not continue to exist. Their interest is centred on their present existence, here and now.

More positively, we may say that the present generation of Buddhists are less interested in karma and rebirth because they are more concerned, at least theoretically, with realization here and now. As a result of this existential emphasis Zen Buddhism gradually replaced the Theravada in popular esteem from about the 1950s. And while Zen has itself now taken second place to Tibetan Buddhism, Western Buddhists seem to remain resolutely uninterested in karma and rebirth and unimpressed by the whole future prospect of life after life after life.

However, the process of karma and rebirth as described in Buddhist tradition, and depicted in the Tibetan Wheel of Life, is worth studying whether or not the question of future lives is an important one for us, because it can be seen not only according to the timescale of lifetimes but on a much smaller scale, reflecting the way life unfolds from day to day, even minute to minute, and suggesting how we can choose the direction our life will take. We will take a brief look at the workings of karma in our chapter on ethics (chapter 10), but here we will focus on the process of rebirth, taking as our guideline the twelve links of becoming, illustrated by the outermost circle of the Wheel of Life.

THE TWELVE LINKS OF BECOMING

The process of rebirth in Buddhism is analysed and understood according to the principle of 'conditioned co-production', otherwise known as 'dependent origination' (or in Sanskrit, *pratitya-samutpada*). As the English translations suggest, this principle explains the origin or production of the various factors of our experience, how they arise in dependence on preceding factors. Thus it represents the application of the general Buddhist philosophical principle of universal conditionality to the process of rebirth. It is analysed down into a number of *nidanas* or 'links' in a series, each of which arises in dependence on, or is conditioned by, the preceding one.

A few texts enumerate five nidanas, and a few others identify ten, but the standard number is twelve.[31] Such inconsistencies may make the whole way the nidana chain is enumerated seem rather contingent, but this is as it should be. Lists of this sort are not to be taken too literally. It is a mistake to think of a particular subject as being literally divided into a specific number of parts. There is not a literal Buddhist path, for example, consisting of literally eight distinct parts. These are divisions just for practical convenience.

So discrepancies between different texts as to how many nidanas to count should remind us that conditioned co-production does not divide itself up into a number of actual 'links' as such. The nidanas should help us to understand the *spirit* of conditionality rather than pin it down in a set, particular framework. There are innumerable factors operating on the individual at any one moment. The nidanas represent simply a selection of crucial ones – and, as conditions do, some of them appear more than once. Of the twelve, the first and second traditionally refer to the previous life, the eleventh and twelfth to the following life, and all the rest to the present life.

(1) Ignorance (*avidya*) is not literally the first nidana, because there is no actual beginning to the chain, but it is in some ways the most important. It is not ignorance in the intellectual sense so much as a lack of spiritual awareness; or even, if you like, a lack of spiritual consciousness, a deprivation of spiritual being. Metaphorically speaking, *avidya* represents a lack of illumination, a state of mental and spiritual darkness. Ignorance in this sense is the direct antithesis of *bodhi* or Enlightenment. Just as Enlightenment or nirvana is the goal of individual human development – the mountain peak ahead of us – so ignorance, lack of spiritual awareness, represents all that lies behind us in that process, the deep valleys swathed in darkness out of which we are gradually emerging.

More specifically, *avidya* is made up of various wrong views – wrong ways of looking at things: e.g. seeing the conditioned as Unconditioned, thinking that anything mundane, anything phenomenal, can last for ever. Such a view is not an intellectual conviction, of course, but an unconscious assumption. In clinging on to things that are subject to decay, and therefore becoming unhappy when we finally have to surrender them, we behave as though we believed that they ought to last for ever.

Another specific instance of *avidya* is belief in a personal god or supreme being. The idea that belief in God is a case of lack of spiritual awareness might raise a few eyebrows; but on this question Buddhism offers the same view as does psychoanalysis. This is that the god figure, the idea of a supreme being, a creator, is a sort of projected father-figure, a glorified representation of the father of our childhood, on whom we depend for help when we get into difficulties. Such belief is seen as a manifestation of spiritually immature dependency and unawareness.

Ignorance can also manifest by way of various beliefs, whether rationalized or not, based upon the assumption that purely external acts such as ceremonies, rituals, and sacraments can have spiritual efficacy or value quite apart from the state of mind with which they are performed. An obvious pitfall to avoid, one might think. However, even today there are, for example, many orthodox Hindus, even educated and Westernized Hindus, who genuinely believe that the waters of the Ganges have a definitely purifying effect, and that if you take a dip in those waters then your sins really will be washed away. And of course it can never be like that at all, as Ramakrishna, the great Hindu mystic who lived at the end of the nineteenth century, used to explain. He didn't like to offend the feelings of the orthodox, but at the same time he didn't like to commit himself to the orthodox belief. He would say, 'Yes, it's quite true that when you take a dip in the sacred Ganges you are purified of all your sins: when you go down into the water, your sins take the form of crows and they perch on the trees nearby; though when you come out of the water the crows disappear and your sins come back to you again.'

Thus it is really quite difficult to dislodge this wrong view, particularly when it is entrenched in a venerable tradition. In the West the sixteenth century Reformation inaugurated by Martin Luther was basically about this question. It was about whether the whole sacramental side of religion (and in particular, the purchase of indulgences, which relieved the purchaser of the burden of their sins) had value and efficacy in themselves, as purely mechanical, external observances. Luther asserted that it was impossible. Yet it is still one of the teachings of the Catholic Church that the sinfulness of the priest in no way impairs the efficacy of the sacrament he administers.

This is *avidya*. Above all it includes ignorance of the law of universal conditionality itself, the law which is exemplified by the principle of conditioned co-production.

(2) Karma formations (*samskaras*) arise in dependence on ignorance, or *avidya*. *Samskara* literally means 'preparation' or 'setting up', and when it appears in the context of the five *skandhas* (i.e. the five aggregates or categories into which the self – or what one thinks of as the self – may be analysed)[32] the term is translated as 'volitions' or 'willed action'. But in the context of the twelve nidanas it is generally rendered as 'karma formations'. This means the aggregate of those mental conditions that under the law of karma are responsible for the production, or preparation, or setting up, of the first moment of consciousness in the so-called 'new life'.

Essentially, the *samskaras* are acts of will connected with particular states of mind. These states of mind – which may be expressed either in physical action, or in speech, or just in mental activity – are either skilful or unskilful. Unskilful mental states are those dominated by greed or craving, by hatred or ill will, and by mental confusion or bewilderment. Skilful mental states are those dominated instead by contentment, generosity, kindness, and clarity of mind.

Unskilful volitions result in what is popularly called a 'bad rebirth', while skilful volitions result in a 'good rebirth'. However, Buddhism takes the radical view that both these kinds of volition, skilful as well as unskilful, are ultimately rooted in ignorance. According to Buddhism, desire for a good rebirth, or even working towards a good rebirth, is just as much a product of ignorance in the spiritual sense as moving more or less unconsciously towards a bad one. This is because rebirth, even a good rebirth, isn't the goal of Buddhism. The goal is the complete emancipation of the mind – or consciousness or whatever one likes to call it – from conditioned existence itself, from the whole round of birth and death and rebirth.

The traditional image given for the relationship between *avidya* and the *samskaras* (whether skilful or unskilful) is a rather pointed one. *Avidya* or ignorance is said to be like the state of drunkenness; while the *samskaras*, the karma formations, are like the actions that you perform while drunk.

In effect, this image suggests that most people in their ordinary everyday actions, even in their so-called conventionally religious actions, are no better – from a spiritual point of view – than inebriates behaving in the foolish ways that inebriates do. This is really the state of most of us. Sometimes it is said that, from a spiritual point of view, we are asleep. But it is just as true to say that we are drunk. We're 'drunk' because we are continuously under the influence of ignorance, so that everything we do, everything we say, everything we think, is the product in one way or another of that lack of spiritual awareness.

A drunkard imagines that whatever he is doing and saying is very clever and witty and wise, when in fact it is simply sottish. We are the same. Whatever we may do or say or think, however we may indulge in all sorts of charitable activities, all sorts of conventional religious practices, it is all done out of lack of spiritual awareness. Which is quite a sobering thought, really. And yet in dependence on this 'drunken' activity arises 'consciousness'. So what does this mean?

(3) Consciousness (*vijnana*) arises in dependence on the *samskaras* or karma formations. But this isn't consciousness in general; it is consciousness in a specific sense, called technically the 'relinking consciousness'. After the death of the human organism it relinks the psyche to the psychophysical process in the form of a new life, a rebirth. According to tradition, three factors are necessary for conception of a human being to take place: first, there has to be sexual intercourse; second, the prospective mother should be ready to conceive; and, third, there must be what is popularly described as a 'being' ready to be reborn.

'Being' here means the last moment of consciousness belonging to the previous existence. In other words, it is the relinking consciousness. According to the Theravada school, there is no interval between death and rebirth. But other schools – the Sarvastivada, and following them the Tibetans – teach that there's an intermediate state, a *bardo*, in between. (This intermediate state forms much of the subject matter of the *Tibetan Book of the Dead*, or *Bardo Thodol*).[33]

Which of these views is correct is open to debate. However, the more important issue is whether or not anyone may be said to be reborn at all. This question exercises many people. In view of the doctrine of *anatman* or no-self, who or what exactly is reborn?

As usual, Buddhism offers no facile solution to this conundrum. All one can do, really, is point out two extreme and thus false positions to be avoided. One extreme view is to maintain that the person who is reborn, who reappears in a new existence, is in some essential way the same as they were before in their previous existence. So, if someone is reborn, well, it's the same Tom or Dick or Harry or Gertrude or Mary as before, only they are kitted out with a new body. This sort of belief is expressed, for instance, in the *Bhagavad Gita*, where Sri Krishna says that rebirth is just like putting on a new set of clothes when you get up in the morning. You cast aside the old worn-out body and take on a new one, but you yourself remain essentially unchanged.

The other extreme view says that no, you must be an essentially different person in your next life. The influence or the conditioning exerted by the body on the psyche as a whole is so profound – i.e. your physical experience is so fundamental to your identity – that you cannot speak in terms of being the same person when you have a different body.

These would appear to be the only alternatives on offer: either the person reborn is the same as the one who died or they are different. However, we can begin to discern the real nature of these two views on rebirth by stepping back to another controversy with which they are connected historically. This is an ancient Indian dispute about the nature of causation, and the two opposing schools survive to this day.

The Satkaryavada school of thought maintains that cause and effect are identical. It says that when a so-called effect is produced, all that has really happened is that the cause has changed its form. They say that if, for instance, you have a lump of gold which you make into ornaments, then the gold becomes the cause of which the ornaments represent the effect. And in that case both cause and effect consist of the same thing. It is the same gold, whether you call it cause or whether you call it effect.

The process is uninterrupted, and there is no specific point at which a cause turns into something different called an effect. Thus cause and effect are one and the same. By contrast, those who follow the Asatkaryavadin line of reasoning say that, on the contrary, cause is one thing, and effect is quite another thing, and they use the example of milk turning into curds to prove their point.[34]

However, both these views, if they are pursued logically, make causation impossible. Whether cause and effect are really identical, or whether they are quite different, either way there can be no relation between them. Hence Buddhists avoid this whole argument. They see it as proceeding from wrong premises.

Buddhism establishes itself on *pratitya-samutpada*, or conditionality. According to this principle, any phenomenon whatsoever, whether mental or material, arises in dependence on, or is conditioned by, a complex of other phenomena. But this relationship – between the conditioning agents and the object of conditioning – cannot be described either in terms of identity or in terms of difference. Neither category fits.

Applying this principle to the question of rebirth, all one can really say on the subject is that in dependence on the karma formations of the last life, consciousness arises. To ask if someone is the same as or different from the person whose karma formations provided the conditioning necessary for their existence is beside the point. The question does not make sense in Buddhist terms. The one who is reborn is neither the same as, nor entirely different from, the one who died. As so often with Buddhism, the really strict, orthodox Buddhist position consists of a paradox: there is rebirth, but there is no one who is reborn. That's the Buddhist position in precise terms.

What no Buddhist should be said to believe in is 'reincarnation' – i.e. getting into a body again and again. This notion assumes that you have a soul, a sort of unchanging essence of yourself that pops into one body after another; such an idea does not conform with Buddhist principles at all. Technically the correct word is not even 'rebirth', but *punarbhava*: 'again-becoming' or 'rebecoming'.

(4) The psychophysical organism (*nama-rupa*) – literally 'name and form', but roughly translatable as 'mind and body' – arises in dependence on the relinking consciousness.[35] *Nama-rupa* comprises the five skandhas: the physical body, feeling, perception, volition, and consciousness. This is a comprehensive link in the chain, representing a basic breakdown of the individual's full experience of himself or herself into these five categories. It is clear from this link that the chain as a whole is not a simple

sequence of causation, but a complex chain of conditionality. So certain factors appear more than once in the chain as the crucial element in a whole complex of conditions.

(5) The six bases (*shadayatana*) arise in dependence on this initially embryonic psychophysical organism. They are simply the five physical sense organs together with the mind, which is treated as a sort of sixth sense organ. Just as our five senses each have their range of objects, so does the mind have its memories, ideas, and projections. The six bases are so-called because they constitute the bases for our experience of the external world, the external universe.

(6) Contact (*sparsha*) arises in dependence on the six bases of the psychophysical organism. Contact or impression represents the mutual impact of sense organ with its appropriate object. The eye comes into contact with visual form, the ear with sounds, and so on – and, of course, the mind comes into contact with mental objects or ideas.

(7) Feeling (*vedana*) arises in dependence on sense contact, and we have already met it as one of the five categories comprising the fourth nidana. Feeling or sensation can be pleasant or painful, or it can be neutral, that is, neither pleasant nor painful; and it is an ever-present element of our experience at whatever level, right up to Enlightenment. However, whereas pleasure may be experienced at any plane of existence, pain is possible only in connection with the gross, sensory level.

(8) Craving (*trishna*) – literally 'thirst' – arises in dependence on feeling. There are three kinds of craving: *kama-trishna*, thirst or craving for sensuous experience; *bhava-trishna*, craving for continued existence, especially continued existence after death, in heaven; and *vibhava-trishna*, craving for non-existence, for annihilation, the desire for oblivion. This particular link is the crucial one of the whole series – why, we shall see shortly – and it appears as the second of the Four Noble Truths: the origin of rebirth and suffering.

(9) Attachment or grasping (*upadana*) arises in dependence on thirst or craving. One might well imagine that this nidana needs no introduction, that we are all familiar enough with attachment: attachment to pleasures of all kinds, to possessions, to people, and so on. However, what we usually think of as attachment represents only one of four kinds of attachment enumerated by the Buddhist tradition.

The second kind is a particularly significant and characteristically Buddhist idea of what constitutes attachment. It is attachment to *drishti*: literally 'view' but meaning also 'opinions', 'speculations', and 'beliefs', including all sorts of philosophical and religious opinions. This is not to say that you shouldn't entertain beliefs or convictions or philosophical or religious opinions – even very strongly – but attachment or grasping or clinging to them is seen as unhealthy.

How then is one to tell the difference between a strong, healthy conviction as to the truth of one's views, and an unhealthy attachment to them? In fact it is quite easy. When we are engaged in argument with someone, and they challenge an idea that for us is axiomatic, if we become in the least bit upset or angry, then that is a sure sign of attachment to *drishti*. If our equanimity is at all disturbed when our belief is challenged, then whether our view is right or wrong is no longer of much consequence. That clinging is a fetter, binding us to the wheel of birth and death. Let us by all means rectify and refine our understanding of the Dharma, and try to put it into practice, but not in such a way that when anyone questions or challenges us, we feel threatened and react in a hostile, unsympathetic manner.

Thirdly, there is attachment to ethics (*shila*) and religious observance (*vrata*). Again, it is not that one shouldn't practise ethics, meditation, and so on. The mistake is to cling on to one's own practice as an end in itself, or to imagine that doing these practices makes one 'different' from other people.

And then, fourthly, there is attachment to a belief in a permanent, unchanging self existing apart from the various and constantly changing elements of one's experience of oneself.[36]

(10) Becoming (*bhava*) arises in dependence upon attachment. *Bhava* is life or existence as conditioned by our attachment, on any plane, on any level, from the lowest hell realms to the highest celestial abodes. The term *bhava* can be taken to mean conception, but it also refers to the whole process represented by the nidana chain in both its passive aspect, consisting of the fruits of action, and its active aspect, consisting of the volitions that result in rebirth.

According to some Buddhist schools, including those of Tibet, this link represents the bardo, the intermediate state between death and rebirth. Others would say that it represents the intrauterine period of human life – that is, the period between conception and birth.

(11) Birth (*jati*) arises in dependence on becoming (in its 'active' volitional aspect). Some would say that this is literally birth in the sense of becoming physically independent of the mother, but it can also be seen as the simultaneous coming together of the five skandhas as a psycho-physical organism in the womb.

(12) Decay and death (*jara-marana*) arise in dependence upon birth – together with, the traditional texts say, 'sorrow, lamentation, pain, grief, and despair'. Once you've been born, well, nothing on this earth can prevent you from decaying, eventually, and dying. We are born out of our attachment to conditioned things, and we must also go the way of conditioned things.

BREAKING THE CHAIN

The Wheel of Life, and this sequence of twelve links, can be taken symbolically to mirror to us the process of actions and their consequences which drive our behaviour from day to day. The very act of reaching for a biscuit can be analysed in terms of these twelve nidanas. But we can also take this sequence as a literal reflection, a pictorial teaching, of the process of birth, death, and rebirth. The twelve nidanas cover a sequence of three lives. The first two links, ignorance and the karma formations, belong to the past life, in the sense that it's because of spiritual ignorance and the actions based on that ignorance that we're born again in this life. Consciousness, name and form, the six bases, contact, sensation or feeling, thirst or craving, grasping or clinging, and becoming all belong to the present life. Birth and subsequent decay and death obviously belong to the future life.

These same twelve links can also be subdivided into two groups, known as the 'action process' and the 'result process'. The word for 'action' here is karma, using the word in its simplest sense. The links belonging to the action process represent what we do – they are *volitional* actions, whether of body, speech, or mind – whereas the links belonging to the result process are passive, representing what we experience as a result of what we have done.

Ignorance and the karma formations constitute the action process of the past life; it is as a result of them that we have come into existence in the present life. Consciousness, name and form, the six bases, contact, and sensation or feeling together make up the result process of the present life. They are the givens of existence, the results of our past actions; there's nothing we can do about them now. Thirst or craving, grasping or clinging, and becoming constitute the action process of the present life, because they are all volitional, and therefore productive of future karmic consequences.

Thus we have, over the three lifetimes – past, present, and future – an alternating sequence of action process, result process, action process, result process. Within this cycle there are three points of transition: the point where the action process of the past life is succeeded by the result process of the present life; the point where the result process of the present life is succeeded by the action process of the present life; and the point where the action process of the present life is succeeded by the result process of the future life.

All these three points are extremely important. The first and the third represent the points of transition from one life to the next. The second point, however, is a point of transition which is in a crucial sense even more important: a point of transition – in the midst of our present life – at which we can potentially move from the cyclical type of conditionality to a completely different, spiral type. This is the point at which the Wheel of Life can cease to revolve altogether, the point at which we can break the chain. But how does this happen?

We have seen that the last link of the result process of the present life is sensation or feeling – pleasant, painful, or neutral. (It is perhaps worth noting at this point that by 'feeling' here is meant no more than the bare sensation. It doesn't mean 'boredom' or 'love' or 'anger', or anything like that; these we could refer to as 'emotions' rather than 'feelings', to make the distinction clear.) There's nothing wrong with feeling, nothing wrong with sensation. In fact, as we have seen, it is part of the 'result process'; we have no choice about whether or not we experience it. Where we do have a choice is in how we respond to that pleasant, unpleasant, or neutral sensation. Of course, we don't usually experience it as a choice. It is usually automatic that in dependence upon feeling arises craving. That's the problem.

Of the three kinds of craving, craving for continued existence and craving for annihilation are impulses – opposite tendencies, really – of which we need to become aware. Generally speaking, each of us tends either to the extreme of eternalism or to the extreme of nihilism – extremes that distort our whole world-view. These tendencies go very deep, but they are clearly in evidence in our everyday life – for example, in that we tend to take either an over-optimistic view of things, or an over-pessimistic one. It is of the utmost importance that we become aware of our own tendency in this respect, and aware that it will be colouring our view of life.

But it is the third kind of craving – thirst or craving for sensuous experience – which gives us the clue as to how we can break the endless circle at this point. Perhaps to speak of 'craving' is slightly misleading, because the connotations of the word suggest that it is simply desire for pleasant experience that is meant, whereas 'craving' here includes three distinct strands. When we experience a pleasant feeling, our usual tendency is automatically to want to hang on to it. When, on the other hand, we experience an unpleasant feeling, our reaction is to push it away, to avoid it. And if we experience a feeling that is neither pleasant nor unpleasant, we are liable just to feel confused. In other words, we are infected by the three root poisons, greed, hatred, and ignorance, symbolized at the hub of the Wheel of Life by the cock, the snake, and the pig. These are the forces that keep the whole Wheel spinning round. When we respond to pleasant feelings with thirst or craving, to unpleasant feelings with aversion, or to neutral feelings with indifference, we set up volitions, we create fresh karma – and round we go again.

This is why this particular link is so crucial. We have to learn to experience feelings and sensations without allowing them to give rise to craving, aversion, or indifference. Here mindfulness – awareness, recollection – is of fundamental importance. It is important that we are able to be mindful or aware of what we are experiencing in the way of sensation or feeling, rather than reacting unconsciously to that sensation and thus setting up unskilful volitions.

Creating this hiatus can be very uncomfortable, because once we become aware at this point, we realize that craving is essentially impossible to satisfy. Although our instinct is to grasp pleasure and push away pain, our longings will not be appeased, nor our pain stilled, in this way. Out of this realization of the essential unsatisfactoriness of mundane things (*duhkha* is the Buddhist term for it), can arise faith in the possibility of something higher; faith, we may say, is the positive counterpart of craving.

This movement from the awareness of unsatisfactoriness to faith is the first step on the spiral path; and this is the starting point of chapter 7, in which we will examine another sequence of twelve links, a sequence that forms not the endless round of the Wheel of Life, but the spiral path – which begins with this moment of awareness between feeling and craving, and which leads us away from the Wheel of Life through more and more positive states of consciousness all the way up to Enlightenment itself.

These twelve 'positive links', as one could call them, have often been forgotten. They are mentioned in only two or three places in the Pali Canon,[37] and as far as I know they are not mentioned in the Mahayana scriptures at all. We hear a lot about the first set of twelve links but we hardly ever hear about this second, positive set. This is unfortunate because it contributes to the impression some people have that Buddhist spiritual practice is primarily negative, consisting simply in getting rid of craving, clinging, and so on. It's therefore important not to forget the twelve positive links. They represent the spiral type of conditionality, and without them our picture of reality – reality as represented by the principle of conditionality – is incomplete. Moreover, without them the spiritual path has no rationale.

There is also a great deal of value in contemplating the twelve links that make up the cyclical trend of conditionality. Indeed, every serious student of Buddhism needs to be well acquainted with them. We should be able to recite them from memory, almost like repeating a mantra. The Buddhist tradition teaches specific methods of reflecting and meditating systematically on the twelve links (see page 194) and we need to make the effort to do this. One could go so far as to say that otherwise there's not much hope of our really understanding what Buddhism is all about.

3

THE TEXTURE OF REALITY

REALITY IS A very big word, but it is not really a Buddhist word. We have *shunyata* or emptiness, we have *tathata* or suchness, and we have *dharmakaya*, the 'truth-body', but there is no true semantic equivalent in traditional Buddhist terminology of the word 'reality'.

Reality is not only a big word; it is also an abstract word (which often means a vague word) and on the whole Buddhists have never been fond of abstract terminology. Tibetan Buddhism, for example, takes a very concrete, and even – if one wanted to be paradoxical – materialistic approach to the spiritual life. And Zen Buddhism goes even further: any indulgence in abstractions or vague generalities is met with a piercing shriek or thirty blows or some other such discommendation.

So when we use this word 'reality' in speaking about Buddhism, we use it in a makeshift and provisional sort of way. It isn't to be taken too literally. Certainly, the connotations that attach to it in general Western philosophical and religious usage cannot be said to apply in a Buddhist context.

It is for these reasons that – while the word 'reality' may be almost unavoidable for an English-speaking Buddhist – I am introducing the idea of its *texture*. This word is almost palpably concrete. Texture is felt, it is handled, it is experienced directly, by touch. Because we have so many nerve-endings in the tips of our fingers, we are able to make very subtle distinctions amongst an enormous range of different textures. We can distinguish between cotton, silk, and wool, or between granite, slate, and marble. And it is possible to discern far more subtle gradations of texture. Chinese experts on jade used to be able to distinguish between hundreds of kinds and qualities of jade – white, black, red, or green jade, 'mutton-fat jade' or 'dragon's-blood jade', or whatever it was – with their eyes closed, simply by feeling their texture under water.

Reality too, in Buddhism, is something to be felt, touched, even handled – because Buddhism is above all else practical. So, continuing to use the word in a provisional sense, we may say that reality in Buddhism is broadly speaking of two kinds: there is conditioned reality and Unconditioned reality – or more simply, there is the conditioned and the Unconditioned.

THE TWO REALITIES

'The Unconditioned' is the usual translation of the Sanskrit *asamskrita*. *Sam* means 'together', *krita* is 'made' or 'put', and *a-* is a negative prefix, so *asamskrita* literally means 'not put together' or 'uncompounded'. 'The conditioned' is therefore *samskrita*, which is a word of particular interest in Sanskrit as it is the name of the language itself – 'Sanskrit' being an Anglicized version of it. According to the Brahmin pundits it is so called because it is the language which has been properly put together, beautifully put together, perfected. It is so designated to set it in contradistinction to the rough, crude, and unpolished 'Prakrit' – including Pali – spoken by the common people (i.e. especially by the non-Brahmins). In modern Indian languages like Hindi, Bengali, and Marathi, *samskriti* means 'culture'. In this way the idea has developed that *samskrita*, the conditioned, is also the artificial, whereas *asamskrita*, the Unconditioned, is the natural, the simple, that which has not been artificially put together.

This connotation to the term 'Unconditioned' receives explicit recognition in Tantric Buddhism. The Tantrics have an interesting word for reality: *sahaja*. *Saha* is 'together', and *ja* is 'born' (as in *jati*, 'birth'); so the literal meaning of *sahaja* is 'born with' or 'co-nascent'. And so reality is said to be that with which one is born, that which is innate, that which does not have to be acquired.

The distinction between the conditioned and the Unconditioned, between the artificial and the natural, is fundamental to Buddhist thought, even though, as we shall see, there is some disagreement amongst various Buddhist schools as to whether it is an *absolute* distinction or not. And it would appear to go back a long way, even to predate the Buddha's own Enlightenment.

In the *Majjhima-Nikaya,* the medium-length discourses of the Pali Canon, there is one discourse that is of rather special interest on account of its autobiographical content. This is the *Ariyapariyesana Sutta,* in which the Buddha describes how he left home, how he became a wandering monk, how he strove for Enlightenment, and, as we have seen, how he deliberated about whether or not to try to teach the Dharma.

What surprises some readers of this sutta is that there is no mention in it of the famous 'four sights', of how Siddhartha Gautama, the future Buddha, sallied forth one fine morning in his chariot with his charioteer, and saw a sick man, and then – on successive occasions – an old man, a corpse, and finally a wandering ascetic; and thus came alive to the existence of sickness, old age, and death, and the possibility of becoming a truth-seeking wanderer.

Instead, this particular account gives a comparatively naturalistic, even humanistic, description of how Siddhartha came to the decision to give up the household life. It is, so far as this account is concerned, a purely internal process, not connected with anything in particular that he saw or heard. Here he is represented – in his own words – as simply reflecting.

The Buddha relates how one day he was sitting at home in the palace, reflecting alone. We should imagine him perhaps under a tree in the compound; it is probably the early evening, when a cool, calm quiet descends over the Indian scene. He is there simply reflecting, 'What am I? What am I doing with my life? I am mortal, subject to old age, sickness, and death. And yet, being such, what do I do? Being myself subject to birth, I pursue that which is also subject to birth. Being myself subject to old age I pursue that which likewise will grow old. Being myself subject to sickness, to decay, I pursue that which is subject to the same decay. And being myself subject to death, I pursue that which also must die.'[38]

Then – as the Buddha goes on to relate to his interlocutor in this sutta, who is a Jain ascetic – there arose in his mind a different, almost a contrary train of reflection. It occurred to him: 'Suppose now I were to do otherwise? Suppose now, being myself subject to birth, I were to go in search of that which is not subject to birth, which has no origin, which is timeless? Suppose, being myself subject to old age, I were to go in search of that which is immutable? Suppose, being myself subject to sickness, to decay, I were to go in search of that in whose perfection there is no diminution? Or suppose, finally, being myself subject to death, I were to go in search of the deathless, the everlasting, the eternal?'

As a result of these reflections, shortly afterwards he left home. There is no great drama in this sutta, no stealing out of the palace by moonlight on muffled hooves. It simply says that although his father and his foster-mother wept and wailed, he put on the yellow robe, shaved his head, cut off his beard, and went forth from home into the homeless life.

This is the story, in brief, of the Buddha's conversion – conversion in the literal sense of a 'turning round', though in Siddhartha's case it was not an external turning round, from one religion to another, but an internal one, from the conditioned to the Unconditioned. Siddhartha realized that he was a conditioned being, and that he was spending all his time and energy in pursuit of conditioned things – that is, in the *anariyapariyesana* or 'ignoble quest'. He realized, in other words, that he was binding himself to the endless round of existence, the wheel of life on which we all turn, passing from one life to the next indefinitely.

So he decided simply to turn round completely and go in search of the Unconditioned instead, to take up the *ariyapariyesana*, the 'noble quest'. In time, he would realize this quest as the spiral path leading from the endless round to the goal of Enlightenment or nirvana. But at this point he identified the course before him with this simple but strong, pre-Buddhistic expression, found in the oldest Upanishads: *esana*, urge, desire, will, search, aspiration, quest, pursuit. He could continue with the 'ignoble quest', or he could undertake the 'noble quest' instead.

The Buddha's conversion was not easy, we can be sure of that, because here and there, in other places in the scriptures, we get indications that a terrible struggle went on in his mind before he made his final decision. But stripped of all the legends and myths that have accumulated around it over the centuries, it was as simple – almost classically simple – as this. And it is in this most simple description of the first great insight of the Buddha-to-be that the essence of the spiritual life is to be found. Here we put our finger on the spring that works the whole mechanism.

This spring is the conditioned in pursuit of the Unconditioned, the mortal seeking the immortal: seeking, that is, not immortality of the self, but a self-transcending immortality. What Siddhartha was looking for was basically the answer to a question, one that we find asked (in the *Majjhima-Nikaya*) by a young monk, Govinda, who spends a rainy season retreat – i.e. of about three months – meditating on *metta* or universal loving kindness, and as a result has a vision of the 'eternal youth' Brahma

Sanatkumara. The question Govinda asks Sanatkumara in this sutta is 'How may the mortal obtain the immortal Brahma world?'[39]

This is the essential religious question. How may the conditioned become the Unconditioned; how may the mortal become immortal? How may I conquer death? Now of course it all sounds very fine put like that, but if one is going to take seriously the question of how to leave the conditioned and go in search of the Unconditioned, one will want a further question answered. What exactly does one mean by the conditioned? How do we identify the conditioned?

According to Buddhist tradition, that which is conditioned invariably bears three characteristics, or *lakshanas*, by which it may be recognized as such. These three characteristics are sometimes called the 'three signs of being', but more properly this should be the 'three signs of becoming', as the nature of the conditioned is nothing as static as a 'state of being'.

The three *lakshanas*, the three inseparable characteristics of all conditioned existence, are: *duhkha*, the unsatisfactory, or painful; *anitya*, the impermanent; and *anatman*, the emptiness of self, of essential being.[40] All conditioned 'things' or 'beings' whatsoever in this universe possess all these three characteristics. They are all unsatisfactory, all impermanent, all devoid of self. Of these three *lakshanas* the first is in some ways the most difficult for most people to come to terms with, emotionally, so we shall look at it in rather more depth and detail than at the other two.

SUFFERING

The Sanskrit word here is *duhkha*, and the usual translation is 'suffering', but a better one – if a bit cumbersome – is 'unsatisfactoriness'. Best of all, perhaps, is to attend to its etymology: though the traditional account of the origin of the word *duhkha* is no longer universally accepted, it still leaves us with a true and precise image.

Duh- as a prefix means anything that is not good – bad, ill, wrong, or out of place; and *kha*, the main part of the word, is supposed to be connected with the Sanskrit *chakra*, meaning 'wheel'. So *duhkha* is said to have meant originally the ill-fitting wheel of a chariot, thus suggesting a bumpy, jarring ride, a journey on which one could never be comfortable, never at one's ease.

So much for a general picture of *duhkha*. As we look closer, though, we see that unease or suffering comes in many different forms – and the Buddha usually speaks of seven.[41] First, he says, *birth* is suffering: human life starts with suffering. In the more poetical words of Oscar Wilde, 'At the birth of a child or a star there is pain.' In whatever way it is expressed, this is a great spiritual truth; it is significant that our life begins with suffering.

Birth is certainly physically painful for the mother, and consequently it is often emotionally painful for the father, while for the infant it is, we are told, a traumatic experience. It is very unpleasant to be suddenly thrust forth from a world of total harmony in the womb out into a cold, strange world, to which one is very likely to be welcomed with a slap on the bottom.

Secondly, the Buddha says, *old age* is suffering. One of the discomforts of old age is physical weakness: you cannot get about in the relaxed, agile way you used to. Then there is loss of memory: you can't remember names, or where you put things; you are not as agile and flexible intellectually as you were. Where this degeneration becomes senility it is a tragic thing to observe, most especially in once eminent individuals. Perhaps most painful of all, when you are very old you are dependent upon others: you cannot do much for yourself, and you may even need constant looking after by a nurse or by your relations. Despite all modern comforts and amenities – and often as a result of modern advances in medicine – many of us will experience this suffering, especially if we survive to an extreme old age.

Thirdly, *sickness* is suffering. Whether it is a toothache or an incurable disease like cancer, no sickness is pleasant. It is not just the physical pain that is suffering: there is also the helplessness, the fear, and the frustration of it. Medical science may sometimes palliate the suffering of sickness, but there is no sign at all that we will ever banish it entirely. It seems that no sooner do we get rid of one disease than another comes along. As soon as one virus is defeated, a new, stronger strain of virus arises. And as soon as we feel physically quite healthy, we start to develop all sorts of mental ailments, more and more complex neuroses and mysterious syndromes, all of which involve suffering. Almost any sense of imperfection in our lives can develop into an illness of some sort: stress turns into heart attacks, fatigue turns into syndromes, habit turns into addictions. So it seems that sickness may change its appearance, but it doesn't go away.

Fourthly, *death* is suffering. We suffer when those dear to us die; we suffer as we watch the life ebbing from a physical body that we have long associated with the life of a loved one. We suffer in the knowledge that our loved ones will die, and we suffer in the knowledge of our own dissolution. Much of our suffering with regard to death, of course, is simply fear. Most of us will put up with a great deal of suffering before we will choose to die, such is our terror of the inevitable conclusion to our own existence:

The weariest and most loathéd worldly life,
That age, ache, penury, and imprisonment
Can lay on nature, is a paradise
To what we fear of death.[42]

People do not always feel ready to die. They are sorry to leave the scene of their labours and pleasures and achievements. Even if they do want to go, even if they are quite happy to pass on to a new life, or into they know not what, there is still the pain involved in the physical process of dissolution. And with this goes, sometimes, a great deal of mental suffering. Sometimes on their death-beds, people are stricken with remorse: they remember terrible wrongs they have done, dreadful harm and pain they have visited on certain individuals; and they may have, in consequence, fears and apprehensions for the future. All this makes death a horrifying experience for many people, and one which, before it comes, they do their best not to think about.

Fifthly, *contact with what one dislikes* is suffering. We all know this. It may be that even in our own family there are people with whom we just don't get on. This is very tragic, especially when it is our own parents or children whom we dislike. Because the tie – even the attachment – of blood is there, well, we have to put up with a certain amount of contact, and this can be painful.

The work we do can also be a source of suffering, if we do it just because we need to earn a living and it is the only work we can get. Again, we may feel that we have to put up with what we dislike, and perhaps work with people we find uncongenial, for periods of time anyway, even though we would rather do something else.

There are, as well, all sorts of environmental conditions which are unpleasant: pollution, noise, weather. It is obviously not possible for everyone to go off and live in a Greek villa. So there seems to be no way of escape – certainly no way of escaping entirely. You just have to live with people, places, things, and conditions that you don't altogether like.

Sixthly, *separation from what one likes* is suffering. This can be a very harrowing form of suffering indeed. There are people we would like to be with, to meet more often – relations, friends – but circumstances interpose and it becomes simply impossible. This happens often in time of war, when families are broken up – men conscripted and taken to far-off battlefields, children sent away to places of safety, and people simply disappearing as refugees.

I myself can remember how, when I was in India during the war as a signals operator, many of my friends used to get letters from home regularly every week or so; and then a day might come when the letters would stop. They wouldn't know what had happened, but they would know that there were bombs falling in England, so after a while they would start suspecting the worst. Eventually, perhaps, they would get the news, either from another relation or officially, that their wife and children, or their parents, or their brothers and sisters, had been killed in an aerial bombardment. This is the most terrible suffering – permanent separation from those we love. Some people never get over such suffering, and brood over their loss for the rest of their lives.

Seventhly, *not to get what one wants* is suffering. There is little need to elaborate upon this. When you have set your heart on something (or someone) and you fail to achieve your goal, when the prize does not fall to you, then you feel disappointed and frustrated, even bitter. We have all known short-lived experiences of this kind, when we fail to get a job we particularly wanted, or fail to be selected for something, or find that someone else has got to something (or someone) before us.

Some people experience a lifetime of disappointment, frustration, and bitterness if they feel that life has short-changed them in some way – and of course the stronger the desire, the more the suffering. But even just in small ways, it is something with which we are acquainted almost every day, if not every hour – for example, when we find that all the cake has gone.

So these are the seven different aspects of *duhkha* identified by the Buddha. The Buddha once declared, 'One thing only do I teach – suffering and the cessation of suffering'[43] – and emancipation from the bondage of suffering is indeed the keynote of his teaching. In the Pali scriptures he compares himself to a physician who attempts to relieve his patient of a tormenting disease – the disease of conditioned existence with which we are all afflicted.[44] Of course, we are not always willing patients, as the Buddha clearly found. But on the many occasions when he spoke about suffering, and tried to get people to see it in perspective, he would apparently sum up his discourse by saying that existence as a whole is painful, that the totality of conditioned sentient experience, comprising form, feeling, perceptions, volitions, and consciousness, is unsatisfactory.

Now most people would say that this is going a bit far, that it is a pessimistic, if not morbid view of life. They would say that human existence can by no means be said to be unsatisfactory and painful all the way through. They will admit to birth being painful, they will agree that sickness, old age, and yes, death, are indeed painful. But at the same time they are reluctant to accept the conclusion which follows from all this, which is that conditioned existence itself is suffering. It is as though they admit all the individual digits in the sum, but they won't accept the total to which those digits add up. They say that yes, there is a certain amount of suffering in the world, but on the whole it's not such a bad place. Why be so negative? There's plenty to smile about. While there's life, there's hope.

And there is, of course. We have pleasant experiences as well as painful ones. But the Buddhist view is that even the pleasant experiences are at bottom painful. They are really only suffering concealed, glossed over, deferred – a whistling in the dark. And the extent to which we can see this, see the suffering behind the gilding of pleasure, 'the skull beneath the skin', depends on our spiritual maturity.

Edward Conze has identified four different aspects of concealed suffering.[45] Firstly, something that is pleasant for oneself may involve suffering for other people, for other beings. We don't tend to consider this, of course. If we are all right, if we're having a good time, we don't worry too much or too often about others: 'I'm all right, Jack' more or less sums up this attitude. The most common example of this is the frank enjoyment with which people eat the flesh of slaughtered animals. They go on merrily plying knife and fork without consciously thinking about the suffering of the animals.

But the unconscious mind is not so easily fooled. You can shut out some unpleasant fact from the conscious mind, but unconsciously you notice everything and you forget nothing. You may never be consciously aware of that unpleasant fact, but it will exert an influence on your mental state that is all the more powerful for being unseen. In this way we develop an 'irrational' feeling of guilt, because in the depths of ourselves we know that our own pleasure has been bought at the expense of the suffering of other living beings. This guilt is the source of a great deal of uneasiness and anxiety.

Conze gives the example of wealthy people, who are nearly always afraid of becoming poor. This is, he says, because unconsciously they feel that they don't deserve to have their money. Unconsciously they feel that it *ought* to be taken away from them, and consciously they worry that perhaps it *will* be taken away from them. By contrast, you notice that poor people who may not know where next week's food is coming from are rarely racked with anxiety over it. They are generally much more relaxed and cheerful than the rich.

Wealthy people may suffer from unconscious guilt feelings because they know, however much they may deny it consciously, that their wealth is 'tainted': its acquisition has brought suffering to other people, directly or indirectly. Consequently, they feel a constant need to justify themselves. They say, 'I earn my money, I contribute to the well-being of the community, I offer a service that people want, I provide employment....' Or else they say, 'Well, if I'm rich and other people are poor, it's because I work harder, I take risks – at least I don't ask to be spoon-fed....'

If the feeling of guilt gets too much then drastic measures are required to relieve it, and the most drastic measure of all is to give away some of that wealth – to the church, or to a hospital or whatever. Hospitals are a favourite option because you can compensate for the suffering you have caused in acquiring the wealth by giving some of it to alleviate suffering. It is called 'conscience money'. If one has anything to do with religious organizations, one soon learns to recognize this sort of donation. Sometimes it is just put through the letter box in an envelope inscribed 'from an anonymous donor'. Then you know that someone's conscience is really biting.

Conze's second kind of concealed suffering is a pleasant experience which has a flavour of anxiety to it because you are afraid of losing it. Political power is like this: it is a very sweet thing to exercise power over other people, but you always have to watch your back, not knowing if you can trust even your best friend, or the very guardsmen at your door. All the time you are afraid of losing that power, especially if you have seized it by force, and others are waiting for their own chance to get their hands on it. In such a position you do not sleep easily.

The traditional Buddhist illustration of this kind of experience is that of a hawk flying off with a piece of meat in its talons. What happens, of course, is that dozens of other hawks fly after it to try and seize that piece of meat for themselves, and the way they accomplish this is to tear and stab not at the meat itself but at the possessor of the meat, pecking at its body, its wings, its head, its eyes.[46] The highly competitive world of finance and business and entertainment is like this. Any pleasure that involves any element of power or status is contaminated by an element of anxiety, by the sense that others would like to be able to replace you at the top of your own particular dunghill.

The third concealed suffering indicated by Dr Conze is something which is pleasant but which binds us to something else that brings about suffering. The example he gives is the human body. Through it we experience all sorts of pleasurable sensations that make us very attached to it; but we experience all sorts of unpleasant sensations through it as well. So our attachment to that which provides us with pleasant sensations binds us also to that which provides us with unpleasant sensations. We can't have the one without the other.

Lastly, Conze suggests that concealed suffering is to be found in the fact that pleasures derived from the experience of conditioned things cannot satisfy the deepest longings of the heart. In each one of us there is something that is *Un*conditioned, something that is *not* of this world, something transcendental, the Buddha-nature – call it what you like. Whatever you call it, you can recognize it by the fact that it cannot be satisfied by anything conditioned. It can be satisfied only by the Unconditioned.

So whatever conditioned things you may enjoy there is always a lack, a void, which only the Unconditioned can fill. Ultimately, it is for this reason that – to come back to the Buddha's conclusion – all conditioned things, whether actually or potentially, are unsatisfactory, painful. It is in the light of the Unconditioned that suffering, *duhkha*, is clearly seen as characteristic of all forms of conditioned existence, and of sentient conditioned existence especially.

IMPERMANENCE

The second fundamental characteristic of conditioned existence, *anitya*, is quite easily translated. *Nitya* is 'permanent', 'eternal', so with the addition of the negative prefix you get 'impermanent', 'non-eternal'. It is also quite easily understood – intellectually at least. It can hardly be denied that all conditioned things, all compounded things, are constantly changing. They are by definition made up of parts – that is, compounded. And that which is compounded, made up of parts, can also be uncompounded, can be reduced to its parts again – which is what happens, of course, all the time.

It should really be easier to understand this truth nowadays than it was in the Buddha's day. We now have the authority of science to assure us that there's no such thing as matter in the sense of actual lumps of hard solid matter scattered throughout space. We know that what we think of as matter is in reality only various forms of energy.

But the same great truth applies to the mind. There is nothing unchanging in our internal experience of ourselves, nothing permanent or immortal. There is only a constant succession of mental states, feelings, perceptions, volitions, acts of consciousness. In fact, the mind changes even more quickly than the physical body. We cannot usually see the physical body changing, but if we are observant we can see our mental states changing from moment to moment.

This is the reason for the Buddha's (at first sight) rather strange assertion that it is a bigger mistake to identify yourself (as a stable entity) with the mind than with the body.[47] But this is the Buddhist position. Belief in the reality of the 'self' is a bigger spiritual mistake than belief in the reality of the body. This is because the body at least possesses a certain relative stability; but there is no stability to the mind at all. It is constantly, perceptibly changing.

Broadly speaking, the *lakshana* of *anitya* points to the fact that the whole universe from top to bottom, in all its grandeur, in all its immensity, is just one vast congeries of processes of different types, taking place at different levels – and all interrelated. Nothing ever stands still, not even for an instant, not even for a fraction of a second.

We do not see this, though. When we look up we see the everlasting hills, and in the night sky we descry the same stars as were mapped by our ancestors at the dawn of history. Houses stand from generation to generation, and the old oak furniture within them seems to become more solid with the passing of the years. Even our own bodies seem much the same from one year to the next. It is only when the increments of change add up to something notable, when a great house is burnt down, when we realize that the star we are looking at is already extinct, or when we ourselves take to our deathbed, that we realize the truth of impermanence or non-eternity, that all conditioned things – from the minutest particles to the most massive stars – begin, continue, and then cease.

EMPTINESS OF SELF

The third *lakshana, anatman*, encapsulates the truth that all conditioned things are devoid of a permanent, unchanging self. So what does this mean exactly? When the Buddha denied the reality of the idea of the *atman*, what was he actually denying? What was the belief or doctrine of *atman* held by the Buddha's contemporaries, the Hindus of his day?

Actually, in the Upanishads alone there are many different conceptions of *atman* mentioned.[48] In some it is said that the *atman*, the self – or the soul, if you like – is the physical body. Elsewhere the view is propounded that the *atman* is just as big as the thumb, is material, and abides in the heart. But the most common view in the Buddha's day, the one with which he appears to have been most concerned, asserted that the *atman* was individual – in the sense that I am I and you are you – incorporeal or immaterial, conscious, unchanging, blissful, and sovereign – in the sense of exercising complete control over its own destiny.

The Buddha maintained that there was no such entity – and he did so by appealing to experience. He said that if you look within, at yourself, at your own mental life, you can account for everything you observe under just five headings: form, feeling, perception, volitions, and acts of consciousness. Nothing discovered in these categories can be observed to be permanent. There is nothing sovereign or ultimately blissful amongst them. Everything in them arises in dependence on conditions, and is unsatisfactory in one way or another. These five categories or aggregates are *anatman*. They don't constitute any such self as the Hindus of the Buddha's day asserted. Such a self exists neither in them nor outside of them nor associated with them in any other way.

THE THREE LIBERATIONS

Seeing conditioned existence, seeing life, in this way, as invariably subject to suffering, to impermanence, to emptiness of self, is called *vipashyana* (Sanskrit) or *vipassana* (Pali), which translates into English as 'insight'.

Insight is not just intellectual understanding. It can be developed only on the basis of a controlled, purified, elevated, concentrated, integrated mind – in other words, through meditative practice. Insight is a direct intuitive perception that takes place in the depths of meditation when the ordinary mental processes have fallen into abeyance. A preliminary intellectual understanding of these three characteristics is certainly helpful, but ultimately, insight is something that transcends the intellectual workings of the mind.

So in meditation, through insight, you see that without exception everything you experience through the five senses and through the mind – everything you can feel and touch and smell and taste and see and think about – is conditioned, is subject to suffering, is impermanent, is empty of self. When you see things in this way then you experience what is technically called revulsion or disgust, and you turn away from the conditioned. It is important to note that this is a spiritual experience, not just a psychological reaction; you turn away not because you are personally repelled by things as such, but because you see that the conditioned is not, on its own terms, worth having. When that turning away from the conditioned to the Unconditioned takes place decisively, it is said that you enter the 'stream' leading to nirvana.

At this point we have to guard against a misunderstanding. Some schools of Buddhism think of the conditioned and the Unconditioned as though they were two quite different entities, two ultimate principles in a kind of philosophical dualism. But it isn't like that. It isn't that on the one hand you have the conditioned and on the other you have the Unconditioned, with a sort of vast gap between them. They are more like two poles. Some Buddhist schools even say that the Unconditioned is the conditioned itself when the conditioned is seen in its ultimate depths, or in a new, higher dimension, as it were.[49] The Unconditioned is reached by knowing the conditioned deeply enough, by going right to the bottom of the conditioned and coming out the other side (so to speak). In other words, the conditioned and the Unconditioned are, in a way, the two sides of the same coin.

This perspective, which is a very important one to take in, is brought into focus by a teaching – common to all schools – called the three *vimokshas*, or 'liberations'.[50] They are also sometimes called the three *samadhis*, or the three 'doors': the three doors through which we can approach Enlightenment.

The first of these liberations is *apranihita*, the 'unaiming' or 'unbiased'. It is a mental state without any inclination in any direction, without likes or dislikes, perfectly still, perfectly poised. Thus it is an 'approach' to the Unconditioned, but it's an approach which is by way of not going in any particular direction. You only want to go in a particular direction when you have a concept of that direction and a desire to go in it. If there's no particular direction in which you want to go, then you just, as it were, stay at rest. This state can be compared to a perfectly round sphere on a perfectly flat plane. Because the plane is absolutely level, the perfect sphere doesn't roll in any particular direction. The *vimoksha* of directionlessness is rather like this. It's a state of absolute equanimity in which one has no egoistic motive for doing – or not doing, even – anything. So this is an avenue of approach to reality, to Enlightenment.

The second liberation, the second door to the Unconditioned, is *animitta*, the 'signless'. *Nimitta* literally means a sign, but it can also mean a word or a concept; so the *animitta* is the approach to the Unconditioned by bypassing all words and all thoughts. This is a very distinctive experience. When you have it, you realize that all words, all concepts, are totally inadequate. Not that they're not very adequate, but that actually they don't mean anything at all. This is another door through which one approaches the absolute, the Unconditioned. The *animitta* is a state in which one prescinds all concepts of reality. In other words, one doesn't think about reality. I don't mean that one 'doesn't think about it' in the ordinary way in which one doesn't think about reality. After all, we could say that most of us, most of the time, don't give much thought to reality at all. But on the attainment of this *vimoksha* one has, as it were, reached the level of reality but one doesn't think about reality. One realizes that no words, no concepts, can possibly apply; indeed, one doesn't even have the concept of non-applicability. This is the *vimoksha* or *samadhi* of signlessness or imagelessness.

And the third liberation is shunyata, the voidness or emptiness. In this state you see that everything is, as it were, completely transparent. Nothing has any own-being, nothing has any self-identity. In the language of the Perfection of Wisdom, the 'Prajnaparamita', things are what they are because they are *not* what they are – one can only express it paradoxically. This is the *vimoksha* of emptiness.

The three liberations represent different aspects of the Unconditioned; that is, they show the Unconditioned from different points of view, which are also different ways of realizing it. You can penetrate into the Unconditioned through the unbiased, through the signless, and through voidness. However, as we have already said, you attain the Unconditioned by knowing the conditioned in its depths. Thus we can also say that you penetrate to the three liberations through attention to the three *lakshanas*. That is, each of the three liberations can be reached through understanding deeply enough its corresponding *lakshana*. In this way the three *lakshanas* themselves can be seen as doors to liberation.

If you look deeply enough at the essentially unsatisfactory nature of conditioned existence, then you will realize the Unconditioned as being without bias. This is because when you see the suffering inherent in conditioned things, you lose interest in the goals and aims and purposes of conditioned existence. You are quite still and poised, without inclination towards this or that, without any desire or direction for yourself. Hence when you go into the conditioned through the aspect of suffering you go into the Unconditioned through the aspect of the unbiased.

Alternatively, when you concentrate on the conditioned as being impermanent, transitory, without fixed identity, then going to the bottom of that – and coming out the other side, so to speak – you realize the Unconditioned as the signless. Your realization is of the emptiness of all concepts, you transcend all thought; you realize, if you like, 'the eternal'

– though not the eternal that continues through time, but the eternal which transcends time.

And thirdly, if you concentrate on the conditioned as devoid of self, devoid of individuality, devoid of I, devoid of you, devoid of me, devoid of mine, then you approach, you realize, the Unconditioned as shunyata, as the voidness. What 'the voidness' is, we shall be going on to consider.

As for the present chapter, however, our aim has been to throw some light on the subject of the three *lakshanas*, the three characteristics of conditioned existence. They are of central importance not just in Buddhist philosophy but in the Buddhist spiritual life. According to the Buddha, we don't really see conditioned existence until we learn to see it in these terms. If we see anything else, that's just an illusion, just a projection. And once we start seeing the conditioned as essentially unsatisfactory, impermanent, and empty of self, then little by little we begin to get a glimpse of the *Un*conditioned, a glimpse that is our essential guide on the Buddhist path.

4

NIRVANA

THE FIRST QUESTION Buddhists get asked when they meet non-Buddhists is, as likely as not, 'What is nirvana?' Certainly, when I was a Buddhist monk travelling about India, I used to find on trains that no sooner had I taken my seat than someone would come up to me (for in India people are by no means bashful when it comes to getting into conversation) and say, 'You seem to be a Buddhist monk. Please tell me – what is nirvana?'

Indeed, it is a very appropriate question to ask. The question is, after all, addressing the whole point of being a Buddhist. You may see Buddhists engaged in all sorts of different activities, but they all have the same overall purpose in view. You may see shaven-headed Japanese monks in their long black robes sitting in disciplined rows, meditating hour after hour in the silence and tranquillity of a Zen monastery. You may see ordinary Tibetans going in the early morning up the steps of the temples, carrying their flowers and their candles and their bundles of incense sticks, kneeling down and making their offerings, chanting verses of praise to the Buddha, the Dharma, and the Sangha, and then going about their daily business. You may see Sri Lankan monks poring over palm-leaf manuscripts, the pages brown with age. You may see layfolk in the Theravadin countries of South-east Asia giving alms to the monks when they come round with their black begging-bowls. You may see Western Buddhists working together in Right Livelihood businesses.

When you see unfolded this whole vast panorama of Buddhist activities, the question that arises is: Why? What is the reason for it all? What is the moving spirit, the great impulse behind all this activity? What are all these people trying to do? What are they trying to achieve through their meditation, their worshipping, their study, their alms-giving, their work, and so on?

If you asked this of any of these people, you would probably receive the traditional answer: 'We're doing this for the sake of the attainment of nirvana, liberation, Enlightenment.' But what then is this nirvana? How is it to be understood, explained? How is it to be fitted in to one's own particular range of mental furniture? One naturally gropes after analogies, of course. If one has a Christian background one will try to envisage nirvana as a sort of eternal life in heaven after death. If one takes it outside the usual religious framework altogether, one may even think of it as a state of complete annihilation or extinction.

But in fact there is no excuse for these kinds of badly mistaken views. It is not really difficult to give a clear account of nirvana, because the ancient canonical texts are pretty clear as to what it is and what it isn't. If one does have the job of presenting the topic of nirvana, one will probably need to begin by discussing the etymology of the word *nirvana* – whether it means a 'blowing out' or whether it means a 'cooling down'. And one will no doubt go on to explain that, according to the Pali texts at least, nirvana consists in the extinction of all craving, all hatred, and all ignorance of the true nature of things.[51]

At some point it is customary to say that nirvana is a state of incomparable bliss, to which the bliss of this world cannot be compared.[52] And if one wants to get a bit technical one may want to describe the two kinds of nirvana: the *klesha nirvana*, consisting in the extinction of all passions and defilements; and the *skandha nirvana*, consisting in the extinction of all the various processes of psychophysical existence, an event that takes place upon the death – as we call it – of someone who has already gained *klesha nirvana* during their lifetime.[53]

One may then go on to the different interpretations of nirvana in the various different schools of Buddhism – the Theravada, the Madhyamaka, the Yogachara, the Tantra, Zen, and so on. Finally, it is always necessary to emphasize that nirvana is neither eternal life in the Christian sense, nor annihilation or extinction in the materialist sense – that here, as elsewhere, one has to follow the middle path between two extreme views.

So this is how nirvana is traditionally delineated. Above all, perhaps, nirvana is conventionally defined as the *goal* of Buddhism. And it is in respect of this particular way of positioning the concept that my approach in this chapter will appear to some people – mistakenly, in my view – to be perhaps rather unorthodox.

THE PSYCHOLOGY OF GOAL-SETTING

There are all kinds of groups of people in the world – religious groups, political groups, cultural groups, charitable groups, and so on – and each of these groups has its goal, be it power, or wealth, or some other satisfaction, and whether it is for their own good or the good of others. And it would seem that Buddhists likewise have their own particular goal that they call nirvana. So let us look at what is meant by this idea of a goal to be attained or realized, and then establish to what extent it is applicable to nirvana.

It should be clear at once where this procedure is going to lead us. The fact is that whenever terms get to be used rather loosely, without any lucid consideration of what they mean, you get the beginnings of serious misunderstandings. This is particularly the case when we transfer terms and expressions derived from mundane experience, like 'goal', to spiritual or transcendental experience, like 'nirvana'. If they don't quite fit then we need to be aware of this, and if they don't fit at all, then we need to think through the whole question afresh.

With this in mind, let us examine the idea of a 'goal' a bit more closely. A goal is an objective, it is something you strive for. You could, if you like, draw a distinction between striving to *be* and striving to *have*. But actually, the two come to the same thing: 'having' is a sort of vicarious 'being'. A goal is in the end something that you want to *be*. Suppose, for instance, your goal is wealth: you can say that your goal is to *possess* wealth, or that your goal is to *be* wealthy, but obviously the possessing, the having, is reducible to the being, the existing.

There is one really crucial (if obvious) precondition for setting a goal: it must represent something you aren't. You don't want to have or to be what you already have or are. You can only want to be what you aren't – which suggests, obviously, that you're dissatisfied with what you are. If you're not dissatisfied with what you are, you will never strive to be what you aren't.

Suppose, just by way of example, your goal happens to be money and material possessions. Well, you will have made these things your goal because you're dissatisfied with being poor. Or if, say, you make knowledge your goal, if you want to add to your understanding, investigate fundamental principles, and so on, then you want to do this because you're dissatisfied with your present state of being ignorant.

We don't always see it in quite these stark terms, but this is the basic pattern or procedure involved in setting ourselves goals; and it is a quite appropriate way of proceeding on its own level. But we get into a tangle when we extend it into the spiritual life – and by this I don't mean some elevated sphere of experience far removed from everyday concerns. By the spiritual life I mean something very close to home.

Any complex of problems we may have can be boiled down to the most basic problem of all, which is unhappiness in one form or another. A case of bad temper, for example, is a problem because it makes us miserable, and one could equally well say the opposite, that being miserable makes us bad-tempered. Even though we don't usually think of the problem we have as one of unhappiness as such, that is what, in the end, it is.

So we try to get away from unhappiness and attain happiness. The way we go about this is to try to ricochet, as it were, from that experience of feeling miserable or discontented into an opposite state or experience of feeling happy; and this usually involves grasping at some object or experience that we believe will give us the happiness we seek.

When we feel unhappy, what we do is set up this goal of happiness, which we strive to achieve. And as we all know, we fail. All our lives through, in one way or another, we are in search of happiness. No one is in search of misery. No one is in search of unhappiness. Everyone is in search of happiness. There's no one who could possibly say they're so happy that they couldn't imagine themselves being a little happier. Most people, if they're honest with themselves, have to admit that their life consists of a fluctuating state of unease and dissatisfaction, punctuated by moments of happiness and joy which make them temporarily forget their discomfort and discontent.

But this possibility of being happy becomes everybody's goal – a goal which can never be realized because happiness is by its nature fleeting. We all continue to set up this phantom goal, however, because the alternative is too challenging for us. The alternative is simply to be aware.

The setting up of goals – which means trying to get away from one's present experience – is really a substitute for awareness, for self-knowledge. Even if we do develop a measure of self-knowledge, we don't tend to maintain it because to do so would be just too threatening. We always end up setting up goals rather than continuing to be aware.

To take a simple example, suppose I have something of a problem with my temper: I get irritated, even angry, rather easily – even a small thing can spark me off – and this bad temper of mine makes life difficult, and perhaps miserable for myself and others. And suppose that I wake up one day and decide that enough is enough, that it's time it came to a stop. What do I do? I set up a goal for myself – the goal of being good-tempered. I think 'Well, here I am now – I'm undeniably bad-tempered: my goal, however, is to be sweet-tempered and amiable, always returning the soft answer, always ready to turn the other cheek.'

What actually happens, though? One almost invariably fails. The intention – even the degree of self-knowledge – is admirable. But after a while one's resolve falters. In the face of the same old provocations, one is back again in the same old rut – and probably blaming the same old people and the same old external circumstances for it. So why is this? Anybody who has ever begun to recognize that their problems are, at least to a degree, of their own making will also recognize that this is what happens. But why does it happen?

The reason is that we are continuing to tackle the symptoms rather than the disease. If we try to get away from our unhappiness simply by trying to be good-humoured, we are still unaware of the fundamental cause of our being bad-tempered. And if this isn't resolved, if we don't know why we are bad-tempered, if we don't know what is prompting the angry answer or the violent reaction, then we can't possibly hope to become good-tempered.

Whatever our problem, we automatically – almost instinctively – set up a goal of being happy in order to get away from our unhappiness. Even if a little awareness, a little insight, does arise, it is not sustained. We revert automatically to setting up a goal of one kind or another rather than continuing to be aware, and trying to understand very deeply why that problem arises. Setting up goals is an automatic reflex to short-circuit the development of awareness and self-knowledge – in short, to get away from ourselves.

How then do we change this? To start with, we need a change of attitude. Rather than trying to escape from ourselves, we need to begin to acknowledge the reality of what we are. We need to understand – and not just intellectually – why we are what we are. If we are suffering, well, we don't just reach out for a chocolate. We need to recognize the fact that we suffer and look at it more and more deeply. Or – as the case may be –

if we're happy we need to recognize that fully, take it in more and more deeply. Instead of running from it into guilt, or into some sort of excitable intoxication, we need to understand why, what the true nature of that happiness is, where it really comes from. And again, this isn't just intellectual; it's something that has to go very deep down indeed.

For some people this sort of understanding, this sort of penetration or insight, will come in the course of meditation. Meditation isn't just fixing the mind on an object, or revolving a certain idea in the mind. Meditation really involves – among other things – getting down to the bedrock of the mind, illuminating the mind from the bottom upwards, as it were. It is about exposing to oneself one's motives, the deep-seated causes of one's mental states, one's experiences, one's joy and one's suffering, and so on. In this way real growth in awareness will come about.

But where is all this leading? What has all this to do with nirvana? It may seem that we have strayed rather from our subject, but in fact we have been doing some necessary preparing of the ground. With some things, if one tackles them too directly, one can easily miss the mark. What we can now do is open up some kind of perspective on the way nirvana is traditionally described – or rather on the effect on us of these traditional descriptions.

Suppose, for example, I have been going through rather a difficult, upsetting period, and am feeling rather miserable. Then one day I pick up a book in which it is stated that nirvana is the supreme happiness, the supreme bliss. What will be my reaction? The likelihood is that I will think, 'Good – that's just what I want – bliss, happiness.' I will make nirvana my goal. And what this means is that effectively I will be making lack of awareness my goal. I will be latching on to nirvana – labelled as the supreme bliss – because it happens to fit in with my subjective needs and feelings at this particular time. Such a reaction has of course nothing to do with being a Buddhist, but it is the way that a lot of us approach Buddhism, and indeed use Buddhism, in a quite unaware, almost automatic way. Unconsciously we try to use nirvana to settle problems which can only really be resolved through awareness.

We do not succeed in banishing unhappiness by pretending to ourselves that we are happy, by shoving our misery out of sight. The first step is to acknowledge the reality of our condition: if there is an underlying unhappiness to our lives, we must face up to the fact. It is certainly good to be cheerful and positive, but not at the expense of fooling ourselves. One has only to look at the faces of the people you see in any city to see the 'marks of weakness, marks of woe'[54] that William Blake saw in

London two hundred years ago, and yet few people will admit to their misery even in their own minds.

No progress can be made till we come to terms with our actual experience, till we get to know our unhappiness in all its comings and goings, till we learn to live with it, and study it. What is it, at bottom, that makes us unhappy? What is its source? We will get nowhere by looking for a way out of our misery, by aiming for the goal of happiness, or even nirvana. It is a mistake, at least, to postulate the goal of nirvana too quickly or too unconsciously. All we can do is try to see more and more clearly and distinctly what it is in ourselves that is making us unhappy. This is the only way that nirvana will be attained.

In this sense nirvana cannot be seen as an escape from unhappiness at all. It is by trying too hard to escape from unhappiness that we fail to do so. The real key is awareness, self-knowledge. One way – a paradoxical way – of putting it would be to say that the goal of Buddhism consists in being completely and totally aware at all levels of your need to reach a goal. We can also say, going a little further, that nirvana consists in the full and complete awareness of why you want to reach nirvana at all. If you understand completely why you want to reach nirvana, then you've reached nirvana. We can go further even than this. We can even say that the unaware person is in need of nirvana, but is unable to get a true idea of it. An aware person, on the other hand, is quite clear about this goal, but doesn't need it. That's really the position.

So there we have the basic drawback to conventional accounts of nirvana as being this or that. We simply accept or reject this or that aspect of nirvana in accordance with our own largely unconscious needs. If the underlying – and therefore unconscious – drive of our existence is towards pleasure, then we will find ourselves responding to the idea of nirvana as the supreme bliss. If on the other hand we are emotionally driven by a fundamental need to know, to understand, to see what is really going on, then almost automatically we will make our goal a state of complete illumination. And again, if we feel oppressed or constrained by life, if our childhood was one of control and confinement, or if we have a sense that our options in life are restricted by our particular circumstances – by poverty, by being tied down to a job or a family, or looking after elderly relatives – then we will be drawn to the idea of nirvana as freedom, as emancipation.

In this way there takes place a half-conscious setting up of goals based on our own psychological or social conditioning, instead of a growing understanding of *why* we feel dissatisfied, *why* we feel somehow 'in the dark', or *why* we feel tied down. Nirvana becomes simply a projection of our own mundane needs.

Hence when we consider the subject of nirvana, the goal of Buddhism, the question we should be asking is not 'What is nirvana?' but 'Why am I interested in nirvana? Why am I reading this book rather than another, or rather than, say, watching television?' Is it curiosity, is it duty, is it vanity, is it just to see how Sangharakshita is going to tackle this thorny topic? Or is it something deeper?

Even these questions will not settle the matter. If it is curiosity, well, why are we curious about nirvana? If it is duty, towards what or whom do we really feel dutiful? If it is vanity, why do we want to preen ourselves in this particular way? What is underneath our interest? If there is something deeper in our motivation, what is it?

This line of questioning might appear unconventional or unorthodox, and in pursuing it we may not learn much about Buddhism or nirvana in the purely objective, historical sense. But we will learn a great deal about what the ideas of Buddhism actually represent. If we follow this particular line, constantly trying to penetrate to the depths of our own mind, we may even get a little nearer to the goal of nirvana itself.

Sometimes we just have to reverse our whole attitude. In the case of this great subject of nirvana, the abstract, ontological approach is of little use on its own. We have to start examining our own relationship to nirvana in the way we conceive of it. This is much more likely to bring us nearer to a deeper awareness, and thus to nirvana, than any amount of purely metaphysical or psychological disquisition. It may also prepare us for something even more profound and important than nirvana itself – the mystery of the void.

5

THE MYSTERY OF THE VOID

PRIMITIVE CHRISTIANITY was a religion not of dogma but of 'mysteries' – and indeed the Eastern Orthodox churches still speak of the mysteries of Christianity. Easter, for example, is a celebration of such a mystery, commemorating, according to Christian tradition and belief, the crucifixion and the resurrection of Christ.

The majority of orthodox, practising Christians take both these events in the same literal sense. They believe that Christ was resurrected in the same physical, historical way in which he was crucified, and that he subsequently ascended into heaven, together with his flesh, blood, and bones, and all that appertains thereto. Most practising Christians believe that the whole of his psychophysical organism went up into heaven quite literally and physically, and sat down, presumably on a physical seat, at the right hand of the Father.

Buddhists do not of course believe this. Whereas the crucifixion may actually have occurred, the resurrection and the ascension, from a Buddhist perspective, are most certainly myths. This is not to say that these myths are not true. When I say that the resurrection, and indeed the crucifixion, are essentially or primarily myths, I don't mean that they are not true. I mean rather that whatever truth they possess is spiritual rather than scientific or historical.

Thus from a Buddhist point of view the crucifixion, the resurrection, the whole festival of Easter in fact, represents a spiritual rebirth after a spiritual death. It represents a triumphant emergence of a new mode of being, even a new mode of awareness, from the old. We may even say that it represents – in Zen Buddhist terms – dying the great death before one can attain the great Enlightenment.[55]

The festival of Easter is, in its origins, a pagan festival. It takes place in the spring, when the trees are bursting into new leaf, when we begin to hear the birds singing again after they have been silent during the long winter months. According to the Venerable Bede, in his *Ecclesiastical History of the English People*, the word 'Easter' is from an old Anglo-Saxon word *eostre*, which he says was the name of a pre-Christian, British goddess – presumably a fertility goddess. And of course there is no biblical warrant for the giving of Easter eggs. The egg, the unbroken egg, is a universal symbol of life, especially of new, renascent life. It is a symbol of resurrection in the widest sense, found in practically all religious traditions.

For example, in Etruscan tomb paintings dating back to 1000BCE the dead are often depicted on the walls of their own tombs reclining on classical couches and holding in their outstretched hands an egg, a symbol of their belief that death was not the end, but would be followed by a new life. The same symbol is found in Buddhist literary sources. The Bodhisattva, the one who is fully dedicated to the attainment of Enlightenment for the sake of all beings, is spoken of by the Buddha in Mahayana scriptures as one who is in the process of emerging from the eggshell of ignorance.

So the mystery of Easter has meaning for all of us if we are sensitive to the many overtones of the festival, even though the crudely literal interpretation of its myths is still officially entertained, and makes it impossible for Buddhists to celebrate it as Christians do. The festival of Easter is a mystery because its myths represent not a doctrine or a philosophy or a dogma but an experience, something essentially incommunicable, a mystery. In its universality, it is the greatest of Christian mysteries.

Buddhism also has its mysteries. And perhaps the greatest of them, the one that represents most uncompromisingly an essentially incommunicable experience, is the mystery of the void, or – in Sanskrit – shunyata. 'Voidness', or 'emptiness' – or even, in Guenther's rendering, 'nothingness' – is an exact translation of shunyata. One could even translate it as 'zero': in modern Indian languages zero in the mathematical sense is *shunya*. But all these more or less literal, philologically correct translations can be most misleading, as we shall see.

Shunyata is a deep mystery not just because it's an abstruse theory or a difficult doctrine or a particularly involved piece of Buddhist philosophy. It's a mystery because it's not a theory or a doctrine or a philosophy at all. One might even say that it's not just a mystery; it's 'a riddle wrapped in a mystery inside an enigma' (to borrow Churchill's famous characterization of Soviet policy). Shunyata or 'voidness' or 'emptiness' is just the word that we use to label an experience – a spiritual, even a transcendental, experience – which we have no way of describing. It is a mystery because it is incommunicable. To speak of shunyata as though it were a doctrine, a theory, a philosophy, and nothing more than that, is a catastrophic mistake, because it precludes all possibility of greater understanding.

There is undeniably a doctrine of shunyata, even a theory or philosophy of shunyata. But we need to remember that these conceptual formulations, like all the others of the Buddhist tradition, are simply for the purposes of communication between the Enlightened (those who have the experience of shunyata) and the unenlightened (those who do not have any such experience). That is to say, they represent, in the first place – historically speaking – the Buddha's communication of his experience to his immediate disciples. And, as well as designating the truth of the Buddha's experience, they all, from within their own different contexts, point the way by which we may ourselves experience that truth. All these so-called doctrines, all these formulations, are just components of the 'raft' whose sole purpose is to take us across the waters of birth and death, across the flood of conditioned existence, to the shore of nirvana. They have no significance apart from that function. They are means to an end, not ends in themselves.

This is something that must always be borne in mind when studying Buddhism, especially in an information-consuming culture like ours. Whatever we may learn about Buddhism, and particularly about the 'philosophy' of shunyata, it is always essentially a mystery, something to be experienced in the equal mystery of one's own personal spiritual life.

However, it must be said that for something that is so quintessentially a matter of experience, shunyata has been the subject of an extraordinary wealth and depth of Buddhist literary treatment. In fact, those scriptures devoted to the investigation of shunyata, known as the Perfection of Wisdom sutras, together represent probably the most important single body of Mahayana canonical literature.

There are thirty-odd Perfection of Wisdom sutras in all, some running to several volumes, while others are very short. The most famous of these are the *Diamond* or *Vajrachchhedika Sutra*, and the *Hridaya* or *Heart Sutra*, both of which are quite short and are recited daily in the Zen monasteries of Japan, and frequently in Tibetan monasteries as well.[56]

But all these sutras, whether they are famous or obscure, deal basically with just one topic: shunyata, the void, emptiness. Furthermore, they all deal with it in basically the same way: not logically, not metaphysically, but as a direct spiritual experience. Most of these texts are presented – as other sutras are – in the form of discourses given by the Buddha, who speaks out of the depths of his own transcendental experience.

They are called Perfection of Wisdom sutras because it is by means of the spiritual faculty of the Perfection of Wisdom, or *prajna,* that the truth of shunyata is perceived (or rather intuited). Or, to put it a little more correctly (that is, less dualistically) *prajna,* the Perfection of Wisdom, represents the subjective pole, and shunyata the objective pole, of what is essentially the same non-dual experience.

However, it would be a mistake to imagine that, because we are talking about 'an experience', we are dealing with something simple or single. What we call shunyata consists of a whole vast spectrum of experiences. Any Tibetan monk should be able to rattle off the names of no less than thirty-two kinds of shunyata, and will be expected to study them as well.

And not only the monks, as I learnt from a friend of mine in Kalimpong (a town in the foothills of the Himalayas where I lived during the 1950s). This gentleman had been at one time governor of the region of Gyantse in Tibet, and he was married to the eldest daughter of the Maharaja of Sikkim, Princess Pema Tsedeun. And I remember her on a certain occasion saying (very good-humouredly), 'When we're in Lhasa my husband is never at home. He's always in the monasteries discussing Buddhism with the lamas. I hardly ever see him.' Intrigued, I said to him, 'Well, what is it that you like to discuss with the lamas?' He thought for a moment, and then said, 'Well, usually, after we've worked through this and that, what we really like to get down to – and sometimes we go on all night – is a discussion on the thirty-two kinds of voidness.' (So one knows where to look first for a husband who is out all night in Lhasa.)

However, to begin with it is probably reasonable enough to confine oneself to just four – the principal and most important – of these thirty-two kinds of shunyata. These four are not literally four different kinds of shunyata as you might have four different kinds of cabbage or daffodil. They really represent four successive stages in our experience of the mystery of the void, four pin-pointings in a continuous ever-deepening experience of reality.[57]

THE VOIDNESS OF THE CONDITIONED

This is the first of the four shunyatas: *samskrita-shunyata*, literally 'emptiness of the conditioned'. To understand this we must appreciate the basic Buddhist distinction between conditioned reality (that which is dependent upon causes and conditions) and Unconditioned reality (that which is not so dependent). Conditioned reality is existence as we know it on this earth, and it is to be recognized by its three fundamental characteristics: it is unsatisfactory, impermanent, and devoid of unchanging individuality or self.

Unconditioned reality (i.e. nirvana), by contrast, has the opposite characteristics – though these are not all quite the opposite characteristics that one might expect. The first of these is straightforward enough: Unconditioned reality is supremely blissful. The second is of course that Unconditioned reality is eternal – though this characteristic should be understood not in the sense of being everlasting within time, but in the sense of transcending time altogether. As for the third, if the conditioned is devoid of self, then the Unconditioned should, of course, be characterized by self. But here there is a difference among the Buddhist schools – albeit largely a difference of terminology.

The Theravadins, for instance, say that not only is the conditioned devoid of self; the Unconditioned, nirvana, is also devoid of self. This voidness of self is obviously not quite the same thing in both cases, but the distinction is not always made clear. Some of the Mahayana schools indeed speak of the Unconditioned in terms of selfhood, – as *maha-atma*, the 'great self',[58] or in the Zen tradition, as the 'true' or 'real' self.

Theravadins usually object strongly to this procedure – and with some justification. There is a very great and real danger of hypostasizing the self, when ultimately one wants to get completely rid of any sense of a separate self whatsoever. Even though it may in a sense be quite legitimate to speak of a higher or greater self – at least in a poetic way – there always remains the danger that instead of aiming at sloughing off the sense of self, one will simply be substituting one self for another, replacing a comparatively gross ego with a more subtle, refined self.

At the same time it is important to bear in mind that all positive predications about nirvana are necessarily analogous: none of them are to be taken literally. We may speak of nirvana as the 'supreme bliss', *nirvanam paramam sukham*,[59] but it's certainly not bliss as we understand it, not by any stretch of the imagination. Not even if we multiply the bliss with which we are acquainted a hundred or a thousand times will we get even the shadow of an idea of what the bliss of nirvana is really like. We're using the term 'bliss' analogously.

By the same token it should be possible to use the word 'self' in the same way, and this is what the Mahayanists do. They don't do it very often, and when they do, they do so very circumspectly. They also have some canonical authority for doing it. The Buddha is to be found in several Mahayana sutras speaking of nirvana as the 'great self' – in, for instance, the *Mahaparinirvana Sutra* (not to be confused with the *Mahaparinibbana Sutta* of the Pali Canon).[60] But in fact the term *maha-atma* can also be tracked down in the Pali Canon. It has been located in a verse from the *Anguttara-Nikaya*, the collection of 'gradual sayings', in which (in its Pali form *maha-atta*) it is used in quite a favourable sense, again as a provisional sort of designation for nirvana.

The Tantras of course go even further than the Mahayana: not only the 'great self', but even the 'great passion' and the 'great anger', appear as synonyms for Enlightenment. This has to be understood in a rather esoteric sense – such terms are employed within a certain traditionally prescribed framework or context, where they may be positively effective rather than dangerous. In the West, where there is not yet a secure tradition in place, there may well be some danger of misunderstanding these usages.

So much for the vexed question of *anatman* or non-self as a characteristic of conditioned existence, and as a different sort of characteristic of nirvana. But we can now begin to see what the emptiness of the conditioned amounts to. Life as we know it, conditioned reality, is empty of the Unconditioned and its attributes. Bliss, permanence, and true selfhood are not to be found in this world, and if we want these things then we have to look beyond this world, we have to look up to a higher dimension of reality. The 'voidness of the conditioned' is in the fact that it is void of the Unconditioned.

THE VOIDNESS OF THE UNCONDITIONED

If the conditioned is empty of the Unconditioned, what is the Unconditioned empty of? Well, it's obvious really: the Unconditioned is empty of the conditioned. In the Unconditioned, in nirvana, there's no suffering, no impermanence, no false selfhood – it is empty of these things. This is the second of the four shunyatas: *asamskrita-shunyata*, 'voidness of the Unconditioned' – which consists in the fact that it is void of the conditioned.

The Unconditioned is also 'the transcendental'. This is not an ideal expression, but it does duty more or less adequately for the Sanskrit and Pali word *lokuttara*. *Loka* means 'world' and *uttara* 'higher' or 'beyond', hence the transcendental is simply that which is above, or beyond, the world. It is not above or beyond in any spatial sense; only in the sense that it is not conditioned. It's beyond all suffering, beyond transience, beyond the sense of self (at least, beyond a false sense of self). It's above and beyond anything we can think of, anything we can imagine or begin to conceive. Contemplating it, the mind stalls and fails. It is almost as if there is only a great blank before us, an unconfined and inapprehensible plenitude.

This is the Unconditioned, the transcendental reality, the goal of the spiritual life, of the *ariyaparyesana*, the 'noble quest' of the conditioned for the Unconditioned. And surely one can't go beyond, or higher, or above, or further than that. Well, as far as some schools of Buddhism are concerned, one can't. The schools of what is called the classical Hinayana – the Sarvastivada – operate with the idea of two mutually exclusive realities, the conditioned and the Unconditioned, a differentiation that provides most of us, if not practically all of us, with a quite adequate basis for our spiritual lives. But the Mahayana, in the Perfection of Wisdom literature, goes even further than this.

THE GREAT VOID

This is the third shunyata: *maha-shunyata*. It is the emptiness of the very distinction between conditioned and Unconditioned, between the world and the transcendental, samsara and nirvana. With this stage we experience and realize that the distinction upon which our whole spiritual life has so far been based is in the ultimate analysis only mind-made, mind-created. It's only a concept, a conceptual distinction, not a real one. All things, the conditioned and the Unconditioned, are equally shunyata. They are all the same voidness, all the same emptiness, all the same *great* shunyata. This *maha-shunyata* embraces within itself all opposites, all distinctions whatsoever.

According to the Perfection of Wisdom teachings all things whatsoever, whether great or small, high or low, pure or impure, Enlightened or unenlightened, all beings whatsoever, are all of them the same unique, ineffable, absolute reality, within which there are no distinctions whatsoever. Not that distinctions are wiped out or obliterated; but they are provisional, not final or ultimate. Thus this teaching takes a very lofty viewpoint – not actually our own viewpoint at all. But it shows us what our viewpoint might ultimately be.

THE VOIDNESS OF VOIDNESS

Shunyata-shunyata, the emptiness of emptiness, is the final, and in some ways most important, level of voidness. It reminds us that emptiness is in the last analysis itself only an operative concept. It's not just the conditioned that is empty, it's not just the Unconditioned that is empty – but even absolute Emptiness, even the Great Void, is itself empty. It is not a final doctrine or dogma to cling on to at the last. It too must be abandoned.

According to the great dialectician of the Madhyamaka school, Nagarjuna, the whole teaching – or rather experience – of shunyata is intended as a medicine for the cure of all possible attachments, whether to the conditioned or to the Unconditioned. It's meant to cure every form of attachment to self, from the most gross to the most subtle, whether it is to the little ego or to the great self. He says that if we then become attached to shunyata itself we have infected the very medicine that should cure us. If the medicine itself becomes poison, our case is hopeless.

So we have to tread very carefully. Nagarjuna goes as far as to say, 'Better be attached to a self as high as Mount Sumeru, than be attached to the idea of shunyata.'[61] If you're attached to the idea of a self, you can always be cured with the medicine of shunyata. But if you're attached to shunyata itself – well, there is no medicine to cure that. And when we begin to consider shunyata as a dogma, or doctrine, or concept, or even as an experience, then we begin to settle down with it, to be attached to it. Therefore we must step warily indeed.

Emptiness is beyond even emptiness. Emptiness cannot even be expressed in terms of emptiness. This is the voidness of voidness, *shunyata-shunyata*. In the end the most appropriate mode of expressing oneself in respect of the fourth kind of shunyata is to give up long and elaborate explanations and commentaries and sub-commentaries, and to say nothing at all. One may be as eloquent and insightful as one likes, but shunyata will always remain ultimately a mystery, even the greatest of all mysteries, so far as the Buddha's teaching is concerned. It cannot be explained or even described.

The idea of writing a neat little chapter on the subject, or giving a smooth, well-rounded lecture on it, is really quite ridiculous. At best one can offer broken hints, little suggestions, and just point in its general direction as one would point a finger at the moon. And if we make sure that we do not mistake the finger for the moon, if we do not take these hints and suggestions too literally, then some of them may help to nudge us towards the actual experience of shunyata, which is conterminous with the experience of supreme Enlightenment itself.

In this way we develop the experience of shunyata to the point at which words can serve no further useful purpose at all. We begin with our experience of the emptiness of the world. This is the deep realization of the fact that the mundane, the world as we know it, contains nothing, quite literally nothing – *repeat, nothing* – of ultimate interest or real value.

Because this world is empty, one directs one's attention to the transcendental, the Unconditioned. One becomes absorbed in it (as it were) and one finds to one's delight that it is empty of everything mundane. What one found in the world one doesn't find here. In the world there was suffering; here one finds bliss. In the world there was impermanence; here one finds eternity. In the world there was no true individual self; here, by losing oneself, one finds one's true individuality.

Eventually one gets to be so absorbed in the Unconditioned that one forgets all about the conditioned. And then one becomes so absorbed in the Unconditioned itself that one forgets all about the Unconditioned. And having forgotten about the conditioned and the Unconditioned, one loses all sense of distinction between the conditioned and the Unconditioned, the mundane and the transcendental. And after that (though in this realization of the nature of reality there is of course no such distinction as 'before' and 'after') one arrives at a state (though it is no 'state' at all) which may be expressed and communicated only by silence. In that silence one experiences the mystery of the void.

PART 2: THE PATH

6

THE GRAVITATIONAL PULL AND THE POINT OF NO RETURN

THE LAST OF THE Indian patriarchs, as reckoned by the Zen school, was Bodhidharma, the founding father of Ch'an or Zen in China. And when he went to China his reputation seems to have preceded him. In those days – we are talking about the fifth or sixth century CE – great Indian scholars and sages would travel every now and then from India, where Buddhism began, to China, where it was just beginning to take root, and people were very interested to meet them and learn something about Buddhism. And it seems that the Emperor of China of those days was quite an ardent Buddhist, though in rather a conventional sense – that is to say he built and endowed monasteries, allowed monks to be ordained (because in those days imperial permission was necessary if one wanted to enter the Order), and generally busied himself with the outward forms of Buddhism.

So when the Emperor came to hear that Bodhidharma, the great Indian sage, had just arrived in China, he was very eager to meet him and talk with him. An invitation was issued without delay, and before long Bodhidharma found himself being ushered into the palace and into the Emperor's presence. And the Emperor apparently wasted no time in getting to the point. He had a rather academic sort of mind, and he was well trained in Buddhist philosophy. He therefore said to Bodhidharma, 'Tell me in just a few words the fundamental principle of Buddhism, upon which everything else is based, from which everything else follows.' And then he sat back and waited to hear what the great sage would come up with.

Bodhidharma said very calmly, very quietly, 'It's quite simple.' He didn't say, 'This being, that becomes', although, as we have seen, that's one answer to the question. Instead he recited a Pali *gatha* or 'verse' from the *Dhammapada*:

sabbapapassa akaranam
kusalassa upasampada
sachittapariyodapanam
etam buddhana sasanam.

which means 'Abstention from all evil, the doing of good, purification of the heart – this is the teaching of the Buddhas.'[62]

When the Emperor heard this he could not conceal his disappointment. 'Is that all?' he demanded. And Bodhidharma matter-of-factly replied, 'Yes, your majesty, that is all.' But the Emperor just couldn't believe it. He said, 'Are you sure? Simply ceasing to do evil, learning to do good, purifying your heart – is there no more to Buddhism than that?' And Bodhidharma said, 'There's really no more to it than that.' So the Emperor, who had apparently expected some abstruse disquisition on Buddhist philosophy, said, 'But even a three-year-old child could understand that.' Bodhidharma replied, 'True. Even a child of three could understand it. But even an old man of eighty cannot put it into practice.'

And that's the difference. That is the degree of incommensurability, as it were, between the theory and the practice of Buddhism. The theory is one thing, the practice is another. Most students of Buddhism, especially in Western countries, are, it has to be said, rather like the Emperor. When confronted with something apparently simple to put into practice, they often say, or at least think to themselves, 'Is that all?' They want a long, learned, elaborate lecture, something they can really get their teeth into intellectually, discuss with their friends, and so on.

Of course, the Buddhist tradition has come up with many more detailed descriptions of the path of Buddhist practice than the terse statement with which Bodhidharma confronted the Emperor. In this part of the book we will be considering the Dharma as path or teaching: the twelve links of the spiral path; the Noble Eightfold Path; the seven factors of Enlightenment; the seven stages of purification; the simplest expression of the path, the Threefold Path; and the six perfections of the Bodhisattva. Although the emphasis is different in each case, these are really all different ways of putting the same thing: the path to Enlightenment. But whichever one tries to practise, sooner or later – and usually sooner – one bumps into the problem that Bodhidharma was so quick to point out. The theory is fine – but why can't we put it into practice? What is it that obstructs our efforts? Why is it so very difficult to do something that sounds so simple? It is perhaps worth having a look at this before we embark on the path itself.

There are various ways in which one might approach the question. One could say, for example, as I have elsewhere, that the central problem of the spiritual life is to find emotional equivalents for one's intellectual understanding.[63] But one can also think in terms of the relationship between the conditioned and the Unconditioned.

The best-known Buddhist symbol of conditioned existence is the Tibetan Wheel of Life. We could say that this is a picture of the nature of life, even a mirror in which we can see ourselves. We have already taken a look at the outermost circle of the Wheel, which depicts the twelve links of conditioned co-production. Working inwards, the next circle is divided into six segments, which represent the six planes of conditioned existence. In the traditional, almost mythological, terminology these are the planes of the gods; of the asuras or titans; of human beings; of animals; of hungry ghosts; and of beings in states of suffering. Then within this circle is another, divided into two halves, one dark, the other light. In the light half are depicted people with happy expressions who seem to be moving upwards towards the realm of the gods, while in the dark half are people tumbling miserably towards the hell realm. And at the hub of the Wheel, keeping the whole thing turning round and round, are three animal figures – a cock, a snake, and a pig – which represent the three root poisons: craving, aversion, and ignorance.

This is what Buddhism calls *samsara*, the sphere of conditioned existence. The Unconditioned is also sometimes thought of as a sphere, called the *Dharmadhatu*. Here *Dharma* means 'ultimate truth' or 'ultimate reality', while *dhatu* means something like 'sphere of operation'. The Mandala of the Five Buddhas of the Mahayana tradition is, one could say, a depiction of the Dharmadhatu.[64] A number of Buddhist traditions also speak of what is called the Buddha-kshetra. *Kshetra* means 'field', so Buddha-kshetra means 'Buddha field', and it refers to the area within which there operates the spiritual influence, the spiritual power if you like, of a particular Buddha. This influence is often referred to, especially in the Tibetan tradition, as his *adhisthana* – an untranslatable word, but it can be roughly rendered as 'grace'. The Pure Land of the Japanese tradition is also a symbol of the Dharmadhatu, being that area within which the infinite light and eternal life of the Buddha Amitabha is the dominant influence.

Thus we have two spheres, each of them governed by its own forces: samsara, driven by the forces of greed, hatred, and delusion, and the Dharmadhatu, where the influence, the *adhisthana*, of the Buddha is the prevailing force. We can extend this analogy by saying that, just as the earth, the sun, and other heavenly bodies have their own gravitational field, their own area within which they will attract to themselves any smaller body, so the sphere of conditioned existence and the sphere of the Unconditioned each exerts its own gravitational pull. The spiritual path, one could say, is the journey from one sphere to the other, a journey, perhaps, from the earth to the sun. This is one answer to the Emperor's question. The spiritual path is hard to follow because, while we are drawn towards Enlightenment, towards the sun, we are held back by the force of gravity that binds us to the earth. There is bound to be conflict.

We could see our movement towards Enlightenment as having three stages: the stage at which we are still very much within the gravitational field of samsara, of conditioned existence; a middle stage, when we are subject to the strong pulls of both spheres; and a final stage, when we are free of the pull of samsara and subject only to the increasingly strong influence of the Dharmadhatu, of Enlightenment. These three stages, one might say, correspond to the three stages of the Threefold Path, the simplest exposition of the Dharma as path: morality or ethics, meditation, and wisdom.[65] We will be looking at each of these three stages in some detail in later chapters; here I will just give a brief introduction.

MORALITY

First, 'morality' – though before going any further it should be said that there is no such word as morality in Buddhism. Buddhists in the East don't talk about morals; they talk about skilful action. Skilful actions are actions expressive of skilful mental states – that is, mental states free from the grosser forms of craving, aversion, and ignorance, and which therefore do no harm either to oneself or others; which may even, on occasion, benefit others. Morality in this sense is of fundamental importance in Buddhism.

At the same time its value is regarded as being strictly limited. Skilful action certainly prepares the way for the experience of the stage of meditation. But – and Buddhism insists on this again and again – skilful action by itself, even skilful mental states by themselves, cannot lead one directly to the experience of the Unconditioned. In the Buddhist view, morality is rather like the launch pad of a rocket. You can't launch the rocket without the launch pad, but once the rocket is launched, once it goes streaking off into the stratosphere, the launch pad is left behind on earth; it doesn't go to the stars. So morality is not identical with the spiritual life. It is only part of it, only a means to an end, the immediate end being meditation, and the ultimate end being wisdom, or even the realization of the Unconditioned.

It should also be mentioned that Buddhism distinguishes sharply between two kinds of morality: 'natural morality' and 'conventional morality'.[66] Natural morality consists of actions expressive of skilful mental states, while conventional morality is simply a matter of local custom or opinion, and has no real moral significance. The first stage of the spiritual path is concerned, of course, not with conventional morality but with natural morality. Morality in this sense, one could say, corresponds to the light half of the second circle of the Wheel of Life, which leads upwards to the periphery of the gravitational field of the conditioned. But that light segment is still inside that gravitational field. Skilful action alone is not enough to move one beyond the Wheel of Life.

Unfortunately, this kind of teaching has led to some major misunderstandings. People sometimes think that the Buddha taught a path exclusively of self-interest; and if one is thinking along these lines, then it may seem that skilful action is being advocated simply as a means to one's own ends, that one is expected to behave kindly and generously towards others only as a way of increasing one's own spiritual chances. It was the Mahayana phase of Buddhism which made it unequivocally clear once and for all, if there was any room for doubt, that there can be no such thing as self-development without care and concern for the well-being and growth of others. Even the pursuit of Enlightenment is not a matter of individual salvation: one seeks it not just for one's own benefit but for the welfare of all beings. It is this which the Mahayana teaching known as the Bodhisattva Ideal is specifically concerned with pointing out (and we will be going into it in chapter 13).

MEDITATION

The second stage of the Threefold Path is usually called 'meditation'. The word meditation is used, even misused, in all sorts of ways, but properly speaking it has three meanings that correspond to three successively higher levels of spiritual experience. To begin with, there is meditation in the sense of concentration of mind, the withdrawal of one's attention from the external world. You no longer see anything – well, your eyes are closed. But you no longer hear anything either, or taste anything, or smell anything. You don't even feel the meditation cushion on which you are seated, or the clothes you are wearing. Your attention is withdrawn from the senses, and therefore also from the corresponding sense objects, and you become centred within. All your psychophysical energies too are no longer scattered and dispersed but drawn together, centred on one point, vibrating, even, on one point.

Next there comes what we could perhaps call 'meditation proper' Attention has been withdrawn from the senses, from the external world. The energies have been concentrated within, unified, integrated. Then, at this second stage, the energies start to rise, and there is a gradual raising of the whole level of consciousness, the whole level of being. One is carried up, away from one's ordinary physical body, away out of the ordinary, physical, material universe that one knows. One ascends in one's inner experience up to successively higher states or stages of 'superconsciousness'.

As one becomes more and more concentrated, more and more peaceful, more and more blissful, the world becomes more and more distant. Even mental activity fades away, until only stillness and silence is left, within which one begins to see with the inner vision and hear with the inner hearing. These stages of superconsciousness are known in Buddhism as the four *dhyana* states. This is 'meditation proper': not just unification of one's psychophysical energies but the raising of them to ever higher levels of consciousness and being, so that one is living in a different world, and is indeed a different person, at least to some extent.

Finally, there comes meditation in the highest sense of all: contemplation – turning this unified, elevated state of being in the direction of the Unconditioned, of reality itself. One sees it, or at least has a glimpse of it, and one begins to move towards it, flow towards it, gravitate towards it. One's unified, elevated consciousness begins to come into contact with the very depths and the very heights of existence and being and consciousness.

Meditation as the second stage of the Threefold Path consists of what I've called 'concentration' and 'meditation proper'; it doesn't include contemplation, which, though it is usually practised within the context of meditation, really belongs to the third stage of the path, the stage of wisdom. Meditation is the intermediate stage of the spiritual path, in which there operate both gravitational forces: the force of the conditioned and the force of the Unconditioned. This, one could say, accounts for two things:

One thing it accounts for is the ease with which we sometimes fall from the heights of meditation right down into the depths of worldliness. Most people who practise meditation have had this experience at some time or other. We enjoy what seems to be a really beautiful meditation. We may begin to think that we're really getting somewhere. We may even think we've really made it at last, spiritually speaking. After all that effort, we've really got up there, we're amongst all these beautiful experiences, floating around us like so many pink and blue clouds. We think, 'This is wonderful, this is going to stay with me all my life, for ever and ever. Here I am, floating on these clouds, timelessly. I'm never going to have any more problems, any more worries. At last I've got there.'

But what happens? Within a matter of minutes – not hours, not days, not weeks, but minutes – we are overwhelmed by what can only be described as highly unskilful mental states. Not only that: we find ourselves even acting in accordance with those highly unskilful mental states, within minutes of floating up there blissfully on those beautiful clouds. In this way we oscillate between the heights and the depths. Sometimes we are right up there with the gods, as it were, thinking, 'I'd like to devote my whole life to meditation,' and the next minute we are right down in the depths.

It is only natural when this happens to start wondering whether meditation is really worth while. One could be forgiven for thinking, 'I make all this effort, spread my wings, and soar up there for a while … then my wings seem to give way somehow, and crash! I find myself back on the earth, maybe with a few damaged feathers. Is it worth it? If I could get up there and stay there, it would be worth it perhaps; but to get up there only to sink down again is so disappointing.' We begin to wonder whether such a thing as spiritual progress is possible at all. Are we just fooling ourselves? Are we doomed to ricochet in this way between the heights and the depths for ever?

Not necessarily. All this trouble is due to the gravitational pull of the conditioned – from which we can become free in the third stage of the path. But until then, we are liable to fall at any time, from any height, regardless of the length of time we spend meditating. We might have stayed up there for a couple of hours, even a whole week. It doesn't make any difference – we come tumbling down just as easily.

In India there are lots of stories about this sort of thing, usually stories about Indian rishis. We are told that thousands of years ago Rishi So-and-so went off to the Himalayas, and he spent thousands of years meditating – meditating in caves, meditating in deep forests, meditating in hermitages, meditating on snowy peaks, oblivious to everything. There are all sorts of wonderful stories about how one rishi's beard grew miles and miles long and went flowing over the whole countryside, and how another rishi was so indifferent to what was going on around him that he just went on meditating even when a colony of ants came and built a great anthill over him.

But of course, eventually any rishi has to end his meditation – or at least he decides to end it – and then what happens? It's the same story every time. As soon as the rishi comes out of his meditation, as he comes down from the mountain or emerges from the forest, he encounters a nymph, a heavenly maiden, and within a matter of minutes, despite those thousands of years of meditation, he succumbs to her temptations and he's back where he started.

What do these stories mean? They all mean the same thing. They mean that meditation is not enough, so far as the spiritual life is concerned. It can only take you so far. But though it's not enough, at the same time it's indispensable. It is the basis for the development of wisdom, just as skilful action is the basis for the development of meditation. If morality is the launch pad of the rocket, meditation, we may say, is the first-stage rocket, from which the second-stage rocket is fired when the first-stage rocket has reached a certain height. This second-stage rocket, of course, is wisdom.

So meditation is indispensable because it is only from meditation that one can reach wisdom. One must reach a certain level of meditation experience and sustain oneself at that level, if one can, for a certain length of time at least, and then try to develop wisdom. Once wisdom has been developed, there is no longer any danger, you're no longer at the mercy of the gravitational pull of the conditioned.

This, then, is one thing accounted for by the fact that at the stage of meditation both gravitational forces operate. The other thing accounted for by this fact is that if we've been meditating fairly successfully for some time, we sometimes feel as though we are about to slide down into fathomless depths, or be carried away by a great stream flowing strongly and powerfully within us and beyond us. At such times usually what we're experiencing, however obscurely, and without necessarily knowing it, is the gravitational pull of the Unconditioned. But what usually happens? When we start feeling this pull, when we start feeling ourselves going, slipping, sliding, being carried away, we usually resist. We usually pull back. This is because we feel afraid. Oh yes, we say we want Enlightenment, we want nirvana, but when it really comes to the point, we don't want to be carried away. We don't want to lose ourselves.

This calls to mind a story about an old woman in Japan, a devout Buddhist. She used to go along to the temple of Amitabha, the Buddha of Infinite Light, who presides over the Pure Land into which – according to Japanese Buddhism – you are reborn after death, if you recite his mantra. She would go along to this temple and she would worship there every morning, bowing down many times and crying, 'Oh Lord, oh Amitabha, oh Buddha of Infinite Light and Eternal Life, please take me away from this wretched, sorrowful, wicked world. Let me die tonight and be reborn into your Pure Land. That's where I want to go, so that I can be in your presence night and day, and hear your teaching and gain nirvana.' In this way, tearfully and with great sincerity, she used to pray every morning and sometimes in the evening too.

A certain monk in that temple overheard her praying and weeping, and he thought, 'All right, we shall see.' The Buddha image in the temple, like many images in Japan, was an enormous one, about thirty feet high. So when the old woman came next, the monk hid behind the image. As she sobbed, 'Lord, please take me now, let me be reborn in the Pure Land. Take me.' The monk called out from behind the image in a great booming voice, 'I shall take you *now*.' At this the old woman leapt up with a shriek of terror and rushed out of the temple. And as she rushed out she called over her shoulder to the image, 'Won't the Buddha let me have my little joke?'

We say that we want to gain Enlightenment, and we say, with complete sincerity, that this is why we meditate. But as soon as we start feeling that pull, feeling that we're going to be carried away, that we're going to lose ourselves, we draw back. Just like the old woman, we are afraid. We don't want to lose ourselves. But this is in fact just what we must learn to do, whether in meditation or in any other aspect of the spiritual life. We have to learn just to let go. This is the most difficult thing in the world: just to let go. We have to give up if you like – not in the ordinary, everyday sense of the expression, but in a more spiritual sense. To use more religious terminology, we just have to surrender to the Unconditioned.

WISDOM

The third great stage of the Threefold Path is wisdom. This isn't, of course, any kind of mental activity; by wisdom here is meant direct sustained awareness of reality or the Unconditioned. As wisdom is the subject of later chapters, we will put it aside for now.

THE POINT OF NO RETURN

These, then, are the three great stages of our journey from samsara, the sphere of the conditioned, to the Dharmadhatu, the Unconditioned. To begin with, we are going to be battling against the gravitational pull of the conditioned, and the pull of the Unconditioned is going to seem very faint – although it must be there, otherwise there would be no question of our moving towards Enlightenment at all. But there comes a crucial point at which the pull of the Unconditioned, of Enlightenment, becomes the stronger force. This we could call the point of no return. Beyond this point our spiritual progress will be assured; there will be no danger of relapse. So clearly this is a very important goal to strive for – remembering all the time that 'striving' for such a 'goal' is this process of continually letting go.

It is said that the ultimate goal of Buddhism is Enlightenment, Buddhahood, nirvana, whatever one likes to call it. But really these are only words. They are quite unable to convey to us an adequate idea of the nature of the attainment towards which we are supposed to be directing our efforts; it is too far beyond us. But we can set our sights on a more immediate, more comprehensible, more accessible aim: to reach the point of no return, the point where the pull of the Unconditioned is stronger than the pull of the conditioned. Once we've reached this point, Enlightenment is in any case assured, and will be attained, according to tradition, within not more than seven more lives.[67]

But although the point of no return is within our reach, we will still need to make a great effort to reach it. We should not underestimate the power of the gravitational pull of the conditioned. It operates at many different levels and applies to all aspects of human life. It is owing to the gravitational pull of the conditioned that an artist may conform, or be tempted to conform, even to betray his or her inner vision. It is owing to the gravitational pull of the conditioned that religions lose any sense of their true mission and become merely a matter of custom and tradition. And it is owing to the gravitational pull of the conditioned that we sink down from the heights of meditation, often as soon as we've managed to gain them, or even stop meditating altogether.

It is very important that we see for ourselves the workings of this great force, both in human history and in our own lives. Once we see it, once we realize how powerful, ubiquitous, and extensive it is, we wake up to the fact that we cannot afford to stop making an effort. If we do, we don't just remain where we were – at least not for long. Once we stop exerting ourselves, the gravitational pull of the conditioned inexorably takes over, and before we know what has happened we are back where we started from, maybe months or even years before. We can perhaps afford to take a breather only when we have reached the point of no return. Until then, there must be no resting on our spiritual laurels, however brilliant. Hence the Buddha's last words to his disciples: *Appamadena sampadetha* – 'With awareness – with mindfulness – *strive*.'[68] He was saying, in effect, that if we can only manage to keep up these two things – awareness and effort – then progress is assured.

The traditional term for the attainment of the point of no return found in the Buddhist scriptures is Stream-entry.[69] The 'stream' is the irresistible force of the Unconditioned once you've got near enough to it. So once again we have the image of a river. Once again we are as though standing on a river-bank which represents conditioned existence. In this image the Unconditioned is represented not by the other shore (as in the parable of the raft) but by the ocean towards which the river is flowing.

We could say that the distance from the point where we are standing to the edge of the river corresponds to the first stage of the path, the stage of morality. Then the distance from the edge of the river to midstream corresponds to the second stage of the path, the stage of meditation. Once we've reached midstream and begin to feel the mighty force of the current flowing towards the ocean, we just have to abandon ourselves to it; this is the point of Stream-entry, the point of no return. And the distance from there to the ocean itself is the third stage of the path, the stage of wisdom.

The image is reminiscent of one of the parables of Sri Ramakrishna, the great modern Indian saint and teacher. He told this parable to illustrate the relationship between 'grace' and 'works', but it has some bearing on this whole question of Stream-entry as well. He said that it is like rowing a boat right out into the centre of the river, to midstream. The process of getting into the boat and rowing, and with great difficulty making progress to the centre of the stream, represents 'works', karma in the sense of activity. But once you're in midstream, you can hoist your sail; and once you've hoisted your sail it will catch the breeze. Then you can rest, you can put up your oars, for no further effort is needed. All you have to do is to steer, as the breeze carries you along. And the breeze represents 'grace' – in other words, the gravitational pull of the Unconditioned.

So, if we are to take Stream-entry as our 'goal', how is it to be attained? This is what the Dharma as teaching or path is meant to explain in detail. We are not simply enjoined: 'be ye perfect'; neither is Bodhidharma's advice to the Emperor the last word on the subject. Throughout his teaching life the Buddha found many different ways of mapping out the journey to Enlightenment, and subsequent Buddhist tradition has added new ways of seeing the same path – not just seeing it, but working out in detail the practical steps one needs to take.

Of all these different ways of describing the path, some make it particularly clear how the point of no return, the point of Stream-entry, is to be recognized. For example, just as we can say that the point of no return in terms of the Threefold Path is the point at which meditation shades into wisdom, so, in terms of the twelve links of the spiral path, the point of no return is reached at the eighth stage, 'knowledge and vision of things as they really are'. Other ways of seeing the spiritual life – the five spiritual faculties, for example – are conceived more in terms of achieving a balance of qualities. But one thing all these descriptions of the path have in common is that they are all about the cultivation of positive spiritual qualities. A rather different way of looking at how one approaches Stream-entry is in terms of the breaking of fetters.

BREAKING THE FETTERS

The Buddhist tradition enumerates ten fetters which bind us to conditioned existence, each one representing a different aspect of the gravitational pull of the conditioned.[70] If we can only burst them asunder, then we become free, totally free, on the spot. But these fetters are strong and binding, and they usually have to be broken little by little, each one gradually filed through over years of spiritual practice. The ten fetters are (1) self-view or self-belief; (2) doubt or indecision; (3) dependence on moral rules and religious observances as ends in themselves; (4) sensuous desire, in the sense of desire for experience in and through the five physical senses; (5) ill will or hatred or aversion; (6) desire for existence in the plane of (archetypal) form; (7) desire for existence in the formless plane; (8) conceit, in the sense of the idea of oneself as superior to, inferior to, or equal to other people, i.e. making invidious comparisons between oneself and others; (9) restlessness and instability; (10) ignorance – that is, spiritual ignorance in the sense of lack of awareness of ultimate reality.

On breaking the first three of these fetters one becomes a Stream-entrant, so that from now onwards one will be subject more to the gravitational pull of the Unconditioned than to the gravitational pull of the conditioned. The fourth and fifth fetters – sensuous desire and ill will – are said to be particularly strong. On weakening – not breaking, but just weakening – these two, one becomes what is called a 'once-returner' (all these terms come from the Theravada tradition). A 'once-returner' has gone well past the point of no return, and is even more strongly drawn by the Unconditioned, feeling the pull of the conditioned comparatively little. As a once-returner you have before you only one more birth as a human being, according to tradition, and you will then gain Enlightenment.

On actually breaking the fourth and fifth fetters, one becomes a 'non-returner'. According to tradition, a non-returner is reborn in one of the 'pure abodes', near the outermost reaches of the gravitational field of the conditioned. The gravitational pull of the Unconditioned is now overwhelmingly predominant; and the non-returner gains Enlightenment directly from the pure abodes without the necessity of another human birth.

These first five fetters are known as the five lower fetters, and they bind one to the plane of sensuous desire, as it is called – in other words, to the innermost circle of the gravitational field of the conditioned, where the gravitational pull is strongest. As for the sixth and seventh fetters, they refer to the 'plane of (archetypal) form' and the 'formless plane'; that is, the middle and the outer circles respectively of the gravitational field of the conditioned. Once the five higher fetters are broken, one is completely free. One experiences only the gravitational pull of the Unconditioned – one is in fact, oneself, the Unconditioned – and there are no more rebirths. Such a person is known, in the traditional terminology, as an arhant – a 'worthy one' or 'holy one'.

This, at least, is the traditional way of putting it in Theravada Buddhism. As we have seen, in the full realization of shunyata one sees that there is ultimately no distinction between samsara and nirvana; so to speak of making the journey from the one to the other is only a manner of speaking – and one that may not suit us if we are wary of anything that seems to suggest an abandonment of the world to its fate. Mahayana Buddhists would speak of what is basically the same process in terms of the arising of the Will to Enlightenment, and the taking of the Bodhisattva Vow, emphasizing that to move towards Enlightenment is not just for one's own sake, but involves – indeed, is inseparable from – great altruism.

But while they perhaps don't give us the full picture, it can be very useful to think in terms of breaking the fetters. The more advanced ones may be beyond us, but we can usefully focus our attention on the first three, the breaking of which is synonymous with Stream-entry. (And it is said that once one of these three fetters is broken, the other two will also go.)

First, then, the fetter of fixed self-view. This is our habitual acceptance of our present experience of selfhood as being fixed, unchanging, and ultimate. It really amounts to a refusal to accept the possibility of change or progress. We are so familiar with ourselves, so used to ourselves, so used to thinking of ourselves in a certain way. We think, 'This is Me. I'll always be like this – I may change a bit but I'll still be recognizably me, very much so.' We just can't believe that this Self, this Me, this 'I' as I am experiencing it here and now, can ever be, as it were, consumed as though by fire, so that out of the ashes of that old self a new self can arise. We refuse to accept that this can happen even once – let alone many times. Fixed self-view is therefore the negation of the spiritual path. We could say, in fact, that it's a sort of rationalization of the gravitational pull of the conditioned.

The second fetter is doubt or indecision. This is not doubt in the intellectual sense; it is not the suspension of belief or judgement. Doubt here means unwillingness to commit oneself, to take the plunge. It means holding back when there's no reason for holding back, even when one sees good reasons for not holding back. And here the gravitational pull of the conditioned is at work with a vengeance. There are lots of people who are interested in the spiritual life, in a way, but they won't commit themselves, they won't throw themselves in. The tendency is just to stretch out one's toe and dip it into the water, then draw it back. Or, if one does venture in, one fastens oneself securely to a good strong post on the shore so that one doesn't get really carried away, so that, perhaps, one can have the best of both worlds. We find it hard just to throw ourselves in. Very often this is simply because we are afraid. We may agree with everything we hear about the spiritual path, but we won't really try to put it into practice, because we are strongly bound by this second fetter, the fetter of doubt and indecision.

The third fetter is 'dependence on moral rules and religious observances as ends in themselves'. There's a lot that could be said about this; but the main point is that it's the dependence that constitutes the fetter. The Sanskrit here is *shilavrata paramarsha*, which is sometimes rendered by the early translators as 'dependence on rites and ceremonies'. Really, however, this has nothing to do with rites and ceremonies. *Shila* means 'ethical precepts', as in the *pancha shila*, the five precepts; *vrata* is 'religious observance'; and *paramarsha* is 'clinging' or 'attachment'. Therefore clinging or attachment to ethical rules and religious observances is according to Buddhism a fetter. Not that these practices are wrong in any way; the problem comes if we come to depend on them too much.

Conventional religiosity, then, is a hindrance to Enlightenment. This is a hard truth for many people to swallow. Indeed, a very great deal, if not the greater part, of ordinary, conventional religious life and activity is simply an expression of this fetter. Religious people tend to become trapped in religion itself. They treat it not as a means to an end – Enlightenment or any other end – but as an end in itself. There's no need to multiply examples; we can find them all around us, even, despite all the Buddha's warnings, within Buddhism itself.

So let us have our pujas; let us have our meditations; let us study our texts. But let us always remember that they are only of value to the extent that they lead us in the direction of Enlightenment. We have to ask ourselves constantly, 'Is what I am doing really helping me in the direction of Enlightenment, or am I going mechanically on week after week, month after month, just like a hamster in a wheel? Have I just got into a sort of religious conditioning? Am I just settling down comfortably in some sort of religious doctrine or practice or group? Or am I using those facilities in such a way that I do get a little nearer to Enlightenment?'

It's not enough to declare that one is a Buddhist. It's not enough even to keep up one's daily meditation. The point is, are we getting nearer to Enlightenment? Are we making some progress? Are these things in which we are engaged functioning as a means to an end, or have they become an end in themselves? We need to be on the lookout in this way throughout our spiritual life, always asking ourselves whether we are continuing to do something not because it's useful to us spiritually, but simply because we have always done it that way.

It is necessary to bear these fetters in mind, because until we have broken them we are always going to be subject to their restraint. We are going to need to keep reminding ourselves that we can change, really change. We will need to look out for those times when we feel like giving up on the spiritual path because we are afraid, because we don't know where it's going to take us. And we will need to notice when we are just going through the motions of spiritual practice, clinging on to a particular habit we've got into.

Breaking these three fetters, and attaining Stream-entry, should be a practicable possibility for anyone within their present lifetime. And once this point has been reached, then one can only rise higher and ever higher on the path. As one does so, one will feel the gravitational pull of the Unconditioned more and more powerfully. One will, in fact, glimpse the Unconditioned, through all the veils, all the hindrances, all the obscurations of the conditioned, and gradually see it more and more fully, more and more clearly, more and more brightly. As one reaches these heights, then the world itself, formerly a veil, formerly a hindrance, formerly an obscuration, will itself be more and more transfigured, more and more resplendent, more and more glorious.

This is the vision before us. But for now we will go right back to the beginning – at least in our imagination – to where it all starts: the first step of the spiral path to Enlightenment.

7

THE SPIRAL PATH

THE NATURE OF spiritual development is perhaps most clearly seen in terms of the spiral mode of conditionality, in which it is represented as a certain sequence of experiences, one experience arising in dependence upon another. Just as out of the bud grows the flower, and out of the flower the fruit, so out of one spiritual experience there grows another, out of that yet another, and out of that another still, each one higher, more refined, more beautiful, a little nearer to nirvana. Each stage is a spiritual experience in the process of transition to another, more advanced experience. The stages aren't fixed or static; you don't proceed up the spiral path like going up the steps of a staircase, even a spiral staircase. We speak of 'the Buddhist path' or 'the spiritual path', but we mustn't be misled by the metaphor. It isn't that the spiritual path is fixed and rigid, and we just go up it; or that *we* move but the path remains stationary. The path itself grows, just like a plant grows, one stage passing over into the next so that there's a constant upward movement.

This is the way spiral conditionality works; spiritual growth, like everything else, unfolds in accordance with this great law. As we have already seen, the law of conditionality functions in two ways, one 'cyclical' and the other 'progressive'. The cyclical mode is the process of action and reaction between opposite factors – say between happiness and unhappiness, or depression and elation, or birth and death; while the progressive, spiral mode is the process of ever-increasing intensity, so that, for example, you get a progression from pleasure to happiness, from happiness to rapture, from rapture to bliss, and so on.

The concern of Buddhist practice is to break the endless cycle of action and reaction illustrated on the Wheel of Life as the chain of conditioned co-production. But how? In Tibetan Buddhism there is said to be something of a hiatus between one life and the next – called the bardo, the 'intermediate state' – and this bardo between lives is said to present a great spiritual opportunity. But we don't have to wait for death in order to find an opportunity for spiritual growth. The chain of conditioned co-production can be broken in the midst of life – indeed, at any moment.

A chain is only as strong as its weakest link. So where is the nidana chain weakest? Where can it be broken most easily? Paradoxically, in this case the weakest link is the strongest. The crucial point is where, in dependence upon *vedana*, feeling, arises *trishna*, craving. It is this link that keeps the whole process going. We don't usually experience feeling in a purely mirror-like way. Craving, aversion, or mental confusion seem automatically to arise in connection with that feeling. But it is in fact possible to break the chain at this point. If we can experience feeling without allowing craving to arise, then the Wheel of Life is broken; it doesn't revolve any more. Or, to put it another way, one is not reborn.

There are two ways of breaking the chain at this weakest and strongest point – a sudden method and a gradual method. Many of the stories in the Pali Canon bear witness to the fact that there *is* a sudden method – we see people who, like Shariputra, hear just a few words and undergo an immediate and irreversible transformation. But to be able to break the chain suddenly is very unusual; the gradual method works better for most people. It is 'gradual' not because it is slow, necessarily, but because it consists of a number of successive stages, the order of which is based on a definite principle. If the cyclical type of conditionality is a circle, then the progressive type is a spiral. All versions of the Buddhist path – the Noble Eightfold Path, the sevenfold path of purification, the six paramitas, and so on – are spiral paths, because they are all based upon this progressive type of conditionality. But where does this spiral path begin? It begins at the crucial point of our experience of *vedana*, the feelings that befall us in the course of our lives.

UNSATISFACTORINESS

Some of the feelings we experience are pleasant, some are painful, and some are just neutral. And our reactions to them are usually pretty automatic. We want to grasp the pleasant experiences and hold on to them for as long as possible. And when our experience is painful, of course we try to escape from the pain. We can't cling on to a pleasant experience for ever, it's invariably interrupted, and that interruption usually causes us pain too. So we oscillate between pleasure and pain, pain and pleasure, and in this way the Wheel of Life continues to revolve.

But we can take a more objective view. If we look at our whole life, all that we've ever thought or known, and then, further, think of all human life, of the way the world is, if we think about it all deeply enough, we see that the whole of it, basically, fundamentally, is unsatisfactory. Yes, there are pleasant experiences. Yes, there are things we enjoy. But there is nothing which is deeply and permanently satisfactory.

This is the sense in which Buddhism says – and it has had rather a bad press for this – that life is suffering. In this context 'suffering' means not just individual painful experiences, like having toothache, or cutting your finger, or being bitterly disappointed by someone. As we have already seen, the Sanskrit word being translated as 'suffering' is *duhkha*, the 'ill-fitting chariot wheel': the sort of discomfort that arises when things don't fit or work together properly, the jarring quality that we experience in the course of our everyday life in this world.

We all know that things are never one hundred per cent right. There's always something, even if it's only a little something, that goes wrong. Even on the most beautiful day, only too often a cloud has to float across the face of the sun. Something goes wrong. Maybe you've been looking forward to this day: you're going to meet someone you like, you imagine things are going to be so lovely. But then some absurd incident happens and it all goes wrong, and you feel utterly jangled. This is how we go through life. Nothing quite lives up to our expectations – or at least not for long. And this is what is meant by *duhkha*, unsatisfactoriness or suffering.

Once one has become sufficiently aware of this, eventually one starts becoming dissatisfied. One may have tried all sorts of things: one may have sought worldly success, or pleasure, or comfort and luxury, or learning. But in the end they are all unsatisfactory. It's a popular belief that material prosperity brings happiness, but only a little contact with people who have it makes it clear that this isn't really true. It's not that you're actually experiencing pain all the time, necessarily, but you're not really happy. You feel a sort of vague discomfort; you can't settle down, you don't feel that you belong. It is a common experience that, in the words of the Bible, 'here we have no abiding city'.[71] It is as though right in the middle of one's heart there is a terrible empty space.

This was certainly the Buddha's experience. If anybody ever had everything, it was the Buddha. Even if we leave aside the legendary additions to his life story, it is pretty clear that he was born into a wealthy, highly-respected family, and that everything was laid on for him from his earliest days. He had beautiful mansions to live in, a wife, a child, social position, and even political power, the possibility one day of ascending the throne, succeeding his father. But despite all this he was not happy. He realized that he had everything, but none of it could last. He, and everyone in his family, everyone who was dear to him, would one day sicken, grow old, and die. And so he left it all – his home, his wife, his parents, his child – and went out into the world to seek the answer to the problem of human suffering.[72]

Philosophy shows us how important it is to investigate the causes of things. If we wish to remove some social injustice we must first of all find out its cause. If there is some disturbance in our domestic affairs – say, for example, the car breaks down – we have to find out why. Unless we discover what has caused the problem, all our efforts will be useless. So if we want to free ourselves from the painful limitations of human existence, we must first ascertain their cause.

Analysis of the problem of suffering produces two widely divergent views. Most of us take the attitude, consciously or unconsciously, that 'I have a number of strong desires that I can't suppress – desires to possess this and to enjoy that. If my desires are fulfilled, I am happy; if not, I am miserable. Happiness must therefore consist in the full satisfaction of my desires, and suffering in the opposite. So I'm going to try as hard as I can to get hold of the things I want, and avoid the painful experiences I don't want. In this way I shall be able to escape pain and suffering.'

But the Buddha, considering the same problem, came to the opposite conclusion. He began by pointing out that all things are impermanent. This none of us can deny, since we experience it in one way or another every day. We may think that happiness and freedom from pain come from the satisfaction of our desires, but we cannot altogether ignore such unpalatable facts of life as sickness, old age, death, and separation – or at least not for long. Whatever we enjoy cannot last, and this is painful to us because we want it to last for ever. We want to be always in good health and spirits, but one day sickness is going to overtake us. We want to retain our youthful strength and vigour, but soon old age will steal imperceptibly upon us. We want to live for ever, but sooner or later we will have to die. Think how many painful separations we have to endure in the course of a single lifetime: from family, from dear friends, from possessions. All this causes us suffering. So our suffering cannot be avoided through the satisfaction of desire. Our solution of the problem is really no solution at all.

Many of us, sooner or later, do have an inkling of this. Of course, we do our best to ignore it. We try to convince ourselves that we are happy, that we *must* be happy, because we've got all the things that make people happy. But then a whisper comes from deep within our heart and says, and keeps on saying, 'But you're not really happy.' We don't like to listen to this little voice. We put our fingers in our ears and go off to drown our sorrows in one way or another, smothering and stifling this nagging feeling. But it's there underneath, building up, painfully pressing, even festering like a secret wound. Stifling it, smothering it, only makes it worse. Rather, we should cherish our dissatisfaction, because it is this that makes us restless, and it's restlessness that makes us go in search of something higher, something more satisfying, some greater happiness.

Of course, we don't know at first what we are looking for. That's the absurdity of it, and the beauty of it too. But even though we don't know what we want, we start looking for it. There's just this vague restlessness, a groping around in all directions for we know not what. And eventually, if we go on looking long enough, we come into contact with something which, for want of a better term, could be called spiritual. (This is not an altogether satisfactory word, but it will have to do.) We come into contact with something higher, or at least a glimpse of something higher, something which is not of this world, even something which is 'out of this world'. It may be a symbol, an echo, a reflection: a book that speaks to you, a picture, a person. And when you come into contact with it, whatever the circumstances, at once you respond. In the depths of your heart you get a feeling, or at least an inkling, that this is what you have been searching for all the time, even though you didn't know it.

FAITH

This response is what, in the context of Buddhist tradition, is called faith. And this is the next step of the spiral path: in dependence upon unsatisfactoriness arises faith. The Sanskrit word is *shraddha*. We translate it as faith, but it isn't faith in the sense of believing to be true something which cannot be rationally demonstrated. *Shraddha* can also be translated as confidence or devotion, and it refers to the whole emotional side of the spiritual life. The word comes from a verb which means 'to place the heart on'. So faith in the Buddhist sense means the placing of one's heart on the Unconditioned, on the Absolute, rather than on the conditioned. It is the reorientation of one's whole emotional life.

It is, in other words, the ethically wholesome counterpart of *trishna,* craving or thirst. In dependence upon feeling – in this case feeling the unsatisfactoriness of the world – there arises not craving but faith – faith in something above and beyond the world, a sensitivity to a higher dimension of truth and reality. Perhaps the best definition of faith is that it is the response of what is ultimate in us to what is ultimate in the universe.

For Buddhists faith means specifically faith in the Three Jewels: the Buddha, the Enlightened teacher; the Dharma, the path leading to Enlightenment; and the Sangha, the spiritual community of those who have realized the higher stages of the transcendental path.[73] They are called the Three Jewels because just as jewels are the most precious things in the material world, the Buddha, the Dharma, and the Sangha are the three most precious things, the three highest values, in the spiritual world.

Faith – this intuitive, emotional, even mystical response to something higher, something supreme, something of ultimate value – is the first step on the spiral path, and the very beginning of the spiritual life. Then, in dependence upon faith, arises joy. This is the next step. You have found what you were looking for. You may not have been able to seize hold of it, but at least you've had a glimpse of it, like the sun through a cloud. So naturally, after perhaps a long period of searching, you are pleased and satisfied and contented.

More than that, this contact with higher values has begun to transform your life. It isn't just a theoretical thing. Your heart has actually been lifted up; this is what the word *shraddha* literally means – a lifting up of the heart. You have been lifted up to something higher, have touched something higher, have experienced, even if only for a moment, something higher. And on account of that contact, however brief, however electrical, as it were, a change begins to take place. You feel that you now have a definite aim in life. Before, you were just swept along aimlessly, driven in pursuit of this or that – education, promotion, marriage, a good pension, whatever it happened to be. But once faith has arisen, you have a definite aim in life: to develop your contact with the higher dimension to which you have become sensitive.

Of course, it isn't, usually, all plain sailing. Faith may arise but it may also subside. After an initial rush of enthusiasm for the spiritual life, and a phase of reading everything we can lay our hands on, and going to talks and meditation classes, we may suddenly lose interest. Perhaps our interest is caught by something else, or perhaps, frankly, we get fed up with trying to be 'spiritual' and just feel like living it up for a while. The pendulum may swing back and forth for quite some while, as our enthusiasm for spiritual life waxes and wanes, but as time goes by it swings less and less violently until it comes eventually to rest in the centre.

As one's faith strengthens, one gradually becomes a little less self-centred. One's egoity has been disturbed, shaken up, and as a result one becomes, or one begins to become, just a little more generous, a little more outward-going. One tends not to hang on to things quite so tightly. What may be described as the lower part of one's nature, the part which is chiefly interested in things like food, sleep, and sex, starts coming under the conscious control of the higher part of one's nature. One begins to live more simply and harmlessly, and this makes one happier and more contented. More at ease within oneself, one doesn't rely so much upon external things. You just don't need them as much as you used to. You don't care if you haven't got a beautiful house in the suburbs, a flashy car and all the rest of it. Sitting loose to all those things, much freer and more detached than you were before, you are at peace with yourself. You may not have explored fully what you have discovered, but you've made contact with it, you know it's there, and that contact has at least begun to transform your life.

You come naturally to start living a more ethical life, especially observing what in Buddhism are called the five precepts: not taking life, not taking what is not given, abstaining from sexual misconduct, speaking truthfully, and abstaining from intoxicating or stupefying drinks and drugs.[74] You have a more or less good conscience. And so you feel joyful. Joy, in other words, is the next stage of the spiral path.

JOY

The Buddhist attitude is that if you're leading a spiritual life, you should be happy, open, and carefree. Religious festivals and celebrations in particular are joyful occasions. When I came back to Britain after twenty years in the East I was surprised to find that the Buddhist movement was on the whole such a serious affair. People hardly dared even to smile when one made a joke in a lecture. But if you have found the precious thing that you were looking for, and if it has really begun to transform your life, why shouldn't you be happy? If you're not happier than other people who haven't found this source of inspiration, what's the use of being a Buddhist? What does being a Buddhist really mean? Joy, one could say, is the hallmark of the true Buddhist.

Buddhism attaches great importance to this stage of feeling happy and carefree and at peace with oneself, having a clear conscience, being able to go about with a song on one's lips. If for any reason one lapses from this state of joy – maybe through having done something one shouldn't have done – and one gets all sad and serious, and starts beating one's breast and thinking one is a terrible sinner, the Buddhist view is that this is a very unhealthy state to be in, and the sooner one can get out of it the better.

It may possibly be that one actually has nothing to regret. In the West people only too often suffer from irrational feelings of guilt, especially perhaps with regard to matters of sex, about which certain beliefs may have been instilled by orthodox Christianity from an early age. Such feelings must be resolved, otherwise there is no real possibility of spiritual progress.

If one really has made a mistake, one needs to admit it, try to make up for it, and resolve not to do it again. But having understood what one has done, and having tried to put it right, one can just put it out of one's mind – just forget it and walk on, leave it behind; it won't do you any good to keep carrying it around.

Buddhist tradition prescribes various ways of bringing about this sort of psychological effect. If one feels weighed down by an unskilful thing one has done, large or small, one can just stand in front of the shrine and bow to the image of the Buddha, then think it all over and say to oneself, 'What a fool I've been. I shouldn't have done that, I really am sorry.' (This is especially important if what you have done has involved hurting someone else.) Then you say to yourself, 'All right, I won't do it again. I shall be very careful, I shall watch myself, I'll be aware, I'll be mindful.' And then you recite some texts, try to focus your mind on the Buddha's teaching, try to recollect the ideal, light some candles if you like, burn some incense, and in this way purge your mind of remorse and restore your clear conscience, your state of joy (the Sanskrit term is *pramodya*) and happiness.[75]

RAPTURE

In fact, you can become even more joyful. In dependence upon joy arises rapture; this is the next stage of the path. Even joy isn't enough; one can become more positive still. 'Rapture' is the nearest we can get in English to translating *priti*, which is a very powerful word in the original Sanskrit. *Priti* is an intense, thrilling, ecstatic joy, which is so powerful that you feel it in your body as well as in your mind. When we listen to a beautiful symphony, or watch the setting sun, or have a heart-warming communication with a friend, we are sometimes so deeply moved that we experience not only an emotion, but also a physical response. One may be so greatly affected, for instance, that one's hair stands on end. Some people shed tears. You see people at symphony concerts wiping their eyes – sometimes in a rather shamefaced way because we're not supposed to do that sort of thing in this country. This is *priti*. In the full sense it is an overwhelming psychophysical experience of rapture and bliss and ecstasy which may even carry one right away; this is the sort of experience that will be generated as we follow the path.

It could be said that there is some resemblance between this rapture and the artistic experience. It is not unlike the surge of inspiration that artists feel welling up within them at the time of creation. What they are doing may be very difficult – it may be giving them all sorts of trouble, whether it's a painting or a poem or a piece of music they're creating – but at the same time there is a sort of rapture, a sort of ecstasy out of which they are creating, on account of which they are creating.

Priti can be of five different kinds. First, there's the 'lesser thrill', as it's called. This is the sort of rapture that makes your hair stand on end, as can happen when you are very moved by something. Then there's the 'momentary rapture'; this is the rapture that comes just like a flash of lightning. It's so overwhelming that you can bear to experience it only for an instant. It touches you, reduces you to ashes, as it were, and then it's gone. You can't stand more of it than that – it just comes and goes. And then there's what's called the 'flooding rapture'. Just as the tide comes in to fill a cave on the seashore, so rapture floods in upon you, especially when you are meditating, and you feel almost carried away by it. Then there's what's called the 'all-pervading rapture', in which you feel just like a balloon, so light, so buoyant, almost as if you were lifted up. And lastly there's what's called the 'transporting rapture', which is said actually to cause levitation.[76]

People are often intrigued by the idea of levitation. It's a rather minor interest in Buddhism, but I have met various people who have experienced it. For example, many years ago I happened to be passing through a place called Kharagpur in India. Kharagpur is near a big railway junction, and I'd gone there from Calcutta to give a lecture. The lecture was scheduled for about eleven o'clock at night – they like to have their lectures late in those parts – so I was waiting for the one o'clock morning train to take me back to Calcutta. I was waiting on the station platform among a crowd of people, and we all got talking to pass the time until the train arrived. Of course, this being India, the train was late.

After a while someone brought forward a certain individual, an ordinary looking man in ordinary Indian dress, from the crowd, and they said 'This man has a problem.' I thought perhaps his wife had run away, or his son hadn't passed an examination, or something of that sort. But they said, 'No. The trouble is that he levitates.' So I said 'Do you mean that he literally levitates?' They said 'Yes. He's a Kabirapanthi.' A Kabirapanthi is someone who follows the sect founded by Kabir, the great medieval Hindu-cum-Muslim yogi. And apparently every morning this man was practising certain breathing exercises, as a result of which he would just float up a few inches, or even a few feet, above the ground.

Naturally I said to these people, a little suspiciously, 'Has anyone seen this happening?' They said, 'Oh yes, we've all seen it every day. He just can't control it. He wants to meditate, but this levitation gets in the way. As soon as he does his breathing exercises he just starts going up into the air. So what should he do? How should he stop?' This, of course, is the sort of question one might be asked at any time in India.

I said, 'According to Buddhism levitation is brought about by excess of *priti* – that is, rapture. So what one must do is cultivate the mental faculty of equanimity or tranquillity, *upeksha*. If one does that, there will be a sort of counterbalancing force to the *priti*, and levitation will not occur.' I never went to Kharagpur again, so I never heard whether the prescription was successful, but let us hope that it was.

I met another levitator when I was living in Kalimpong, up in the Himalayas. I was once entertaining to lunch an American couple and a Tibetan lama, rather a distinguished one. In the course of the lunch the American man said, with a rather knowing smile, 'I suppose you haven't heard of anyone who can levitate?' So the lama said modestly 'Yes. In fact, I do a little myself.' At this the two Americans nearly fell off their chairs. They said, 'You can do it *yourself*?' He said 'Yes. I don't think I could do it right now, but if I spend about six months meditating alone in the jungle, or in a secluded monastery, at the end of that time I can levitate.'

He was not really unusual – although my visitors certainly thought so. I have met a number of Tibetans who have either seen levitation done or who can do it themselves. It is all said to be due to an excess of *priti*, or rapture, when one's experience, especially in meditation, becomes so intense that the body is quite literally lifted up. One finds records of this sort of thing not only in Buddhist life and literature, but also in the lives of some comparatively recent Christian mystics. But Buddhists would say it isn't a very important phenomenon or experience. This is still only the third stage of the path – it's essentially a mundane experience. If it happens one shouldn't take too much notice of it. It just means that one has accumulated rapture of sufficient intensity to produce this particular psychophysical effect.

To use modern terminology, one could say that rapture comes about as a result of the release of blocked energy – energy that is short-circuiting itself, as it were, or as if locked up. In the course of one's spiritual life, especially when one practises meditation, these blocks get dissolved. One digs down, one uncovers certain depths within oneself; little complexes are resolved, so that the energy locked up in them is released and surges up. It's due to this upsurge of energy, felt throughout the nervous system as well as in the mind, that one experiences *priti*.

CALM

Then, in dependence upon rapture there arises calm or peace. In Sanskrit this is called *prashrabdhi*. The word means 'calm, tranquillity, serenity', and it is the calming down of the physical side effects of rapture, so that you're left with a purely mental and emotional experience.

The physical experiences calm down not because the rapture is less but because it has become greater, beyond all possibility of physical expression. A text from the Pali Canon illustrates this with the simile of an elephant stepping into a pond. In India, of course, there were and still are lots of elephants, and elephants are very fond of bathing. Almost every day, sometimes several times a day, they like to go down into a pool, pond, lake, or river and bathe, squirting water over themselves and one another. But suppose an elephant goes to bathe in a small pond, a pond which is perhaps not much bigger than the elephant himself. When this great beast gets into that little pond, because the elephant is so big, and the pond, in comparison, is so small, the water goes splashing out at the sides. This is like rapture. The experience is so great, and our capacity to receive it is so small, that some of it spills over, as it were, in the form of these physical side effects.

But then, suppose the elephant steps into a great pool of water, a huge lake, or even an enormous river. Then, even when he fully immerses himself in the water, there's hardly a ripple, because although the elephant is so big, the body of water is immeasurably bigger. In the same way, in this stage, even though the experience of rapture may be very great, you're more able to receive it, more able to bear it. The physical innervations therefore die down, leaving just the inner, purely mental experience of rapture.

BLISS

In the fifth stage, in dependence upon calm – calm in the sense of this purely mental experience of rapture – there arises bliss, *sukha*. *Sukha* has various meanings in Buddhism. It can refer to pleasant bodily feeling, or to pleasurable emotion or happiness, whether hedonic or spiritual. Here it means the feeling of intense happiness that wells up within you when bodily awareness is transformed. The physical side of rapture has been refined away, and a purely mental or spiritual experience of bliss or happiness is left.

Given this progression of ever more positive mental states, from joy to rapture to calm or pacification, and now even to bliss, it seems extraordinary that some of the early books written in the West on Buddhism described it as a gloomy, pessimistic, negative religion. Here we see the exact opposite. Bliss is described as a state of intense happiness that represents the complete unification of all our emotional energies. They are not divided, there's no split. They are all flowing together strongly and powerfully in a single direction, like a great river. There are no negative emotions. By the time you've risen to this stage there is no craving, no fear, no hatred, no anxiety, no guilt, no remorse, no negative emotion whatsoever. Whatever energy you had invested in those negative emotions now flows positively in the form of bliss, this intense happiness. In this way we rise higher and higher in the spiritual scale.

This points to an extremely important aspect of the spiritual life: the fact that we owe it to ourselves and to others to be emotionally positive whenever possible. In this way we shall contribute not only to the raising of our own level of consciousness and being but also to that of everybody with whom we come into contact. Unfortunately it is possible to be so bound up with negative emotions, so riddled with fear, anxiety, jealousy, possessiveness, hatred, and suspicion, that one's whole life is passed in a sort of dark cloud. To stop this from happening, one has to be very quick to prevent negative emotions from developing, and actually cultivating and encouraging only the positive emotions of love, joy, compassion, peace, and so on.

Only too often even religious life, organized religious life, is bound up with negative emotion. Without wishing to harp on this sort of theme – because preoccupation with negative emotion is itself negative – one has only to look back on the history of Europe, with its hundreds of years of religious persecution and witch-hunts, to see that this is so. The lesson to learn from all this is perhaps not to get caught up in group emotion, especially 'religious' group emotion.

It is no accident that what could be described as the motto of Buddhism is the phrase *sabbe satta sukhi hontu*, which means 'May all beings be happy.' In a way, this is the sole wish of Buddhism – it's as simple as that. It's not just words, not just something to repeat and recite. The aspiration is that all beings should be emotionally positive, that everyone should be free from negativity, free to become happy, blissful, full of love, compassion, peace, joy, devotion, and faith.

SAMADHI

Then sixthly, dependent upon this intense happiness arises *samadhi*. The word has several different meanings, but here it means concentration. This does not mean a forcible fixation of the mind on a single object, but a concentration which comes about quite naturally when, in that state of intense happiness, all one's emotional energies are flowing in the same direction. In other words, when we are completely happy, when all our emotional energies are unified, we are concentrated in the true sense. A concentrated person is a happy person, and a happy person is a concentrated person. The happier we are, the longer we shall be able to stay concentrated; and conversely, if we find it difficult to concentrate for very long, the reason will be that we are not happy with our present state. If we were truly happy we wouldn't need to do anything else – we could just stay still. But we are unhappy, dissatisfied, so we get restless and go searching for this or that, looking for some distraction, some diversion.

This connection between happiness and concentration is illustrated by another story from the scriptures. We are told that one day there was a discussion between a certain king and the Buddha. The king came to the Buddha to ask him about his teaching, and as they talked a question cropped up – the question of which of them was happier. Was the Buddha happier than the king, or was the king happier than the Buddha? Of course, the king was quite sure that he was the happier of the two by far. He said, 'Well, look, I've got all these palaces, I've got this army, I've got this wealth, I've got all these beautiful women. I'm obviously happier than you. What have *you* got? Here you are sitting underneath a tree outside some wretched hut. You've got a yellow robe and a begging-bowl, that's all. Obviously I'm far happier than you.'

But then the Buddha said, 'Well, let me ask you a question. Tell me, could you sit here perfectly still for an hour, enjoying complete and perfect happiness?' The king said, 'Yes, I suppose I could.' Whereupon the Buddha said, 'All right. Could you sit here without moving, enjoying complete and perfect happiness, for six hours?' And the king said, 'That would be rather difficult.' Then the Buddha said, 'Could you sit for a whole day and a whole night, without moving, absolutely happy the whole time?' And the king had to admit, 'No, that would be beyond me.' Then the Buddha said, 'Well, I could sit here for seven days and seven nights without moving, without stirring, all the time experiencing complete and perfect happiness without any change, without any diminution whatsoever. So I think I must be happier than you.'[77]

The Buddha's happiness arose out of his concentration, and his concentration arose out of his happiness. Because he was happy he was able to concentrate; because he was able to concentrate he was happy. And the fact that the king could not concentrate showed that the king was not really as happy as he had thought, certainly not as happy as the Buddha.

This relates closely to the practice of meditation. We know that meditation begins with concentration, but many of us find this very difficult. It's really no use thinking that concentration can be gained by force of will; although, of course, a lot of people do think this. It's quite usual to experience a train of thought along the lines of 'Here I am. This is my time for meditation. I've got a concentration technique I can use. My mind is buzzing, full of idle thoughts. There's traffic going up and down outside. I'm sure there's going to be a knock on the door at any minute. But I'm going to concentrate. I don't particularly want to, but I've made up my mind to do it, so I will.' Most people's approach to meditation is more or less like this. We try to fix the mind forcibly on a certain point, but then all sorts of disturbances arise – we get distracted – because there is a split within us, and our emotional energies are not integrated. But meditation is not just a question of the application of techniques, not even the right techniques. It's much more a matter of gradual growth.

It has to be said that the Buddhist scriptures don't always seem to bear this out. They recount many instances in which a monk goes along to see the Buddha, the Buddha says a few words, and the monk – or sometimes the lay person – becomes Enlightened. Or they describe a monk living in the forest who sees a leaf fall from a tree, and from that gains an intense realization of impermanence which leads almost immediately to his becoming Enlightened. So why doesn't this kind of thing happen to us? Why don't the Buddha's words, or the falling leaves, affect us in this way?

Partly, at least, it's because the ground has not been prepared. It's full of rocks and stones and weeds and garbage. Even if a few seeds are scattered haphazardly here and there, they don't stand a chance, even before considerations of rain and light come into play. So the ground must have been prepared. Faith, satisfaction, delight, rapture, and so on must be cultivated (both within and without the meditation practice) before any concentration technique can be really fruitful. If concentration doesn't grow in this natural, spontaneous way, if we insist on making it a business of the forcible fixation of the mind on an object, the unregenerate or unsublimated portions of our psyche are liable to react against what we are doing.

We may manage through force of will deliberately, consciously, to hold the mind on a certain object – the breath, or an image of the Buddha, or a mantra. We may even succeed in keeping the mind on that object for a while. But we've done it with the energy of the conscious mind. The unconscious mind isn't co-operating, and sooner or later there's going to be a reaction, or even a sort of breakdown.

This doesn't mean that concentration exercises are not useful; they are. But they're much more effective when the ground has been cleared. If we haven't really stopped to think about the unsatisfactoriness of life, if no faith has arisen, if there isn't much joy, and certainly not much rapture or calm or bliss or anything like that, there's not much possibility of real concentration. It's significant that concentration in the sense of samadhi arises only at the sixth stage, halfway up the path. It's only then that we can really begin to concentrate, because our emotional energies have been unified, and we are now, perhaps for the first time in our lives, happy. So really one's whole life needs to be a preparation for meditation.

It is also important to prepare well for each individual meditation session – the same gradual approach applies here, although the timescale is different. You can't just sit down and switch your mind on to the object of concentration; you have to pave the way. First of all, you have to disengage your energies from other things, and direct them into one channel; then, when your preparations for meditation are complete, the concentration exercise – the mindfulness of breathing or whatever it is – will just put the finishing touch, and you're away.

But however elevated our meditation practice, however concentrated we are, at this point we are still on the level of the mundane. We're on the spiral but we're still subject to the gravitational pull of the round. However, with the arising of the next stage in the series we come to the second part of the spiral, which is purely transcendental and from which there is no possibility of regression.

Although this stage represents a radical change, it still arises in dependence on the previous stage of the path. There's a saying of the Buddha that comes into its own here: 'The concentrated mind sees things as they really are.' When the mind is full of thoughts, when it isn't calm or harmonized or balanced, but pulled this way and that, it can't see things as they really are. But the concentrated mind – not the mind which is straining to stay on an object of concentration, but the mind which is naturally concentrated, with or without the help of a concentration exercise – is able to see the true nature of things.

KNOWLEDGE AND VISION OF THINGS AS THEY REALLY ARE

When the waters of a lake are still, they can reflect the face of the moon without distortion. But when the wind blows, making lots of tiny ripples, or even great waves, the reflection of the moon is broken up and distorted. The way we see things is like that – all in bits and pieces, broken up, twisted. It's only the concentrated mind that sees things as they are, which sees the full moon as it is, full and perfect and round. And this is the stage we come to next: in dependence upon samadhi, concentration, there arises *yathabhuta-jnanadarshana*: 'knowledge and vision of things as they really are'. This stage is of the utmost importance, because it marks the transition from meditation to wisdom, from the psychological to the spiritual. Once we've reached this stage, the stage of Stream-entry, there can be no falling back. According to the traditional teachings, the attainment of Enlightenment is now assured.

One way of putting it is to say that this 'knowledge and vision' is insight into the three characteristics of conditioned existence. First of all, one sees that all conditioned things are impermanent, that they're constantly changing, that they don't remain the same for two consecutive instants. Then, one sees that all conditioned things are ultimately unsatisfactory. They may give us some pleasure for a time, but they can't give permanent and absolute happiness, and to expect that from them is a delusion. And then, thirdly, one sees that all conditioned things are insubstantial, ultimately unreal. Not that we don't experience them, not that they're not there, empirically speaking, but we see them only superficially, we don't penetrate into what they really are.

Consequently this stage represents a direct perception: you actually *see through* the conditioned. Not only that; you see through the conditioned to the Unconditioned. Piercing through the impermanence of the conditioned, you see the permanence of the Unconditioned; piercing through the unsatisfactoriness of the conditioned, you see the perfectly satisfying nature of the Unconditioned; and piercing through the insubstantial, the unreal, you see that which is eternally and everlastingly real, that which Mahayana Buddhism calls the *dharmakaya*, the 'body of spiritual truth'.[78]

When you begin to see things in this way, your whole outlook changes radically. You are not the same as you were before. In Shakespeare's play, once Hamlet has seen the ghost stalking along the battlements he's a changed man, because he's seen something from another world, another dimension. In the same way, but in a much more positive sense, once you've glimpsed something beyond, once you've seen through the passing show, once you've had a glimpse of that higher dimension, call it what you will, higher reality, the Absolute, even God if you must, once you've had a glimpse of that – not just an idea of it, not a concept, not a speculation, but a real glimpse, a real contact, a real communication – then you'll never be the same again. A permanent change takes place in your life. To use the Yogacharin expression, you've turned about, or begun to turn about, in the deepest seat of consciousness.[79]

WITHDRAWAL

Then, dependent upon knowledge and vision of things as they really are, there arises *nirveda*. This is sometimes translated as 'revulsion' or 'disgust', but that's too strong, too psychological a way of putting it; at this level you're far above and beyond any psychology in the ordinary sense, because you're above and beyond the psyche, the mind, in any ordinary sense. It's a purely spiritual withdrawal – calm, deliberate, and natural. This stage represents the clean, even serene, withdrawal from involvement in conditioned things. It's just like seeing a mirage in the desert. At first, seeing those palm trees and that oasis, you may hasten in their direction. But when you see that it's a mirage, you stop in your tracks. There is no point in going towards what isn't really there.

Similarly, when you deeply see, when you really realize, on the basis of your experience of samadhi, that conditioned things, all the things with which you normally come into contact, are unsatisfactory, that they're going to pass away, and that there's no real truth or reality in them, you become less and less attached to them. You withdraw from them, you lose interest.

This stage of withdrawal is a sort of sitting loose to life. You still play the games that other people play – or at least some of them – but you know that they're games. A child takes his game very seriously because to him it is real, but the adult can join in the child's game while knowing that it's a game. If the child wins, the adult doesn't get upset, because it's only a game. In the same way, once you've seen through the games people play, you can go on playing the games, but you know that they're just games and you can withdraw from them, at least inwardly. You may be doing what is necessary objectively, but subjectively you're not caught up in it. This is what is meant by withdrawal. You're still part of the conditioned, but in your heart you've withdrawn from it.

In India fishermen sometimes catch fish in their hands. They just poise themselves on the bank at the edge of a flooded rice-field, and they look down into the muddy water between the rice plants, watching for a sign of movement. Then suddenly they reach down and grasp. But sometimes, when they bring what they have caught out of the water, they see that it isn't a fish at all, but a poisonous snake – and, of course, they drop it at once. The Buddhist texts say it's just like this with conditioned things. We grab hold of them, just as the fisherman grabs what he hopes is a fish. But then, just as the fisherman sees the marks that show that what he thought was a fish is a poisonous snake, so, when we see on all these mundane things that we've grasped the three marks of unsatisfactoriness, transitoriness, and insubstantiality, we just let go.

DISPASSION

In dependence upon withdrawal arises *vairagya*, which can be translated, approximately at least, as 'dispassion'. This stage differs from the previous one in that while withdrawal is the movement of detachment from conditioned existence, dispassion is the state of actually being detached. In this state you can't be moved or stirred or touched by any worldly happening. This isn't hardness or insensitivity, but a state of serene imperturbability, like that exemplified by the Buddha just before his Enlightenment.

According to legend, when the Buddha was sitting under the bodhi tree along came Mara, the embodiment of evil – or, it would be more accurate to say, the embodiment of *samsara* – with his forces. In depictions of this episode in Buddhist art you see Mara leading his army, with elephants and horses and soldiers and all sorts of monstrous demon figures, and they're throwing great rocks and spitting fire and releasing arrows against the Buddha, hundreds and thousands of them swarming and swirling around. But the Buddha doesn't take any notice. He doesn't even see them, doesn't even look, doesn't even listen. He's in a state of complete imperturbability, complete dispassion.[80] And this is what this stage represents. You're so firmly fixed in the truth, your mind is so absorbed in the Unconditioned, that nothing can touch you.

There's a beautiful touch in these representations of the defeat of Mara in Buddhist art. As all the arrows, all the stones, all the flames that are hurled by these demon hosts close in on the Buddha, as they whizz through the air, when they touch the edge of his halo they just turn into flowers and fall to the ground. So this is the state of dispassion. All the forces of Mara may rise up against you, all these weapons may come hurtling through the air, but as soon as they touch the edge of your halo, they just turn into flowers.

FREEDOM

In dependence upon dispassion there arises freedom – spiritual freedom, *vimukti*. Nowadays there's quite a lot of talk about freedom, and most people, it seems, think that it means the freedom simply to do as one likes. But the Buddhist conception of freedom is rather different. In the earliest Buddhist teaching it is twofold. Firstly there's *cheto-vimukti* – freedom of mind – which means complete freedom from all subjective emotional and psychological bias, from prejudice, from all psychological conditioning. And secondly there's *prajna-vimukti* – the 'freedom of wisdom' – which means freedom from all wrong views, all ignorance, all false philosophy, all opinions.[81]

This complete freedom of heart and mind at the highest possible level is the aim and object of Buddhist life and practice. The Buddha once said, 'Just as the ocean has one taste, the taste of salt, so my teaching has one taste: the taste of freedom.'[82] This is the final objective, if you like, the end of Buddhism, this taste of complete spiritual freedom, freedom from everything conditioned, even from the very distinction between the conditioned and the Unconditioned, as the Mahayana goes on to say.

KNOWLEDGE OF THE DESTRUCTION OF THE ASHRAVAS

But this freedom is not the culmination of the spiral path – not quite. Next, dependent upon freedom arises the stage called 'knowledge of the destruction of the *ashravas*'. It isn't even enough to be free. The next stage is to *know* that one is free. And one knows that one is free when one realizes that the *ashravas* have been destroyed. This is another of these untranslatable terms; it's a very expressive word which means a sort of mental poison that floods the mind. There are three *ashravas*: *kamashrava*, which means the poison of desire or craving for experience through the five senses; *bhavashrava*, craving for any form of conditioned existence, even for existence as a god; and *avidyashrava*, the poison of spiritual ignorance.[83] When these poisons are extinct, and when one knows that they are extinct, then at last thirst or craving, *trishna*, the emotional counterpart of spiritual ignorance, has been destroyed. You've broken the chain at its weakest and its strongest link. In dependence upon feeling there no longer arises any craving whatsoever. And at that stage you have reached the end of the spiral path, you have gained Buddhahood.

A NATURAL PROCESS OF GROWTH

The spiral path shows us that the spiritual life is a natural process of growth, each succeeding stage arising from the overflow, as it were, of the preceding stage. As soon as one stage reaches its fullness, it inevitably passes over into the next. One finds this in meditation. Sometimes people wonder how, when you've got to a certain stage in meditation, you go about progressing to the next stage. But there's really no need to ask. If you get to a certain stage and you go on cultivating that, so that it becomes more and more full, more and more complete, then out of its very fullness it will move forward, under its own momentum, to the next stage. Similarly, as each stage of the path reaches a point of fullness, it gives birth to the next stage. We don't really have to worry about the next step; we just need to cultivate the stage we're at. It's quite useful to have a theoretical idea of what lies ahead, but one doesn't need to bother about it too much. Once one stage is fully developed it will automatically pass over into the next.

The principle of conditionality isn't just an idea. Being aware that this is how life works can have a transforming effect on every aspect of the way we live. When any experience befalls us – when someone says something to us, or we read something, or we experience something through the senses – we can always ask ourselves whether our reaction is cyclical or progressive. If there's a cyclical reaction – say from pleasure to craving – then we go round and round on the Wheel of Life. But if there's a progressive response, however faint, however feeble – say from an experience of the unsatisfactoriness of life to a feeling for something higher – then at that very moment we place our foot, however hesitantly, upon the first step of the path to Enlightenment.

8

THE JOURNEY TO ENLIGHTENMENT

THE TRANSCENDENTAL EIGHTFOLD PATH

THE FACT THAT in terms of the spiral path permanent transformation begins with 'knowledge and vision of things as they really are' suggests that usually we do *not* see things as they really are. We see them only as they appear to be; we see them the wrong way round; we even see them upside-down. The Buddha identified four 'upside-down views' (*viparyasas*) that represent the way we usually see things.[84] One of these views is seeing the painful as pleasant; another is seeing the impermanent as permanent; the third is seeing real selfhood where there is no real selfhood; and the fourth is seeing the ugly as beautiful. And these four upside-down, topsy-turvy views stand between us and reality.

Let us, for instance, take a closer look at impermanence. In the case of something quite obvious, quite tangible, like a house or a car, we can become attached to it and start behaving as though that object – that house or that car – is going to be there for ever. We start treating it as though it were permanent. And this applies, of course, to our relations with people as well. Not that we actually *think* that our house or our car is permanent. If we were asked we would say, 'Well, of course it isn't permanent. I know that very well.' But our emotional attitude towards it is that it is permanent. And it's the emotional attitude, primarily, that constitutes the topsy-turvy view. When we are deprived of something to which we have become attached, towards which we are in the habit of behaving as though it will always be there, we experience suffering, to a greater or lesser degree, and this tells us that we have been seeing at least that particular thing, or indeed person, the wrong way up.

Similarly, we see what is really insubstantial, without selfhood or own-being – and this very much includes our view of ourselves – as having a self, something substantial and fixed amid, or somehow standing behind, the changing processes of life. And we imagine that what is in reality unsatisfactory is giving us satisfaction – or at any rate we imagine that it will give us satisfaction in the future. These three 'topsy-turvy views' of course are connected with the three *lakshanas*, the three characteristics of conditioned existence.

The fourth *viparyasa* – seeing what is in reality ugly as being beautiful – requires a little more explanation. The teaching isn't saying that we should regard a flower, say, as being essentially ugly. It is more that in comparison with the beauties of a higher plane of reality, the beauty experienced within conditioned existence pales into insignificance.

So we need to turn our view of things the right way up, or, as the Buddhist expression has it, to cultivate 'right view' or even 'Perfect Vision'. If you have Perfect Vision, you see the painful as painful, the impermanent as impermanent, and so on. You also see the truth of the Four Noble Truths, and the truth of conditioned co-production. In other words, you see reality, at least to some extent.

Perfect Vision is the first step of the Buddha's Noble Eightfold Path, which, as it happens, was the Buddha's first ever description of the path to Enlightenment. We have seen how, having decided to teach the Dharma, he sought out his old companions with the intention of unfolding to them his great discovery. The way he put it to them, which resulted eventually in their realization of the truth, was in terms of the Four Noble Truths: that life is unsatisfactory; that this is because of our craving; that it is possible to reach a state of complete peace and freedom from the painful tug of craving for things to be otherwise; and that one can reach that state by following a path. In this connection the Buddha outlined what has become known as his 'Noble Eightfold Path'.[85] Here I want briefly to introduce this formulation of the path – perhaps the best known throughout the Buddhist world – as well as two much less well-known descriptions: the seven factors of Enlightenment, and the seven *visuddhis* or purifications.

The first thing to say about 'the' Eightfold Path is that in fact there are two: the mundane Eightfold Path and the transcendental Eightfold Path.[86] You may perhaps have been thinking that Perfect Vision of reality is a strange place for a spiritual path to start; it's rather reminiscent of the Zen phrase, 'If you want to climb a mountain, start at the top.' But strictly speaking, it is the transcendental path to which one refers when one speaks of the aryan Eightfold Path ('aryan' here means 'noble' or 'holy') and it is this path that starts with Perfect Vision. The mundane Eightfold Path is an Eightfold Path but it's not an *aryan* Eightfold Path. Most accounts of Buddhism deal only with the mundane Eightfold Path, but they deal with it as though it was in fact the transcendental Eightfold Path, which can be rather confusing. Here I want to focus specifically on the transcendental Eightfold Path.

It is divided into two great sections. The first section consists of the first step only – that is to say, Perfect Vision – while the second section consists of all the other steps: Perfect Emotion, Perfect Speech, Perfect Action, Perfect Livelihood, Perfect Effort, Perfect Mindfulness, and Perfect Samadhi. These two sections are also known as the two paths: the Path of Vision or Path of Reality; and the Path of Transformation. The Path of Vision represents our initial vision of things as they really are – a glimpse that is sufficient to start in us the process of real, radical transformation – and the Path of Transformation represents the gradual transformation of every aspect of our being, every aspect of our life, in the light of that glimpse. At the same time, the more we are transformed – the more our life is transformed – the brighter that glimpse becomes.

Let us see, just briefly, how this works out in detail. Once one has taken the first step, Perfect Vision, then the Path of Transformation begins with – and I'm translating interpretively here – Perfect Emotion. This represents the transformation, in the light of Perfect Vision, of our entire emotional and volitional nature. Greed is transformed into generosity; we don't grasp or grab – we give. Aversion is transformed into loving kindness, cruelty into compassion, and so on.

The third step of the path is Perfect Speech. Only too often speech is untruthful – not only that, it's often harsh, often frivolous, and often divisive. Perfect Speech is the exact opposite. It's truthful, of course, but it's also pleasant, affectionate, meaningful, and genuinely beneficial. In the *Dhammapada* the Buddha says 'Better than a thousand meaningless words collected together is a single meaningful word on hearing which one becomes tranquil.'[87] Perfect Speech is also conducive to harmony, in the sense of bringing people together, creating friendship between them rather than dividing them.

The fourth stage of the transcendental Eightfold Path is Perfect Action. This consists in behaviour that is thoroughly ethical. It consists in abstention from violence, from misappropriation, and from unchastity; and in more positive terms it consists in actions expressive of love, generosity, and contentment. On the mundane Eightfold Path, this is a matter of conscious discipline. But Perfect Action as a factor of the transcendental Eightfold Path is natural and spontaneous; it is action as transformed in the light of Perfect Vision.

All these stages – Perfect Emotion, Perfect Speech, and Perfect Action – involve other people, at least to some extent. One can't be generous without someone to give to; one can't speak the truth without someone to speak it to. Thus Buddhist ethics is not just self-regarding, but also other-regarding. Indeed, we cannot really separate self from other in any case – and this is especially true of the next stage, Perfect Livelihood. Perfect Livelihood consists in earning one's living – in supporting oneself and one's family, if one has a family – in a way that does no harm to any living being. In contemporary terms we could say that Perfect Livelihood is livelihood that is ethically and ecologically sound. Buddhist tradition gives quite a number of examples of wrong livelihood: for instance, selling alcohol, manufacturing weapons, dealing in poisons, and so on.[88] Nowadays, of course, the list would be much longer, but the principle remains the same.

Modern economic life has become extraordinarily complex. Our livelihood, only too often, depends on the livelihoods of so many other people, and it's sometimes very difficult for *us* to be ethical if *they* are not ethical. So it's not enough for us to be *personally* ethical; we also have to try to transform the society in which we live into an ethical society. It's very difficult to be perfectly ethical in an unethical society. What this means in principle is that the Buddhist has not only to transform himself or herself. We have to try to transform the world in some degree, at least the society in which we happen to live, in collaboration with other like-minded people.

Then, sixthly, there's Perfect Effort. This is the effort, basically, to eliminate and prevent unskilful mental states as well as to develop and initiate skilful ones. This is an extremely important aspect of the spiritual life. Though it is spoken of as the sixth step of the Path, Perfect Effort really enters in at every stage. In fact, one could almost speak of the spiritual life itself as a life of Perfect Effort because there is never anything passive about it.

The seventh, penultimate step is Perfect Mindfulness or Recollection. This consists in knowing what we're doing, whether mentally, verbally, or physically, and also why we are doing it. In other words, this step consists in our being *aware* – aware of ourselves, aware of other people, aware of our environment, even aware of reality.[89]

And then, eighthly and lastly is Perfect Samadhi. I'm using the Pali/Sanskrit word here because in the context of the transcendental Eightfold Path the term samadhi is really quite untranslatable. It usually means mental one-pointedness or concentration but here it represents the total absorption of one's subjective being in reality.

This, then, is the Path of Transformation. First we develop the Path of Vision – we obtain a glimpse of reality, the Dharma-eye opens at least a little,[90] we even enter the stream – and *then* we enter upon the Path of Transformation, transforming our own lives and the society in which we live. Of course, even if we have not developed the Path of Vision in the transcendental sense, we will have had at least a glimpse of a glimpse of reality – or we would not have set out on the path at all. At the least, we can cultivate the intellectual counterpart of Perfect Vision, usually known as right view. And we can still work to transform ourselves in the light of what we have seen. We can still follow the mundane Eightfold Path. Our aim, however, should be to enter upon the transcendental Eightfold Path, to enter the stream that leads ultimately to the ocean of nirvana.

THE SEVEN FACTORS OF ENLIGHTENMENT

The seven factors of Enlightenment, or *bodhyangas*, are: awareness; sorting out of mental states; energy; joy; calming down; samadhi; and equanimity.[91] After a brief glance at this list, one might be forgiven for concluding that we are now dealing with a very different path from the Eightfold Path we have just – at least in imagination – traversed. Gone are overt references to such matters as speech and livelihood; instead we are asked to consider 'sorting out mental states' and 'calming down'. And indeed, this formulation of the path to Enlightenment is more akin to the spiral path, with which, indeed, it shares several stages.

Bodhi means 'Enlightenment' (the word 'Buddha' comes from the same root) and *anga* means 'limb' or 'shoot'; so the seven *bodhyangas* are the seven limbs or branches of the spiritual life, all of which are to be developed if *bodhi* is to be attained. Their name reminds us that we should not take the image of a path too literally as a description of the spiritual life. Sometimes it may help to see in one's mind's eye a path stretching ahead of one, or spiralling up the mountain and out of sight. But it is just as valid – and may be more useful sometimes – to see spiritual growth as being akin to the unfolding of the petals of a flower, or the growth of a sturdy tree. We are reminded of this by the fact that the 'factors' of Enlightenment are seven 'limbs' or 'shoots' – and in fact the eight aspects of the Eightfold Path are designated by this same word, *anga*.

The first of these 'limbs' is *smriti*, which is usually translated 'recollection' or 'awareness'. The spiritual life, one could say, begins with awareness: simply knowing what is happening, knowing what is going on. Not that it is simple to do this. Four kinds of awareness are usually distinguished. In the first stage we are aware of what we are doing – that is, we are aware of bodily movement, and also of what we are saying. We are rarely fully aware of what we are doing; very often we don't really know what we are saying either, because our minds are elsewhere – but this is a crucial aspect of awareness.

Then, we also need to know what we are feeling: whether we are happy or sad, greedy or contented, angry or loving. And we also need to become aware of what we are thinking. At first it may not be obvious that we need to make an effort to do this; surely we know what we're thinking, at least most of the time? But very often we don't. At this very moment, even, you may not really know what you are thinking. You may think you are fully absorbed in what you are reading – but are you? Or are you thinking about what you need to do next, or what you did yesterday, or what to have for supper? Unless we know what we are thinking from moment to moment, the mind will be scattered and confused. The fourth kind of awareness to be practised is awareness of the Dharma. Once we know – at least intellectually – the truth of how things really are, we must try never to forget it. Whatever we do, we must keep the Dharma in mind.

But we can start with the basics. We may find it impossible to keep the Dharma in mind much of the time. We may find it hard to stay aware of what we are thinking and feeling. But we can begin by at least trying to stay aware of what we are saying and doing. There's a story that illustrates the fundamental importance of this level of mindfulness. It's about a young Japanese Buddhist who wanted to learn meditation. Deciding he needed a meditation teacher, he searched for some months, and travelled many hundreds of miles, until he came to a temple where – so he had heard – a great meditation teacher lived. Having been granted an interview, the young man entered the teacher's room. First, though, he folded up the umbrella he was carrying, and put it to one side of the door.

The teacher asked him what he wanted, and he said, 'I want to learn to meditate. Please teach me.' The teacher said, 'All right. But first I want to ask you one or two questions.' The young man was quite pleased to hear this, thinking that he would be questioned about the theory of meditation. But the teacher asked, 'When you arrived just now, was it raining?' The young man replied, 'Yes, it was raining quite heavily.' Then the guru asked, 'Did you come carrying an umbrella?' The young man thought this rather an odd question. Why wasn't the teacher asking him anything about meditation? But anyway, he thought he'd better reply. 'Yes,' he said. 'I was carrying an umbrella.' Then the teacher asked, 'When you came into my room, on which side of the door did you leave it?' Try as he might the young man couldn't remember. There was nothing he could say. So the teacher said, 'You are not yet ready to practise meditation. First you need to learn mindfulness.' And away the young man had to go.

Of course, we need not really put off learning to meditate until we have learned to be mindful. Indeed, meditation – especially the mindfulness of breathing – will help us to cultivate mindfulness. But our practice need not be – *should* not be – restricted to when we're sitting in meditation. We can practise mindfulness in all situations. Whatever we do, we should do it carefully, with proper thought. We may be studying, or cooking, or sweeping the floor, or mending the car, or driving, or talking with our friends – but whatever it is, we can try to do it with a clear mind, with *smriti*, with recollection and awareness.

The second *bodhyanga* is *dharma-vichaya*. Usually the term Dharma or Dhamma means the Buddha's teaching, but, as we have seen, it can also mean 'mental state', and this is what it means here. Having become aware of your mental state, with *dharma-vichaya* you take the process a step further. *Vichaya* means 'distinguishing' or 'sorting out'; so this stage or limb of the path involves not just being aware of your mental states, but distinguishing them from one another, in particular distinguishing 'skilful' (*kushala*) states from 'unskilful' (*akushala*) ones.

The Buddhist meditators and scholars of certain traditions have made something of a speciality of the identification of different mental states; in its most systematized form, this is known as the Abhidharma.[92] But the crucial distinction is between skilful – that is, ethical – states, and unskilful states. It isn't enough just to let mental states happen. We have to keep watch over the mind; we have to sort out the skilful states we wish to develop from the unskilful ones we wish to get rid of.

We can think of it as a process of sifting or sorting out. In India one of the most time-consuming household tasks – and of course it is almost always done by the women of the house – is cooking. And more often than not, the meal involves cooking rice. So – you see this done everywhere in India – what the cook will do is spread the rice out on a kind of wicker tray, and then go over it very carefully, putting the grains of rice on one side and the stones and bits of dirt on the other, until eventually there is a big heap of nice clean rice and a small pile of dirt and stones.

Of course, in the West our rice usually comes pre-packed and spotless, but the idea of this kind of sorting out persists in our language in phrases such as 'separating the wheat from the chaff'. And we can think of sorting out our mental states in a similar way. We can literally say to ourselves, 'This is skilful; that is unskilful. This I must cultivate and develop; that I must get rid of.' Just as rice is sorted from stones, one can purify one's mind by getting rid of unskilful mental states.

The third factor of Enlightenment is *virya,* which means 'energy'. Buddhists may sometimes be imagined to be rather passive and ineffectual, but in fact a Buddhist is properly the embodiment of energy: physical energy, mental energy, emotional energy, and spiritual energy. Of course, this energy must be put to good use. The great Buddhist poet Shantideva defines *virya* as 'energy in pursuit of the good'.[93] If you have a lot of energy but use it for a purpose that is not worthwhile, you are not practising *virya*.

Shantideva likens a person with *virya* to an elephant – not a tame elephant but a wild elephant. The wild elephant is a playful beast, and one of the things he likes doing in hot weather is plunging into a pool, especially a lotus pool. After plunging into one pool and spending a few minutes there he comes out and plunges into another pool. Thus he goes on plunging into one pool after another, and in this way enjoys himself. Shantideva says that the Bodhisattva is like that. As soon as one task is finished he plunges into another.

The fourth factor of Enlightenment is *priti* – which, of course, we have already encountered as a stage of the spiral path. *Priti* is joy or enthusiasm, and its development follows naturally from the development of energy. That energy radiates in all directions, so that you are full of life, bubbling over. You feel really wonderful. For an illustration of this we can look to Buddhaghosa, the great commentator on Pali texts. *Priti,* Buddhaghosa says, is like a great silken bag filled with air.[94] I suppose our modern equivalent is a balloon. When you are full of *priti,* you feel very light, as though you were floating through the air. You feel very happy. And you get this sort of feeling especially when you meditate.

The fifth factor is *prashrabdhi*, 'calming down'; again, this is also a stage of the spiral path. The excitement, as it were, of the *priti* has died away, and you are left with a calm, steady feeling of pure happiness. To use a homely image, it is like what happens when a bee collects nectar from flowers. First it locates the flower, then it alights on it with a loud buzzing sound and crawls within the petals. So long as the bee has not found the nectar the buzzing sound continues, but as soon as it finds it, the sound stops. *Prashrabdhi* is like that.

Samadhi is the sixth factor. Of course, as we have seen, the word means much more than just 'one-pointedness of mind', but it does include this. We find an example of one-pointedness in the life of the Buddha himself. After his Enlightenment the Buddha was a wanderer all his life, and even when he was an old man he continued to walk from place to place, teaching the Dharma. And sometimes, of course, he felt quite tired and quite thirsty. On one such occasion he sat down at the side of the road and asked Ananda to fetch some water from a nearby river. While Ananda was away the Buddha passed the time in meditation. After a while Ananda returned and told the Buddha that he was unable to get any water, because five hundred bullock carts had just crossed the river and made it very dirty. They had, in fact, passed along the road by the side of which the Buddha was sitting. But to Ananda's surprise the Buddha said, 'I heard nothing at all.' Five hundred bullock carts had passed by right in front of him, but he had not heard a thing. This is what is meant by one-pointedness.[95]

As part of the process of developing samadhi, one makes a start by cultivating one-pointedness of mind. It's not necessary to adopt a wandering lifestyle or go and live in a cave in order to do it; it can be done in the affairs of everyday life, by trying to give one's whole mind to whatever one is doing, whether it is washing the dishes or contemplating the Dharma.

The seventh and final factor of Enlightenment is *upeksha*, which is usually translated 'equanimity'. The word sometimes connotes no more than a psychological state of security, but here it is synonymous with Enlightenment itself. If you have *upeksha* you are like a mountain: solid, massive, and unshakeable, even if the winds blow from all the corners of the earth. Whichever of the eight worldly winds – happiness or sorrow, praise or blame, loss or gain, fame or infamy – is buffeting us, we needn't let it affect us. We can be just like the mountain. With the development of *upeksha* in its fullest sense, the last of the seven factors of Enlightenment is present; and we become as unshakeable as the Buddha himself.

THE SEVEN VISUDDHIS

Towards the end of the fourth century CE a boy was born into a brahmin family in the city of Magadha. Magadha was near the place which had become known as Buddha Gaya because, hundreds of years before, a man called Siddhartha Gautama had sat to meditate beneath a tree by the river there, and had gained Enlightenment. But the brahmin boy did not hear the Buddha's teachings until, as a young man well versed in the Hindu scriptures and keen on discussion and debate, he met a Buddhist elder called Revata. It was Revata who got him interested in Buddhist doctrine, especially the Abhidharma, which by that time had been in the process of development for more than five centuries. When the young man wanted to know more, Revata told him he could take things further only if he accepted ordination into the Buddhist tradition. This the young man did, eager as he was to learn, and he soon mastered the teachings of the three pitakas of Buddhist doctrine.

The young man became known as 'Buddhaghosa' – 'he whose speech is like that of the Buddha' – and he went on to become the greatest of all commentators on Theravadin Buddhism. Of his many works, the most famous is the *Visuddhimagga*, or 'Path of Purity'.[96] The work amounts to a complete exposition of Theravada teaching, focusing particularly on meditation practice and technique. It is based, as its name suggests, on yet another formulation of the Buddhist path. The *Visuddhimagga*, the 'Path of Purity', is divided into seven stages which are outlined in the *Rathavinita Sutta* of the *Majjhima-Nikaya*, the collection of middle length sayings.[97]

So here is a way of thinking about the path to Enlightenment that emphasizes the point that spiritual practice is all about purifying the mind. In fact, we find that the path of the seven *visuddhis*, the seven purities, corresponds to the Threefold Path of ethics, meditation, and wisdom. The first *visuddhi* (they are listed in this chapter in their traditional Pali form) is *sila visuddhi*, purity of ethical conduct; the second is *chitta visuddhi*, purity of mind, gained especially through meditation; and the remaining five *visuddhis* are a progressive approach to wisdom through five stages.

But before we investigate the seven *visuddhis*, it is worth having a look at a point that crops up in the *Rathavinita Sutta*, in which they are mentioned. The sutta recounts a dialogue between two of the Buddha's disciples, Shariputra (whom we have already met) and Punya. It describes how Punya, having listened to the Buddha teaching, 'gladdened, roused, incited, and delighted', goes to meditate in a certain grove. Shariputra follows Punya to the grove, hoping to converse with him, and when the two men have spent the day meditating beneath the trees of the grove, they start to talk. The subject Shariputra chooses to raise is that of the seven *visuddhis*.

In particular, he is concerned with a kind of question that might well be asked about any formulation of the path to Enlightenment. He wants to know, 'Do we get to nirvana by means of *sila visuddhi* (that is, the first of the seven stages of this particular path)?' And Punya answers no. Then Shariputra asks, 'Do we get to nirvana without *sila visuddhi*?' And again the answer is no. Then: 'Do we get to nirvana by means of *chitta visuddhi*?' No. So he asks, 'Well, do we get to nirvana without *chitta visuddhi*?' and again the answer is no. He asks the same question about all the other *visuddhis*, but each time the answer is no. You don't get to nirvana with them, and you don't get to nirvana without them. Punya – who at this stage doesn't know he's talking to the revered Shariputra – chooses to make the matter clear with the help of an illustration called the 'Relay of Chariots'. (This is how the sutta gets its name, incidentally; *Rathavinita Sutta* means 'Discourse on the Relay of Chariots'.)

In ancient India, in the Buddha's day, most people had to walk everywhere, but if you were rich you might have a chariot, drawn by two or maybe four horses. The illustration given in the sutta is this. There is a king, and he wants to get to a certain city, but it is a long way away. So he gets into his chariot and drives his horses for many miles. When the horses are tired he jumps out of his chariot and gets into another which is waiting with some fresh horses, and drives on again. Some miles later, these horses too get tired, so he jumps out and gets into another chariot. In this way he changes chariot and horses seven times.

Hence the question arises, does the first chariot take the king to his destination? No, it does not. Does the second chariot take him to it, or the third? Again, the answer is no. But does the king get to his destination without the help of the first chariot, the second chariot, and so on? No, he does not. What happens is that the first chariot takes him to the second chariot, the second chariot to the third, and so on, until the seventh chariot carries him to his destination. In just the same way, *sila visuddhi* takes you as far as *chitta visuddhi*, *chitta visuddhi* as far as *ditthi visuddhi*, and so on. Then the seventh *visuddhi*, *nanadassana visuddhi*, takes you as far as nirvana. Thus one doesn't gain nirvana by means of *sila visuddhi* and so on, but one doesn't gain nirvana without it.

Shariputra is well pleased with this answer – although Punya is rather embarrassed to discover that he has been holding forth to such a great Dharma teacher as Shariputra. And the story is a useful illustration of the point that none of the stages of the path can be regarded as ends in themselves.

So let us return to consider the first of these seven 'chariots': *sila visuddhi*. *Sila* means 'ethical conduct', so at this stage of purification one pays attention to one's ethical life. Basically, there are five *silas*, five ethical precepts: not to harm living beings, not to take what is not given, not to commit sexual misconduct, not to speak falsehood, and not to take intoxicants.[98] If one can observe all these five precepts, one's ethical conduct is purified, giving one a strong basis for one's individual development, as well as the basis of a harmonious social life.

Once you are leading an ethical life, you find that it begins to have a purifying effect on your mind, so this first stage naturally flows into the second, *chitta visuddhi*. *Chitta* means 'mind', and this purification is somewhat similar to the stage of *dharma-vichaya* in the Seven Factors of Enlightenment. It means getting rid of *akushala chittas*, unskilful states of mind – anger, jealousy, fear, ignorance – and replacing them gradually with positive, friendly, clear states. This is, of course, a central purpose of meditation.

If you purify your mind, it becomes very clear. No longer mentally confused, you can think clearly and straightforwardly. This leads to the third stage of purification, *ditthi visuddhi*. This is the first of the five stages of purification which involve the progressive realization, in terms of actual experience, of the true nature of phenomenal, conditioned existence on the one hand, and nirvana on the other. *Ditthi* (Sanskrit *drishti*) simply means 'views'. Developing *ditthi visuddhi* involves getting rid of wrong views and cultivating right views.

The Buddha had a lot to say about wrong views; he enumerated sixty-two different kinds.[99] Of these, three of the most fundamental are: 'everything is made by God'; 'everything is the result of fate or destiny'; and 'everything happens by chance'. Ultimately these wrong views can be traced back to our belief in a fixed, unchanging self or soul. Traditionally, therefore, the purification of views involves reflection – in the context of meditation – on the three characteristics of conditioned existence, the five skandhas, or another of the formulations of the Dharma that reflect the way things really are.

When you practise *ditthi visuddhi* you purify your mind of these three wrong views. You see that when things happen, they happen because of certain definite causes and conditions – and that this holds good not only of the external world, but also of your own mind. This realization – that we are not fixed beings, but can change if we make the effort, and that if we set up appropriate conditions, desirable consequences will follow – is the key to spiritual development. But if you don't realize this – if you think that your life is not in your own hands but controlled by God or fate or random circumstance – you can't take the spiritual initiative. We may think that 'abstract ideas' don't impinge much on 'real life', but in fact it is very important to establish right views.

The next stage of purification is closely related to the previous one. Having purified one's views, one may still be reluctant to act on the basis of right views. So the next step is 'crossing over by the overcoming of doubt' – *kankhavitarana visuddhi*. Here, doubt doesn't mean just enquiring into things. It is perfectly valid, indeed desirable, that one should doubt in this sense; one shouldn't take things on trust. But this is not what is meant here. This doubt is an unwillingness really to find out about things. You don't take the trouble to find out the truth because, to put it bluntly, you don't want to. If you find out the truth you may have to put it into practice, and that is going to mean change – by which it is natural to feel threatened. And one strategy one may use to defend oneself against change is to raise all sorts of unnecessary difficulties and objections. Underneath it all is the desire to keep things vague and unclear. If one allows to emerge a clear vision of how things are, one is going to have to act, one is going to have to change.

Highly educated people tend to suffer a lot from this sort of doubt because, with their active minds, they can raise all sorts of problems and difficulties. They enjoy the sort of talking that goes on all night and never comes to any conclusion – because if it doesn't come to any conclusion you don't have to take any action. It's very important to overcome this kind of doubt. It's not so difficult to see through wrong views (Pali *miccha-ditthis*), but if you're not careful, even after you have apparently got rid of the view, you bring it all back with your doubt. Unless one can overcome this sort of doubt, one's will is going to be completely paralysed.

The next *visuddhi* is 'knowledge and insight into what is the path and what is not the path'. (In Pali this is *magga-amagga-nana-dassana*.) This, again, is a very important stage. It is one thing to be convinced, at least provisionally, that you can take responsibility for your own spiritual life, having cleared away doubt and confusion, at least for the moment. But if you are going to make spiritual progress, the next thing you need to do is commit yourself to a specific path, a specific line of approach. And this is not easy in a world that offers so many spiritual and pseudo-spiritual options. Not only that. Once you have committed yourself, it isn't necessarily going to be obvious whether or not any particular action, practice, or initiative is actually conducive to spiritual growth.

Here one needs to bear in mind the Buddha's advice to his aunt Mahaprajapati Gautami: that a reliable teaching will lead one towards dispassion, not passion; towards freedom, not bondage; towards simplicity of lifestyle, not covetousness; towards contentment, not discontent; towards energy, not laziness; towards solitude, not company; and towards delight in good, not delight in evil.[100] These are the criteria we need to apply and keep on applying, if we are to be able to distinguish the right path from the wrong path.

The next *visuddhi*, 'knowledge and vision of the path' (*patipada-nana-dassana*), clearly follows from the previous one. Once you have established what is the right path and what is the wrong path, the next step is actually to tread the path for yourself. Then from your own experience you come to know that it is the path. It's no good distinguishing the right path from the wrong path if you don't then follow the right path. And, of course, this is easier said than done. Even when one can see clearly which is the right path to take, one is still held back by all the forces within one that resist change. This is what could be called the battleground of the spiritual life. As the *Dhammapada* says, 'Though one should conquer in battle thousands upon thousands of men, yet he who conquers himself is [truly] the greatest in battle.'[101]

The seventh and last of the *visuddhis* is called simply 'knowledge and insight' – *nana-dassana*. This is not ordinary knowledge, but an elevated, pure, supremely clear knowledge – the knowledge that sees things exactly as they are. It's a sort of *prajna* – a sort of wisdom – and of course it is joined with *karuna*, with compassion. It is a knowledge that fills you with energy and enables you to work for the benefit of other people, even for the benefit of the whole world.

These seven stages of purification will carry us along the whole course of human development, to Enlightenment itself. Or rather, if we develop them, we will move under our own steam in the direction of Enlightenment. Above everything else, the Dharma is something to be practised. This is why it is spoken of as a path – a path which, as we have seen, is described in so many different ways. The idea is that we don't just gaze admiringly at the signpost that says 'Nirvana this way'; we actually begin to follow the path to which the sign points. Whether we think in terms of the transcendental Eightfold Path, or the seven *bodhyangas*, or the seven stages of purification, the idea is the same: that here is a path we must actually travel.

There are still more ways of thinking of the path. Sometimes, for example, it is called the *madhyama marga*, or 'middle way' – that is, the middle way between extremes, especially the extremes of self-torture and self-indulgence;[102] of course, each of the formulations of the path we have considered is a middle way. Each of these formulations has its own use, its own emphasis. Perhaps the little-known path of the seven stages of purification in particular deserves to be more widely known, especially because it emphasizes that the Buddhist path is a path of beauty. As well as ethical purity, *visuddhi* means 'brightness, splendour, excellence'. It doesn't just mean purity in the ordinary sense; it means something much more than that. It means a beautiful path, a path that we should enjoy following. It's just like going along a track among beautiful hills. The higher you go, the more beautiful the view, the more open everything becomes, the more you enjoy it and the more free you feel.

9

THE PATTERN OF BUDDHIST LIFE AND WORK

THE SUBJECT OF this chapter is the 'five spiritual faculties'. The chapter title is intended to emphasize the overall purpose of these faculties, which is the living of a Buddhist *life*. Buddhism is concerned with life. One might even say that Buddhism is itself life – life in the sense of growth, in the sense of realizing the potential of one's life. A Buddhist is someone who is first and last alive – awake to life.

We often come across people who, while they may be present in body, do not seem to be really mentally or emotionally present. They're not fully alive to what is going on, not really alive to other people – not alive even to themselves. But the most basic characteristic of a Buddhist should be that they positively vibrate with presence, with spiritual life, with a wakefulness to life. Everything else on the spiritual path is secondary to this and follows from it.

I may say that this is one of the reasons why, when I was in India, I was so much attracted to the movement of conversion to Buddhism among the ex-Untouchables, and why I became so deeply involved in it.[103] They were very poor and largely illiterate, and indeed many of them still are, but one thing at least they had – and still have – and that is life. They are completely alive. Their involvement with Buddhism means a sort of enhancement, a refinement, of that life which they do already have.

Travelling to an Indian village usually involves a journey by train followed by a ride on a bus or a bullock cart; then you finally approach your destination on foot. It's a laborious business as a rule, but if you have been invited to speak to the people of the village about the Dharma, then they certainly do everything they can to make the engagement a memorable and joyful one. You are often still a couple of miles out from the village when you are met by an enthusiastic party of twenty, thirty, perhaps forty men – young and old – who proceed to dance you into the village, such being their traditional mode of welcome for an honoured guest. A long brass trumpet is sounded, there is much banging of tambourines and rattling of castanets, and they dance and stamp energetically all the way to the village. There, some of the houses will be decorated in various ways – for example with chalk designs in front of the doors – and flags will be hung everywhere, especially the five-coloured Buddhist flag. And when they finally come together for the meeting, usually very late at night, everyone is agog to hear something about Buddhism. In short, everyone is alive to the occasion.

In the West we do things differently. We tend to lead rather separate, routine-filled lives. We are dominated, gripped, by routines and responsibilities, and in such circumstances how is it possible to be spontaneous, to bubble with spiritual life? Routine – by which I don't mean a carefully thought-out, balanced programme of activities, but a dull, mechanical daily round – kills spontaneity, and without spontaneity there is no life in any meaningful sense. You might even go as far as to say that life *is* spontaneity, that spontaneity is life. This is why I am here characterizing the traditional Buddhist teaching of the 'five spiritual faculties' as the 'pattern of Buddhist life and work'. The five spiritual faculties should amount, in the end, to a spontaneous and enthusiastic engagement with life, and the work of life, in the fullest and deepest possible sense.

What, then, are these 'faculties'? In Sanskrit and Pali they are called *indriyas*, and if we look at the etymology of this term we will find that it throws a great deal of light on the subject. *Indriya* denotes 'that which belongs to Indra' – Indra being, in Indian mythology, the ruler of the gods. So the *indriyas* are those things that pertain to Indra, the ruler, and thus the word translates as 'the governing – or controlling – principles'.

What is really interesting about this word, however, is its application to what we call 'the senses'. In the Indo-Aryan languages *indriyas* is the term given to the five senses (or six, if you include the mind). They are given this name, meaning 'governing, controlling, dominating principles', because the whole of human life as we normally live it is governed, controlled, dominated, by these senses.

Every living thing, whether vegetable or animal or human, belongs to a certain level of development. Every living thing, from the lowest to the highest, from the humblest to the most exalted, has its own place in the scale of evolution. And every sentient being is organized to function on its own particular level – which it does through the operation of its own particular range of senses: the *indriyas*.

This is quite a sobering thought, really. Most of the time we are controlled, dominated, governed completely by our senses – though these do include, according to the usual Buddhist way of reckoning them, the mind as a sense-faculty. We can see that this is the case most clearly, perhaps, first thing in the morning. During sleep the senses have been more or less in abeyance. But eventually we wake up, we open our eyes, sleepily turn over, and start becoming aware of the external world. As we do so the senses all begin to look for their respective objects and we start to act on the impulses to which they give rise: we make tea, we switch on the radio, we look for the newspaper, we decide to have another five minutes in the warmth of the bed. The senses of sight, hearing, smell, taste, touch, and mind are all moving out towards, and engaging with, various objects (including mind-objects), and this goes on all through the day. All the time we are being pulled by the senses, and therefore we identify ourselves with the senses and with the psychophysical organism to which they belong. And we function most of the time largely on that basic psychophysical plane of the *indriyas*.

However, this word *indriyas* denotes also the five *spiritual* faculties.[104] Edward Conze calls them the five 'cardinal virtues', but this translation fails to register the fact that it is the same word as for the sense-faculties. The fact that the same word is used for both sets of faculties is significant because it indicates the overriding importance of the five spiritual faculties to the spiritual life. The suggestion is that the two sets of *indriyas* perform an analogous function. Just as the five sense-faculties govern and control and dominate mundane life, so, in the same way, the five spiritual senses govern and control and dominate spiritual life. Just as we find our way about the physical world with our sense-faculties, so, in the same way, we find our way about the spiritual world with the five spiritual faculties.

If our various senses are – to the extent that we have them at all – more or less fully functioning, our spiritual faculties are embryonic and in need of development. It is the development of these five spiritual senses or faculties that makes up the pattern of Buddhist life. They are: *shraddha* or faith; *prajna* or wisdom; *virya* or energy, vigour; *samadhi* or concentration; and *smriti* or mindfulness. Let us take them one by one.

FAITH

I have known people who have been surprised to find that there is any such thing as faith in Buddhism. They have come into contact with Buddhism under the initial impression that it is essentially rational, that emotion is not really involved at all. This confusion arises out of two mistaken ideas: that emotion is essentially irrational, and that faith is the same thing as belief.

Belief – in the sense of accepting as true on authority something that one can never verify, or something that is even inherently absurd – is not faith, at least not in Buddhism. In Buddhism, as we have already seen in connection with the spiral path, *shraddha* or faith covers the entire devotional or feeling aspect of spiritual life. Faith in Buddhism could never be said to be contrary to reason – or even beyond reason. Faith is the emotional counterpart of reason. What you understand with your intelligence you must feel also with your emotions. The two go together, and you can't really separate them.

Shraddha in Buddhism is faith in the Three Jewels: the Buddha, the Dharma, and the Sangha. But it is especially faith directed towards the Buddha himself, because – at least from our point of view – the Buddha comes first. Even though the Dharma represents immemorial Truth, we would know nothing of it without the Buddha, and there would certainly be no Sangha without him. In Buddhism faith is essentially faith in the founder of Buddhism himself.

However, it's not just belief; it's not even just feeling. Faith in the Buddha is the sort of emotional response that you have when you are confronted by the embodiment of Enlightenment. This confrontation can take place in various ways. You can of course be confronted personally by some living human being who is the embodiment of Enlightenment. Alternatively, you can be confronted through literature, by reading about someone who was such an embodiment – if not the life of the Buddha himself, then perhaps the biography of the great Tibetan yogi, Milarepa, or that of Hui Neng, the sixth patriarch of Ch'an or Zen Buddhism. With any of the great masters or teachers, there is the possibility of an immediate emotional response to accounts of their lives – whether historical or legendary – a response that is not just sentimental, but engaged, challenging, personal, real.

Then again, you can be confronted by an image, an artistic representation – a painting or a statue – of someone who was Enlightened. And here I am reminded of a French Buddhist nun whom I knew in Kalimpong in the 1950s. She told me that in her student days in Paris she used to like visiting museums and art galleries, which is how she found herself eventually in the Guimet museum of oriental art. She was a rather militant, aggressive woman; she told me that she used to go around with a pair of ice-skates with which to defend herself if she was attacked. 'Well, I thought if I carried these skates with me, if anyone tried to attack me I'd slash the blades across his face.'

But as she strode along the galleries of the Guimet – having left the skates in the cloakroom – looking to left and right rather fiercely as she usually did, suddenly she encountered an image of the Buddha. From her description I gather that it was an image from ancient Cambodia. She just turned a corner and there was the celebrated smile – faint and delicate and rather withdrawn – so characteristic of this Khmer style of sculpture. The whole expression of the face is intensely peaceful.

This image – the face of this image – just stopped her in her tracks. She told me that she stood looking at it without moving, almost without blinking, for forty-five minutes. She couldn't take her eyes off it. The impression of peace, tranquillity, and wisdom that emanated, that streamed as it were, from those features, was so strong that she couldn't pull herself away. She hadn't yet studied anything about Buddhism, but as soon as she saw this image, she felt compelled to ask herself, 'What is it that gives its expression to this image? What is it trying to tell me? What depths of experience does it come from? What could the sculptor have experienced, to be able to express something like this?'

Confronted by this embodiment of Enlightenment, she could not move away unchanged. In fact, it determined the whole subsequent course of her life. This is the kind of emotional response we can have to an embodiment of Enlightenment simply rendered in stone, let alone one in the form of a living person. And it is a response that amounts to faith.

What it is in fact is the response of our potential Enlightenment – our own deeply hidden capacity for Enlightenment – to the actual Enlightenment with which we find ourselves confronted. There's something deep down within us that has a sort of affinity with what is fully realized, fully expressed, fully achieved, in that embodiment of Enlightenment. There's a sort of kinship. It's as though you have two stringed instruments side by side: if you sound the strings of one, the other starts softly vibrating too.

And what this response gives rise to is devotion. There are all sorts of different ways of expressing devotion, but traditionally it is done by means of prostration or worship, the offering of flowers, the lighting of candles and incense, and so on. Some people in the West are a little shy of Buddhist devotional practices. They would like to think that Buddhism had no truck with the kind of apparently superstitious activities that they were trying to get away from when they abandoned Christianity. They feel, perhaps, that these are practices for children, and that it is time to be grown-up and stop bowing and scraping and offering candles and the like.

However, if you leave out devotion you are closing the door on any emotional engagement with your spiritual ideal. A healthy spiritual life, just as much as a healthy psychological life, must include the expression of emotion.[105] Having said that, there is a balance to be maintained. Faith and devotion can go to extremes, and when they do so they become superstition, fanaticism, or intolerance. It is for this reason that, according to this teaching of the five spiritual faculties, faith – the whole emotional and devotional side of the spiritual life – should be balanced by wisdom.

WISDOM

Broadly speaking, in Buddhism *prajna*, wisdom or knowledge, is conterminous with the Dharma understood as truth, principle, reality. More specifically, it consists in seeing things as they really are rather than as they appear to be. It consists in seeing all worldly existence as conditioned, and thus as unsatisfactory, impermanent, and without an ultimate and unchanging self. At the same time it involves seeing the Unconditioned, by contrast, as being blissful, permanent, and characterized by true individuality, unimpeded by the illusion of a separate and substantial self. Wisdom is further seen, in the Mahayana development of Buddhism, as consisting in the realization of the great shunyata or voidness – that is, the essential non-difference between the conditioned and the Unconditioned.

Technically speaking, wisdom is of three kinds. Firstly, there is *shrutamayi-prajna*: wisdom or knowledge or understanding that is derived from hearing (or reading). You are sufficiently interested to take the trouble to listen to someone speak about the Dharma or to pick up a book and read about it, and you are receptive enough to derive some understanding from what you hear or read. It makes sense to you and you take it in.

Secondly, there is *chinta-mayi-prajna*: prajna or wisdom 'based on thinking', i.e. your own individual thinking. You start reflecting on the Dharma, chewing it over rather than just swallowing it undigested. You start thinking on your own account, seeking to arrive at an understanding based on your own thinking, working out the implications of the Dharma yourself, rather than having it interpreted for you by someone else.

Thirdly, *bhavana-mayi-prajna. Bhavana* means 'calling into being' or 'cultivating', and it is conventionally translated as 'meditation'; so this is wisdom based on one's reflections in the context of the experience of higher states of consciousness. It is not arrived at through intellectual excogitation. It is realized, intuited, seen, as a result of meditation, as a result of one's own spiritual – and especially transcendental – experience.

Most of us have had some experience of all three kinds of wisdom. We have all come to some understanding as a result of hearing about the Dharma, or at least reading about it. We have all developed our understanding as a result of independent thought, however rudimentary. And many of us have had moments of direct vision, some glimpses of the truth as mediated by a higher state of consciousness, especially in meditation. But it is important to be clear about which category of wisdom our experience falls into, and especially about whether it is our own wisdom or actually someone else's. It's easy to imagine that we have reflected upon something ourselves when all we have done is juggle with someone else's thoughts and insights.

A useful and illuminating exercise is to survey one's ideas and views and perceptions and assess how many of them can be found to be the result of one's own individual reflections. Unless one is a very exceptional individual, it won't be many. Nearly everything we know comes by hearing, or reading, so ninety-nine per cent of our knowledge and understanding we get at second hand. Nearly all of us tend to consume large daily quantities of facts and opinions, without giving much time to really thinking about them. Unless we earn a living by thinking, we probably feel we can't afford the time simply to sit and reflect upon things in such a way as actually to come up with a truly original thought.

Can one honestly say that one has ever had a truly independent thought? Has one ever really thought something out for oneself from beginning to end without any help at all? Has one ever thought something through and come up with an original idea? Has one ever had a significant thought – even a shade of a variation of one – that no one else has ever had? It happens of course, but *chinta-mayi-prajna* is quite rare.

As for *bhavana-mayi-prajna*, this is even more rare. We may imagine that we have had a direct, intuitive insight into something when all we have done is achieve a certain depth of reflection that has given us a clearer idea of it. The wisdom that almost any of us is likely to have garnered while in higher meditative states is infinitesimal.

All of which may sound unnecessarily discouraging, but it is in fact the reverse. If we never make these distinctions, we may flatter ourselves that the ideas and insights we embrace are our own thoughts, even our own experience. But by doing so we will not be allowing ourselves the option of actually moving on to a deeper and more personal investigation of reality, and even perhaps eventually the possibility of an actual experience of the Truth, a truly transformative wisdom.

Prajna represents the whole intellectual and doctrinal side of Buddhism. At least the first and second levels or kinds of wisdom do – the third, strictly speaking, is neither intellectual in a narrow sense, nor emotional either, but represents a sort of fusion of the two. But the first two definitely represent an intellectual – as opposed to an emotional or devotional – approach to the goal of Buddhism. The development of prajna can therefore, when taken to extremes, become a merely academic sort of knowledge. It can become, as a friend of mine once described the writings of a famous scholar of Buddhism, 'as dry as the last ounce of dust in desiccation'.

Unfortunately some people have a definite taste for this sort of thing. Another old friend, Lama Govinda, who originally came from Germany, said of his own countrymen that their idea of a good lecture on Buddhism would be a discussion of all the different possible meanings of a certain term according to various dictionary definitions, and follow this with a close analysis of its meaning according to at least a dozen Buddhist scholars, before concluding judiciously that all these views were wrong. This, he said, was the way to fascinate a German audience. And he said that the English liked a different sort of lecture. What they wanted was the complete picture, a single perspective on the whole subject. Whether this would still be the case today is another matter, but it does illustrate the way that a strength – in this case the German tradition of intellectual rigour – can become a weakness when it is not balanced by anything else. For this reason, in the five spiritual faculties, faith and wisdom form a pair. The one must be balanced by the other. Neither must be allowed to preponderate over the other; they must work together in harmony.

VIGOUR

As we saw when we considered *virya* as one of the seven factors of Enlightenment, it is defined by Shantideva in the *Bodhicharyavatara*, the 'Guide to the Career of the Bodhisattva', as 'energy in pursuit of the good'.[106] Energy in the usual sense of the word – as applied to people who dance all night or pursue money and power vigorously – is not *virya* at all. *Virya* is energy applied to the goal of nirvana.

Virya can be of two kinds – objective and subjective. The objective aspect of *virya* consists in doing things to help others, things that may involve a certain amount of physical effort and trouble, even difficulty. In its subjective sense, that is, as applied to one's own mental content, it corresponds to *samyak vyayama*, right effort or Perfect Effort, the sixth step of the Noble Eightfold Path. Right effort consists of the 'four great efforts': firstly, the effort to eradicate unskilful states of mind; secondly, to prevent the arising of unskilful states that have not as yet arisen; thirdly, to maintain skilful states of mind that are already present; and fourthly, to bring forth skilful states that have yet to arise. This is the fourfold right effort.[107] It is the effort to eliminate all unskilful states of mind, all states that are rooted in greed and hatred and bewilderment or delusion, and to cultivate all skilful states, all states rooted in generosity, love, and wisdom.

Both these aspects of *virya*, objective and subjective, need to be cultivated, as the Buddha himself never tired of pointing out. His discourses quite often get on to this subject of the importance of maintaining the momentum of one's practice. One presumes that he must have noticed his own followers tending to let things slide from time to time, to stop putting in the effort, to stagnate.

There is quite an arresting story from the Jataka tales that would evidently have been recounted in order to awaken energy that was beginning to flag in this way. The Jataka tales are a collection of stories about the virtuous activities of the Buddha-to-be in his previous lives, both human and animal. They're a kind of Buddhist folklore. This story concerns the god Indra, who happens to be on a journey when he comes to the banks of a great river, a river so broad that he can hardly see the further shore. Just down by the edge of the water he finds a squirrel that is behaving in a rather extraordinary manner. It is repeatedly dipping its big bushy tail into the water, and then lifting it up and sprinkling the water on the dry land.

Seeing this, the king of the gods is intrigued, and says to the squirrel, 'What on earth are you doing?' The squirrel replies quite cheerfully, 'I'm emptying all the water of the river on to the dry land.' Indra of course is totally bemused at the scale of this ambition: 'You foolish creature. Do you really think you can fulfil such a task?' But the squirrel looks at him, unabashed: 'Certainly – it's only a question of going on long enough.' Indra is quite impressed by that, and the Buddha comments that – yes, there may appear to be little progress taking place, we may not seem to be getting very far, but if we carry on long enough, anything may be achieved.

If we keep putting one brick on top of another, a house may be built. If we keep reading one page after another, a particular subject will eventually be mastered. If we keep doing a regular meditation practice, day after day, our overall mental state will change. Indeed, it is the only way these things can be done, by steady persistence. From moment to moment, even from day to day, we may seem to be progressing by such infinitesimal amounts that it can all seem to be a waste of time. But in the spiritual life, that is how we achieve anything: by regular, sustained, long-term effort.

However, there is no doubt that, like the other faculties, true vigour can turn into something much less helpful. It can become restlessness: energy in pursuit, not of the good, but of anything that will take us away from our experience of ourselves, anything that will distract us from our deeper task. If we can't settle down, if we're always wanting to be on the move, on the go, busy doing something – anything – then this is not vigour but a neurotic inability to sit still, a neurotic compulsion to avoid any kind of relaxed attentiveness to what is present before us. The result is activity that tends to be restless, agitated, and jerky, whereas real vigour is relaxed, easy, and smooth. Real vigour is achieved by not allowing one's energy to be one-sided – in short, by counterbalancing it with the spiritual faculty of samadhi.

ONE-POINTEDNESS OF MIND

As we have seen, samadhi covers the whole field of what we generally call concentration and meditation. Samadhi literally means the fixation of the mind on a single object – in other words, one-pointedness of mind. However, there is nothing forced about this concentration; it is more accurately described as a unification of the total energies of the psyche. Our energies are generally quite scattered – it is rarely that we are at once mentally, emotionally, and physically fully concentrated. Samadhi consists in drawing all of ourself together into a single focus of energy.

The Buddhist scriptures describe samadhi in terms of the four *dhyanas*. These represent progressively purer and clearer states of superconsciousness, which are attained as one's energies progressively become more and more unified. They are usually described, especially by scholars, in rather a dry, analytical manner – all one gets, very often, is a catalogue of different mental functions. But this is unfortunate, because it does need to be emphasized that these are actual experiences attainable by living human beings like you and me. And in fact the spirit, the actual human experience, of these higher or more unified states of consciousness is brought out very well by the Buddha himself in four famous similes.

Of the first dhyana, the Buddha begins, 'Suppose you take a plateful of soap powder....' By the way, this soap would have come – this may come as a surprise – from a soap tree: the tree has a large fruit that would have been dried and powdered, as it still is in parts of southern India, and used as soap. And the Buddha goes on, 'Suppose you then gradually mix your soap with water and knead it all together until you have a ball of soap absolutely saturated with water, so that there is not a single speck of soap powder that is still dry, and not a single drop of water trickling free of the ball....'

When you sustain this level of meditative concentration you are saturated with this higher consciousness: a blissful peace fills every part of your psychophysical organism. You are permeated by that super-subtle sense-experience, just as the powder is permeated by the water. There is no unintegrated energy draining away or drifting off.

'Well', the Buddha says, 'the first stage of dhyana is like that.' It is a state of unified consciousness, the union of positive and negative forces – the yin and the yang principles, as the Chinese tradition would say – within one's conscious mind. It is a state of harmony, integration, peace, in which the energies of the conscious and the energies of the unconscious mind are brought together, unified, and harmonized, just like the soap powder and the water in the Buddha's simile.

For the second dhyana, the Buddha proposes the image of a pool of water – perfectly clear, pure water – being constantly refreshed and replenished by a subaqueous spring. So the second dhyana is a clear pure state of consciousness into which rapture and joy are bubbling up all the time from deep within you.

As for the third dhyana, this is likened to lotus flowers immersed in a pond of fresh water: their stalks, their leaves, flowers, blossoms, seedpods – everything lives immersed in the water, permeated by the water, but still separate and distinct from it. Similarly we experience our consciousness as completely pervaded and fed by an all-encompassing bliss.

Finally, the Buddha comes at the fourth level of higher consciousness through another typically Indian image. He invites you to imagine that in the heat of the day when you are very hot and dusty you go and bathe in a pool or a river, and then, on emerging from the clear fresh water, you wrap yourself in a clean, cool, white sheet, and you just sit there like that, enveloped from head to toe. In the same way, in the fourth dhyana you wrap yourself in a purified consciousness that insulates you from all harm. The dust of the world cannot touch you.

Such are the Buddha's comparisons for the four successively purer and clearer states of samadhi.[108] However, although these are intensely positive and beneficial attainments, they too can be taken to extremes if they are practised on their own, without reference to anything or anyone else, without being balanced by energy and vigour. What you can end up with is inertness or passivity, even laziness or drowsiness. You find this particularly in the case of people who sit naturally and comfortably in meditation posture, and are happy to sit there, more or less undisturbed by gross mental activity, but not putting any effort into really deepening their awareness.

So samadhi must be balanced by *virya,* especially work that benefits other people, and especially physical labour. In the Zen monasteries of Japan, as in the pre-communist Ch'an monasteries of China, you get your full share of both meditation and work. However many hours of meditation you do, you will be expected to do almost an equal number of hours of hard physical work. And this means down on your knees floor-scrubbing or up to your elbows pan-scouring rather than deliberating over the arrangement of a couple of flowers or taking a delicate paintbrush to a porcelain bowl.

A friend of mine, Peggy Kennett, who became a Zen teacher in Japan after many years of difficulties (being foreign and female), once wrote to me describing the daily programme in her small monastery, where she had three or four disciples. They began at four in the morning with hard physical work until nine, and then had a simple meal, after which they got down to four or five hours of meditation, and finally they had another light meal in the afternoon. That was their life, she said: physical labour and meditation.

If they had been spending all their time in meditation you can be quite sure – in the case of the comparative novices, anyway – that they would have become just lazy. On the other hand, if they had been spending all their time in physical labour they would eventually have become – unless exceptionally gifted – more or less brutalized: just hewers of wood and drawers of water. So both must be there, at least to some extent: so much meditation, so much physical effort – a balance between the two.

Most people are naturally inclined either towards activity or towards meditation, depending on their psychology – on whether they are extrovert or introvert. Some people have suggested that Buddhism is particularly suitable for introverts because of its emphasis on meditation, but this is to fail to take account of the balance of qualities called for by this teaching of the five spiritual faculties.

Besides, once an individual has made some definite spiritual progress, they are beyond this sort of classification. You can say neither that they are introvert, nor that they are extrovert. It is important to balance a natural introversion, which may express itself in an affinity for meditation, with outward-looking activity and healthy work (or vice versa) – certainly in the earlier stages of one's spiritual career.

MINDFULNESS

In the Buddhist tradition, as we have seen, mindfulness, or the development of awareness, is practised with regard to four areas of experience. Firstly, as regards the body and its movements and attitudes, one is mindful of whether one is walking, standing, sitting, or lying down. One brings full awareness to the whole body, whether moving or still, and one is mindful of what each hand and foot and every other part of the body is doing. Secondly, one practises mindfulness as regards feelings, whether pleasant, painful, or neutral – whether one is happy or sad, elated or depressed, pleased or displeased. Thirdly, one tries to sustain mindfulness of thoughts: whether one is thinking about dinner or friends or relations or the work to be done the day after tomorrow, one should know exactly where the mind is going, where it is straying, from minute to minute.

The fourth area of one's experience of oneself to which mindfulness is applied is one's higher spiritual ideals. Whatever one may be doing, wherever one may be going, even in sleep, one keeps up at least a sort of undercurrent of awareness or mindfulness of one's ultimate goal. This of course is one of the purposes of mantras.[110] Repeating a mantra to oneself throughout the day is a means of keeping in touch all the time with one's ideals. One may be out shopping or sitting down with a cup of tea, or talking to someone – but if the mantra is always there in the background, one never completely loses touch with one's ultimate objective. So this is what the practice of mindfulness entails – maintaining some level of awareness of all these different areas all the time.

Nor is there any danger of getting caught up in an unbalanced over-enthusiasm for the practice of mindfulness. Unlike the other spiritual faculties, mindfulness or awareness does not need to be balanced by something else. If faith is not balanced by wisdom it becomes blind and fanatical. If wisdom is not balanced by faith it turns cold and dry as dust. If energy is not balanced by meditation it degrades into mere restlessness. And if meditation is not balanced by vigour it degenerates into sloth and apathy. But in the case of mindfulness and awareness there is no such danger. By its very nature it is incapable of degenerating when left to itself. It does not need to be balanced.

In fact, mindfulness is itself the balancing agent. It is only through mindfulness that you can balance faith and wisdom, energy and meditative concentration. And mindfulness is so pivotal to Buddhism because balance itself is so pivotal to Buddhism. Indeed, the Buddhist spiritual life is the balanced life at the highest possible level, in the broadest possible sense. If we're not trying to be balanced then we're not really practising Buddhism. Being Buddhist really means always trying to avoid slipping into extremes, or rather rising above the tendency to slide to one extreme or the other. It means looking for a point of balance, the pivot or fulcrum, as it were, between, or rather above, the extremes. And we do this through the exercise of mindfulness.

All this is not to say that mindfulness can be said ever to stand alone in any literal sense. In practice you can't really have any one faculty without also having the others, even if in a lesser degree. They are all present. One of them may predominate, but the fact that it is there at all means that the others are there, at least embryonically. And the spiritual effectiveness with which any faculty operates will depend on the degree to which it is balanced by the others.

For instance, you may have a lot of devotional feelings – you may be fond of offering flowers, lighting candles, and waving sticks of incense – but this will not constitute faith in any real sense without some understanding of the significance of it all. Thus there is no faith, properly speaking, without wisdom – and vice versa. There is no faith without spiritual energy, either, because when you participate in any devotional exercise a certain amount of effort is involved – at least you have to turn up. The same goes, too, for concentration: devotional practice and concentration go hand in hand. In the process of making offerings or chanting a mantra or reciting a puja or performing prostrations, you will, if you do these things with the appropriate faith and devotion, develop concentration – sometimes a deeper level of concentration than you might normally get even in meditation. And finally, of course, mindfulness must be there with faith, otherwise there can be no continuity to your faith, no possibility of sustaining it beyond a series of fitful impulses, unconnected to one another and therefore going nowhere.

So the pattern of the Buddhist life lies in the development of all the five spiritual faculties equally: faith and wisdom, energy and concentration, and above all mindfulness. In this respect it is interesting to compare these five spiritual faculties – or at least four of them – with the four principal yogas of Hinduism.

The word *yoga* in Hindu systems of thought means 'union' – that is, union with the higher self (according to the Vedanta), or union with God (according to the theistic forms of Hinduism). Thus each of the four yogas is a particular path to union with the higher self or with God. At the same time they correlate quite closely with four of the five spiritual faculties of Buddhism. *Bhakti* yoga, the yoga of devotion, corresponds to the spiritual faculty of faith. *Jnana* yoga, the way to union through knowledge, is the Hindu equivalent of the spiritual faculty of wisdom. *Karma* yoga, the way of selfless work, matches up with the Buddhist faculty of spiritual vigour or energy. And *raja* yoga, union through the royal science of concentration and meditation, is of course the Hindu version of the spiritual faculty of meditative concentration. The correlation is quite exact.

However, the significance of this comparison is to be found where the two systems part company, which is in the way they are applied. A Hindu teacher will tell a disciple who is very emotional to take up *bhakti* yoga – that is, to leave aside *jnana, karma,* and *raja* yoga, and seek liberation simply through being a devotee. Someone who is very intellectual, on the other hand, will be told to follow just the path of *jnana,* the path of knowledge and study. Then again, a person who is very active will be advised to take up the spiritual path of unselfish work. In modern India politicians are often accorded the courtesy title of '*karma* yogins', because of course there is no one so unselfish, if we go by the tenor of their pronouncements, as a politician: they give up all their time, all their energy, for the public good. Someone, finally, who is introspective, and perhaps a bit uncommunicative – a loner – will be picked out as a natural *raja* yogin, and will be set to meditate and not bother with knowledge, devotion, or outward activity.

Thus the Hindu approach is to follow the line of least resistance; they say that if your natural bent is towards, say, devotion, then you should specialize in that. However, Buddhists take the opposite – and more demanding – approach. They say that one should pay attention to the faculty which is weak. If one's faith is strong, then one needs to cultivate wisdom – and vice versa, otherwise one's strength will become a weakness. If one is meditative, then one needs to get up and cultivate some outward-going energy – and vice versa. Developing one's strong point fully will actually depend upon developing one's weak point. Indeed, all four faculties – faith, wisdom, energy, and meditation – need to be developed; otherwise one's spiritual development will be lopsided.

The reason for this difference in approach may well lie in the one faculty that is missing from the Hindu system. It is quite astonishing to note that mindfulness is not stressed in Hinduism at all – but this is my own personal experience, having heard Hindu teachers and pandits speaking on hundreds of occasions. Amongst many addresses and discourses about devotion, spiritual knowledge, meditation, and so on, not once have I heard mindfulness or awareness mentioned. It just wasn't there. This may be one of the reasons why in Hinduism you have to choose between the four yogas. You can't unify them because they can be unified only through mindfulness or awareness. There was one great Hindu teacher, Sri Aurobindo, who did blend all the four classical yogas into what he called an 'integral yoga' – but even he says nothing about mindfulness or awareness. Mindfulness does seem to be a distinctively Buddhist emphasis.

The environment for Buddhist life and work, for the growth and development of the five spiritual faculties, is provided by the spiritual community, the Sangha in the broadest sense.[111] It provides spiritual friends to help us identify where we need to put our energy, whether into meditation, beneficial work, devotion, or study. (As for mindfulness, this is to be practised constantly as an aspect of everything we do.) The Sangha also provides opportunities for us to help set up, support, and make use of facilities by which the spiritual faculties may each be developed. Traditionally, these facilities would have centred around viharas where the monks lived and practised and taught, but today in the West they often consist of public centres, retreat centres, Right Livelihood businesses, libraries, and so on.

NURTURING THE FIVE SPIRITUAL FACULTIES

The spiritual community is, we may say, like a greenhouse. Seeds are sown in trays under glass during the cold weather, to be transplanted outside when they have germinated and the weather is a bit milder. Likewise, it is in the more favourable environment of the spiritual community that our spiritual faculties will best develop. Of course, the plants remain in the greenhouse only while they're comparatively vulnerable, and in a way it is the same with us: the point of the spiritual community is not to provide a closed shelter from the world. But our spiritual faculties are always liable to be crushed, or frozen, or dried and withered, or burnt up, if we do not have the spiritual community – a favourable context for intensifying spiritual practice – to support us.

This image of spiritual development as being like the growth of a plant is of course a very traditional one, going right back to the Buddha's vision of humanity as being like a bed of lotuses. It can be useful to think in terms of nurturing our spiritual faculties, helping them to grow and develop by making sure we have appropriate conditions. I would say that, just as there are five spiritual faculties, so there are also five conditions for spiritual growth – though this is a list of my own, not a traditional one.

For the growth of a plant, obviously, five things are needed. First of all there needs to be a seed; and then the seed needs soil, warmth, light, and water. Similarly if we are to grow, if we are to develop our spiritual faculties, five things are necessary.

First of all, the seed is the potentiality for Enlightenment – and according to traditional Buddhist teaching, all human beings, even all living beings, do possess that. The seed is there. We can all become Enlightened if we make sufficient effort – of course, the effort involved is very great – and if conditions are propitious.

Then, just as the plant needs soil, we need circumstances that are favourable to spiritual growth and development. We can still develop to some extent if circumstances are unfavourable, but it's much more difficult. In particular we need leisure, health, and facilities of various kinds; and in the West we're very fortunate that usually these facilities do lie ready to hand.

Many Buddhists in India, for example, do not have access to the facilities that we enjoy. For them it's not easy to follow the spiritual life, for all sorts of reasons. I heard about a young woman who became a Buddhist and who wanted to take up meditation. But she came from a family who all lived together in a hut that had only one room – and there were eighteen members of the family. But she was determined to meditate. So she meditated every morning – she got up very early – sitting on a shelf to one side of the hut, and in that way she kept up her meditation practice. Not many of us in the West ever have to meditate sitting on a shelf in a small room occupied by seventeen other people, but this is what she did. I also heard of the case of an old woman who wanted to go on a week's retreat. The cost of a retreat in India is very small, but this old woman just didn't have that money. So what did she do? She worked for a month as a farm labourer, digging and carrying stones – this was at the age of seventy – and she saved up her money, and then she went on a week's retreat.

We don't have such difficulties anywhere in the West, certainly not outside some of the Eastern European countries, or perhaps some parts of South America. We have it very easy, and we don't always appreciate that. We have access to books. We have free time. We have health. We have leisure. So we have to ask ourselves, do we really make the best use of all these facilities?

Then, corresponding to the warmth the seed needs, we need the warmth of spiritual friendship; this is very important in Buddhism. I usually distinguish between two kinds of spiritual friendship: what I call 'vertical' spiritual friendship, between the less and the more spiritually experienced, especially between pupil and teacher; and 'horizontal' spiritual friendship, the spiritual friendship that springs up within the Sangha among those who are practically on the same level. And we really need both. We can't always be in personal contact with our teacher – if we have one. Perhaps he or she has many disciples and doesn't have much time to spare for us. But in any case we need just friendship, human friendship – and this we get from our peers. We all need this warmth in our spiritual lives.

And then, corresponding to the light that the seed needs if it is to grow, we need intellectual clarity, clear thinking. Not all Western Buddhist teachers, it has to be said, are celebrated particularly for clarity of thought; only too often one comes across serious misunderstandings and misrepresentations, even about quite basic Dharmic matters. Hence we need the light of intellectual clarity; we need clear thinking.

And then of course, more than anything we need the rain of the Dharma. And the rain of the Dharma must be pollution-free. It must not be an acid rain. In other words, the Dharma must not be mixed with non-Dharmic or even anti-Dharmic elements. Buddhist teachers in both

East and West are becoming increasingly aware of this danger. Yes, we need to engage in creative dialogue with the adherents of other religions and philosophies. But we need to be very clear about what the Buddha taught, what Buddhism teaches. We need the rain of the Dharma, desperately, more than ever before. But that rain needs to be pure, unmixed with Catholicism or Vedanta or secular ideologies. We need to saturate ourselves in the rain of the pure Dharma. In that way our spiritual faculties will grow and develop, and bear fruit: the precious fruit of Enlightenment.

10

THE THREEFOLD PATH: ETHIC

NO ONE WHO HAS READ in the Pali scriptures the
of the life of the Buddha and his disciples can dou
supremely happy people. Their love, compassion,
ness, and contentment profoundly impressed all w
orbit of their influence. Kings and courtiers, pries
widows, soldiers and scholars, farmers and artisans
the Buddha in order to learn the secret of that radia
wonder that among the many epithets by which he
Sugata, 'the happy one'.

But even during the lifetime of the Buddha there
who did not relish a reward as abstract as the pea
nirvana, but craved a teaching that would show the
human desires and aspirations. The Buddha wou
who felt like this by pointing out that there wer
which they could be reborn as a reward for vir
feeding the poor, providing for the sick, digging
shady trees under which travellers could rest. But
them that these celestial realms were temporary ab
of merit is exhausted, the inhabitants of these heav
in the ceaselessly revolving wheel of change, to be

10

THE THREEFOLD PATH: ETHICS

NO ONE WHO HAS READ in the Pali scriptures the glowing descriptions of the life of the Buddha and his disciples can doubt that they were all supremely happy people. Their love, compassion, renunciation, happiness, and contentment profoundly impressed all who came within the orbit of their influence. Kings and courtiers, prostitutes and virtuous widows, soldiers and scholars, farmers and artisans, all sat at the feet of the Buddha in order to learn the secret of that radiant happiness. It is no wonder that among the many epithets by which he is known is the title *Sugata*, 'the happy one'.

But even during the lifetime of the Buddha there were many people who did not relish a reward as abstract as the peace and blessedness of nirvana, but craved a teaching that would show them how to satisfy their human desires and aspirations. The Buddha would encourage people who felt like this by pointing out that there were various heavens in which they could be reborn as a reward for virtuous deeds such as feeding the poor, providing for the sick, digging wells, and planting shady trees under which travellers could rest. But he did not omit to warn them that these celestial realms were temporary abodes. When their stock of merit is exhausted, the inhabitants of these heavens are caught again in the ceaselessly revolving wheel of change, to be born once more in the human realm, and live and suffer as before. Perhaps, the Buddha would point out, once one had experienced these vicissitudes a few times, one would become weary of transient happiness and resolve to win the lasting bliss of nirvana.

The Buddhist ethical system also envisages a series of hells in which those who have behaved unskilfully are reborn as a result of their unskilful actions. But the hells are as transitory as the heavens. When their misdeeds have been expiated, the inhabitants of hell are born once more in the human realm, and have yet another opportunity to find the path that leads beyond the Wheel of Life."[12] In the Buddhist vision, all beings – even the bird and the flower, some would say – will ultimately become Enlightened.

THE LAW OF KARMA

All this, of course, follows from the law of karma. In its simplest and most widely accepted form, the doctrine of karma is merely an expression of the universal belief that as we sow, so do we reap: ultimately we ourselves will feel the effects of our actions. The doctrine of karma helps in some degree to explain the apparent discrepancies of fortune that exist in the world; but one has to be very careful here. Someone's suffering – or happiness – is not necessarily the result of their past actions. The law of karma is often much misunderstood in this respect. Here we come back again to the basic truth: conditionality. The Buddha identified five orders of conditionality, five *niyamas*, as Buddhaghosa subsequently called them: physical inorganic; physical organic (i.e. biological); psychological; karmic; and transcendental."[13] Unless one has the insight of a Buddha, one cannot be sure which niyamas have brought about what particular effect.

The example usually given is that of a fever. If one gets a fever, it may be a chill caused by a sudden change in temperature; or one may have caught a viral infection; or perhaps one has succumbed to illness as a result of some kind of mental strain; or it may have been caused by an unskilful action committed in the past; or it may even be the effect on one's system of transcendental insight. Thus the same end result may have been brought about by something physical, something biological, something psychological, something karmic, or something transcendental – or a combination of two or more of these.

Causality is a complex web; anything that happens or comes into being does so as a result not of one cause, but of many. Indeed – and this is an aspect of the Buddha's insight into reality – if one reflects on the factors that have produced the coming together of any phenomenon, there is simply no end to them. Consider, for example, what has 'caused' the loaf of bread (or the bag of rice) in your kitchen. Think of the people involved – and what 'caused' them. Think of their ancestry, stretching back into beginningless time. Think of the sun and the rain and the earth; think of transportation and packaging materials. Really, there is nothing, and no one, who has not been involved in the coming into being – and into your kitchen – of that loaf of bread. This is, incidentally, another way of coming at the truth of *anatman*, 'no separate selfhood'. Reflection shows us that nothing has an 'own-being' separate from everything else; everything and everyone is interconnected. To illustrate this, Mahayana Buddhism gives us the image of Indra's net – an infinite net of jewels each of which reflects all the other jewels in the net.[114]

The many-stranded complexity of causality means that if someone is suffering in some way, it cannot be assumed that this is inevitably the result of unskilful behaviour on their part. It may be, but you just can't tell. Hinduism adopts a fatalistic view of the law of karma, and some Buddhists seem to say something similar, but the Buddhist doctrine of the five niyamas makes it clear that someone's present suffering cannot be assumed to imply past unskilfulness.

What we can be sure of is that present unskilfulness is almost certain to result in future suffering (although some minor unskilful actions are 'cancelled out' by skilful ones); and skilful action will bring us joy. Our *locus classicus* here is the very beginning of the *Dhammapada*:

> *[Unskilful] mental states are preceded by mind, led by mind, and made up of mind. If one speaks or acts with an impure mind suffering follows him even as the cart-wheel follows the hoof of the ox.*
>
> *[Skilful] mental states are preceded by mind, led by mind, and made up of mind. If one speaks or acts with a pure mind happiness follows him like his shadow.*[115]

This is the basis of Buddhist ethics, sometimes summarized as 'Actions have consequences.' So here we have the law of conditionality as applied to the ethical sphere. The Buddhist tradition has many sets of precepts or training principles, the most universally practised of which is the list of five ethical precepts. They are not rules in any narrow, literalistic sense; it is more accurate to describe them as principles of ethical behaviour. They reflect the way an Enlightened person would naturally behave, so that in trying to behave in that way oneself, one moves gradually towards Enlightenment.

THE FIVE PRECEPTS

There are four basic precepts – together with a fifth which is equally basic but upon the practice of which not all Buddhists agree. This is the way they are expressed:

> *I undertake the training principle of abstaining from taking life.*
> *I undertake the training principle of abstaining from taking the not-given.*
> *I undertake the training principle of abstaining from sexual misconduct.*
> *I undertake the training principle of abstaining from false speech.*
> *I undertake the training principle of abstaining from taking drink and drugs that cloud the mind.*[116]

These five precepts enshrine, broadly speaking, the principles of non-violence, non-appropriation, chastity, truthfulness, and mindfulness.

The principle of non-violence is that we should refrain from harming or hurting others and, in particular, from killing or injuring them. Fundamentally, violence is the assertion of one's own ego at the expense of another. In its most extreme form it means the physical elimination of another in one's own personal interest. Violence towards another human being thus represents a denial of fundamental human solidarity, a radical assertion of separative selfhood, and a failure to identify imaginatively with another person.

If you are capable of violence towards someone, it is because you are failing to put yourself in their position, to empathize with them, to feel their feeling as your own. To a violent person, another person is simply an object, a thing. Violence is thus the ultimate negation of ethical and spiritual life; and non-violence in some ways represents the fundamental principle of Buddhism. There is one text, in fact, the *Mahavastu* of the Lokottaravadins, which says this – that non-violence is the supreme dharma. The implication is that if you sincerely try to practise non-violence you will find, in the long run, that you are practising every other Buddhist virtue. In principle they are all contained in non-violence.

Non-violence means not just that we should abstain from acts of violence, but that we should work for the welfare and happiness of mankind by every means in our power. This it is impossible to do unless our hearts are full of love towards people. Non-violence – *ahimsa* – may be defined as 'love in action'. If we want our actions to be harmless and helpful we should at all times cultivate a loving state of mind. Without this it is impossible to do any real good. A hateful thought can work untold harm in the world; all deeds of violence were once hateful thoughts, just as all acts of charity were once thoughts of love. Love is the only force strong enough to overcome hatred, and for this reason it is the most powerful weapon in the world. Clearly the practice of *ahimsa* on an international scale would entirely preclude the possibility of war or any other form of bloodshed or butchery, including capital punishment and the slaughter of animals for food. The ideal of *ahimsa* is that it should be universal in practice and universal in application.

A clear statement of this is to be found in the *Metta Sutta*, or 'Discourse on Divine Love', which is expressive of the very essence of *ahimsa*.

Now, may every living thing, or weak or strong,
Omitting none, tall, middlesized or short,
Subtle or gross of form, seen or unseen,
Those dwelling near or dwelling far away,
Born or unborn – may every living thing
Abound in bliss. Let none deceive or think
Scorn of another, in whatever way.
But as a mother watches o'er her child,
Her only child, so long as she doth breathe,
So let him practise unto all that live
An all-embracing mind. And let a man
Practise unbounded love for all the world,
Above, below, across, in every way,
Love unobstructed, void of enmity.
Standing or moving, sitting, lying down,
In whatsoever way that man may be,
Provided he be slothless, let him found
Firmly this mindfulness of boundless love.
For this is what men call 'the State Sublime'.
So shall a man, by leaving far behind
All wrongful views, by walking righteously,
Attain to gnostic vision and crush out
All lust for sensual pleasures. Such in truth
Shall come to birth no more in any womb.[117]

The second great principle of Buddhist ethics is the principle of non-appropriation. Violence is based on a strong sense of 'I' and appropriation is based on a strong sense of 'mine' – the two go together. So we must not take what belongs to others, either by force or by fraud – in other words, we must not steal. The traditional phrase is that we should not 'take the not-given'.

This is obviously going to mean not appropriating things that belong to other people – and this includes acquiring debts that one is unable to repay, and borrowing things without asking. But one can also take the not-given in the sense of taking people's time or energy without checking with them that they are willing to give it.

When it comes to the non-appropriation of material things, this includes the kind of thing that many people these days would hardly think of as theft at all. Living as we do in a world governed, even dominated, by institutions and multinational corporations, it is easy to feel that cheating them – perhaps fiddling our tax return or claim for social welfare, or taking home stationery from the office – is ethically insignificant, even justifiable in the face of what we may perceive as an unjust system.

This kind of attitude, though, fails to take into account the true nature of Buddhist ethics. Morality is not an end in itself. The altruistic aspect of ethical behaviour is obvious; what may not be so obvious is that our actions have their effect on us too. Each of the five precepts is expressed not just in 'negative' terms – 'I undertake the training principle of *abstaining* from taking the *not*-given,' for example – but also in positive terms:

With deeds of loving kindness I purify my body.
With open-handed generosity I purify my body.
With stillness, simplicity, and contentment, I purify my body.
With truthful communication I purify my speech.
With mindfulness clear and radiant I purify my mind.

Here we are reminded that practising these precepts involves the cultivation and expression of positive qualities as well as abstention from doing harm. We are also reminded, through the emphasis on purification, that in behaving ethically we are refining and purifying our own mental states, and thus preparing the ground for the practice of meditation and the development of wisdom.

Whether we feel that our appropriation of what belongs to the government or our employer is going to make any difference to 'them' is, viewed from this perspective, neither here nor there. If our aim is to see things as they really are, an aspect of this is going to be the attempt to break down the barrier between self and other. The practice of ethics gives us constant opportunities to do this, to go beyond the strong sense we have of the separation between 'me' and 'the world', or 'other people'. And, of course, we are reminded all the time these days that even actions that seem so small as to make no difference can in fact have a devastating cumulative effect: on wildlife, on weather systems, on the whole world.

The third precept relates to the principle of chastity. This is, obviously, about our sexual behaviour, and it means in the first place that we should not exploit others sexually, should not obtain sexual satisfaction by means of force, fraud, or misrepresentation. Sex, as everybody knows, is a very powerful urge indeed; the Buddha once said something to the effect that if there was another samsaric force that was as strong, we would have no hope of spiritual development. If one takes one's practice of Buddhism seriously, therefore, one will naturally find oneself relegating sexual activity to the periphery of one's life rather than allowing it to occupy a central position, and one's aim will be eventually to achieve complete chastity of body, speech, and mind, even though – to be realistic – for many people this may be possible only towards the end of life.

But we can all aim to cultivate 'stillness, simplicity, and contentment' in this area of life, aiming to be contented with our situation, whether we are 'married' or single, homosexual or heterosexual, and whether we choose to be sexually active or not. The Buddha had no pronouncements to make about sexual orientation or behaviour; nothing is singled out either for special approval or for condemnation. What is important is that we should bring a spirit of non-harming to our sexual activities, and that we should steer clear of the modern Western tendency to glorify the sexual relationship – a tendency that has manifestly caused a great deal of unhappiness.

The fourth principle is that of truthfulness. We should never in any way, either directly or indirectly, give our consent or approval to what we know is false. Truthfulness in its widest sense may be defined as unity of thought, word, and deed. In the Pali scriptures the Buddha is often referred to not as 'the Buddha' but as 'the Tathagatha'. There are various explanations of the meaning of this title, but one of them is that a Tathagatha is one who acts as he speaks and speaks as he acts. That this achievement constitutes almost a definition of Enlightenment itself shows how rare a quality complete truthfulness really is.

Without truthfulness there can be no such thing as commerce, no such thing as the administration of justice, and no such thing as politics in the true sense of the term. It is interesting that in the Pali scriptures, when the Buddha refers to truthfulness, the illustration he chooses is from the judicial context.[118] If a witness commits perjury even after taking an oath, justice cannot be administered, and if justice cannot be administered the whole social fabric collapses. The speaking of truth in the courtroom is an example – almost a paradigmatic example – of truthfulness, because unless the truth is held to be sacred in such a context, there's really no social, human life. And, one might add, untruthfulness consists not merely in telling lies, but also in refraining from speaking the truth when this might remove ignorance and misunderstanding.

In Swift's satire *Gulliver's Travels*, when Gulliver visits the country of the Houyhnhnms, he discovers that they are so virtuous that they don't have a word for 'lie'. Gulliver has to take great pains to explain what a lie is, and in response the Houyhnhnms coin a term in their own language: 'to speak the thing that is not'. So we 'speak the thing that is not' – we tell lies. But why? Untruthfulness is always based on negative mental states. We tell lies or suppress the truth, we exaggerate or minimize, either out of greed – to get something we couldn't otherwise get – or out of fear of punishment, or just out of vanity.

In some very rare circumstances, one may need to give up truthfulness for the sake of a still greater virtue. The classic illustration given by the Buddhist tradition is that of a monk who saw a man running to hide himself behind some bushes. Presently a band of ruffians with swords in their hands came dashing along the road in hot pursuit and asked the monk if he had seen the man they were looking for. And, of course, the monk said he had not. In such a case one can be excused from telling the truth since if one did so, one would incur responsibility for murder.

But most of us are unlikely ever to be caught on the horns of such a dilemma. The alternatives between which we are forced to choose are usually: to tell the truth and so lose something; or to tell a lie and so be enriched. In modern life there are many occasions when one may be tempted to bend the truth, particularly, again, when dealing with tax forms or other official business. This is another area of ethics in which it is easy to feel that the institutions of the state or the multinationals, impersonal as they are, will not feel the effect of our actions. This may or may not be true; but we ourselves will feel the effects of unskilful behaviour. We need to bear in mind the alienating effect of untruthfulness on our own mental states.

The fifth precept is broadly speaking the application of the principle of mindfulness. But – and this is why it is controversial in Buddhist circles – it is expressed in terms of abstention from 'drink and drugs that cloud the mind', and of course the most common of these is alcohol. There is some difference of opinion among Buddhists, even in the East, regarding this precept. Some believe that a Buddhist should abstain from alcohol totally. Others would say that one can take alcohol in moderation – that is to say, to the extent that it does not cloud one's awareness.

Personally I think that it is better if, as Buddhists, we can abstain totally. Even if the occasional drink doesn't do *us* any harm, what about the example we set? One has only to open the newspapers to see how much harm, how much damage, how much misery, how much loss of life, is caused by the abuse of alcohol. So I think that Buddhists really need to set an example here. Some years ago one of my students, touring around some of the Buddhist centres in America, was shocked to find that some centres actually had their own bar, so that, whether before or after the meditation, you could just go and have a drink, a cocktail or whatever. I think that, at the very least, alcohol should not be available at Buddhist centres or at Buddhist functions.

But, of course, there is more to this precept than the question of whether or not we drink alcohol, important though that question is. Mindfulness, one could say, is the characteristic virtue of the thinking or mental part of our make-up. It goes far beyond such practices as doing the washing-up mindfully, answering the telephone with awareness, and so on, although all such practices are valuable. Mindfulness means, above all, that every day of the week, every hour of the day, and every minute of the hour, we continually bear in mind the true nature of our situation. We need, in other words, to bear in mind the Four Noble Truths: suffering, the cause of suffering, the cessation of suffering, and the way leading to the cessation of suffering.

We have seen – in the chapter on the gravitational pull – that virtuous behaviour alone cannot take us to Enlightenment. This is symbolized not just by the second circle of the Wheel of Life, with its light and dark halves, but also by the third circle, with its depiction of the six realms. Skilful action will result in pleasant consequences for us, symbolized by the realm of the gods, and unskilful action will have unpleasant consequences, symbolized by the hell realm. But in the Buddhist vision both heaven and hell are still within the round of mundane existence, within the conditioned; once we have experienced the karmic consequences of our actions, we will still be faced with the necessity of finding the way beyond the Wheel of Life. This is why ethics or morality is only the first stage of the Threefold Path.

At the same time, this idea that mindfulness can extend to mindfulness of our purpose in life – indeed, that this is a crucial aspect of the practice of mindfulness – suggests that practising ethics fully is going to take us on to the further stages of the path. In practice skilful behaviour as conceived by the Buddha only makes sense in the context of a commitment to the spiritual path. There is no God in Buddhism insisting on our following a list of commandments 'because he says so'. Ethics is conceived not as an end in itself but as a means to the attainment of Enlightenment.

THE THREE REFUGES

This connection between skilful behaviour and commitment to the path to Enlightenment is made explicit in a practice that is followed by Buddhists of all schools: the recitation of the Refuges and Precepts. The Three Refuges are the Three Jewels of Buddhism: the Buddha, the Dharma, and the Sangha. The recitation of the Refuges is an expression of one's commitment to the Three Jewels, traditionally called 'Going for Refuge to the Three Jewels'. And then, straight after reciting these verses of commitment to the spiritual path, one chants or recites the Five Precepts. It is in the context of Going for Refuge, in other words, that ethical practice is most meaningful.

I want, therefore, to go into this question of Going for Refuge to the Three Jewels in a bit more detail. It presents us with another way of regarding the path to Enlightenment – indeed, I would say that it presents us with the most important, or at least the most fundamental, way of regarding that path. Going for Refuge to the Three Jewels, one could say, is the fundamental act of the Buddhist spiritual life.

Of course, to make sense of this one needs to understand what the Buddha, Dharma, and Sangha really are. For example, a Buddhist is one who goes for Refuge to the Buddha *as* the Buddha; he or she has faith in the Buddha as the Enlightened One, not something else. This may seem obvious, but it isn't to everyone. If, for example, one spends any time in India, one is sure to meet with Hindus, pious, religious-minded Hindus. And if, in such company, one mentions the name of the Buddha, they say, 'Oh yes, we know all about him. He is the ninth incarnation of the Hindu god Vishnu.' As a Buddhist one has to disagree with this view of the Buddha. When I lived in India myself I frequently found myself having to say, 'No. The Buddha was not an incarnation of a god. He was a human being, a human being who gained Enlightenment by his own efforts.'

Similarly, we don't go for Refuge to the Buddha if we consider him to have been just a wise man like Socrates, or just an ethical teacher like Epictetus. If we have that sort of idea about the Buddha – if we have any idea about him other than that he is the Enlightened One – there's no

Going for Refuge. Similarly, there's no Refuge if one simply admires the Buddha's personality from a safe distance, saying, 'Oh, how wonderful! The Buddha was so kind, so compassionate, so wise,' while not allowing oneself actually to be moved by his Enlightened qualities. No amount of simple admiration constitutes Going for Refuge.

In the same way, one has to understand what is really meant by 'Dharma' in order to go for refuge to the Dharma. The Dharma is the transcendental path to Enlightenment. If one regards it just as a source of interesting and useful ideas, or of merely academic interest, then even if one knows quite a lot about it, especially in its historical manifestations, one is not Going for Refuge to the Dharma, one is not actually a Buddhist. Academic knowledge about Buddhism certainly has its own definite, though limited, value; but Going for Refuge to the Dharma is quite another matter.

Going for Refuge to the Sangha means Going for Refuge to the Arya-Sangha, those men and women who have personally realized the higher stages of the transcendental path – Stream-entry and beyond. Sometimes it's said that one goes for refuge to the bhikkhu sangha, to the order of monks, but this is not at all correct. The Sangha to which one goes for Refuge consists of both monks and lay-people; indeed, on this level the distinction between monastic and lay doesn't have much relevance.

By the way, I am quite deliberately using the expression *going* for Refuge, not *taking* Refuge. Many Western Buddhists talk of taking refuge with Bhikkhu So-and-so or Lama So-and-so, but the original expression is definitely 'I *go*' – *gachchhami*. This is quite an important difference, I think. The implication is that Going for Refuge is an action, something one does. It's a movement towards something infinitely greater than oneself. One can even speak of Going for Refuge as a surrender of oneself. But 'taking' Refuge has a rather different connotation. It suggests appropriation; it suggests trying to make the Three Jewels yours in an egoistic sense – even trying to grab them – rather than trying to make yourself theirs.

It may seem like quibbling to insist on saying 'Going for Refuge' rather than 'taking Refuge', but the use of the latter expression may be symptomatic of an unhealthy trend in contemporary Buddhism. Nowadays we are presented with marvellous opportunities for understanding and practising many different forms of Buddhism. Things were very different when I came in contact with Buddhism more than fifty years ago. At that time there was only one Buddhist group in London – and it was probably the only one in Britain – and it had perhaps a dozen active members. I can remember us meeting during the war, in a little room in central London not far from the British Museum. On one occasion we were sitting there, meditating – well, at least we were sitting there with our eyes closed, trying to experience some inner peace – and suddenly there was a terrific noise and the windows rattled. Of course, a bomb had fallen. But I am glad to say that nobody moved. Whether this was Buddhist equanimity or British phlegm I'm not sure – perhaps we were all waiting for somebody else to move first – but nobody moved. We just sat there and finished our meditation. That was Buddhism in Britain fifty years ago.

Things are very different these days. There are at least a couple of dozen flourishing Buddhist groups just in London, and hundreds more throughout Britain, while in America there are probably several thousand groups representing nearly all the Eastern Buddhist traditions. These have all come to the West, at least as addressed to Westerners – I'm not referring here to the so-called ethnic Buddhist communities – within the last twenty or thirty years, in what amounts to a tremendous, radical cultural development. Before this happened, our knowledge of religion was pretty well limited to Christianity. Perhaps we'd just about heard of Islam, if we'd read about the Crusades. But now, well, not to speak just of Buddhism, we know, or at least we've heard of, so many different religions. There's been this vast expansion of our spiritual horizon.

But there's a danger – a danger of what could perhaps be called 'pseudo-spiritual consumerism'. Nowadays we're consumers almost by definition. 'I shop, therefore I am' just about sums up our philosophy. And there's a danger that we will bring this consumerist attitude with us when we approach Buddhism, especially when it is presented to us in so many tempting varieties, in so many mysterious, exotic, and fascinating forms. Only too often, I'm afraid, we just can't wait to get our sticky little paws on them. There's a sort of smorgasbord of spiritual goodies, just waiting to be devoured, and the temptation is to pick and choose as the fancy takes us.

If we do this, we become not Buddhists, not people who go for Refuge, but consumers of Buddhism. And to be a consumer of Buddhism is the very antithesis of the transformation that Buddhism is all about. As 'consumers' we assimilate Buddhism to ourselves, at least in its externals, assimilate it to our own greed, hatred, and delusion. But if we are to transform ourselves, we need to assimilate ourselves to Buddhism.

This commitment to transformation is a progressive thing. In the process of a deepening commitment, a deepening Going for Refuge to the Three Jewels, it is possible to identify a number of levels, and I have come up with my own terms for these, to paraphrase the equivalents in Pali and Sanskrit.

LEVELS OF GOING FOR REFUGE

The first level is what I would call cultural Going for Refuge, or even ethnic Going for Refuge. In the Buddhist East there are tens, scores, perhaps even hundreds of millions of Buddhists, and in a sense they all go for Refuge. At least, they all repeat 'To the Buddha for Refuge I go; to the Dharma for Refuge I go; to the Sangha for Refuge I go,' either in Sanskrit or Pali, or in their own language, so they all consider themselves to be Buddhists. But usually they repeat the refuge-going formula without attaching any great significance to it; it's just a formality.

I have seen this myself many times. In the East, at the start of any Buddhist meeting, someone, usually a monk, recites or chants the Three Refuges and Five Precepts, and everybody repeats them after him. But rarely do people ask themselves, 'What are we doing? What does this mean?' It's just part of their culture, something they always do. It's the respectable thing to do, even; it's respectable to be a Buddhist and recite the Refuges and Precepts from time to time. But not much thought is given to it. It's something that you've inherited, something you do because your parents do or did, or because your grandparents do or did. This is cultural or ethnic Going for Refuge. Its significance is not really spiritual, but mainly cultural, or even sociological. This is the first, and lowest, level of Going for Refuge. And, of course, one need not depreciate that level. It's a start, a starting point.

The next level is that of 'provisional' Going for Refuge. This is the level of someone who is genuinely interested in Buddhism – but only up to a point. They may try to observe the Precepts – sometimes. They may meditate a little, or even quite a lot – sometimes. They may read books on Buddhism, even take a degree in Buddhist studies. Many Western people who would describe themselves as Buddhists go for Refuge on this sort of level. At this point they are not making a serious effort to develop insight into the truth, nor are they really orientating their lives towards the Three Jewels. In fact, on the contrary, they may well be trying to fit Buddhism into a quite ordinary, probably quite affluent, probably middle-class, lifestyle. This is provisional Going for Refuge – Going for Refuge up to a point.

Then comes 'effective' Going for Refuge. When your Going for Refuge is effective, you have given some thought to the matter. You know what is meant by the Buddha, Dharma, and Sangha, and you really and truly wish with your whole heart, your whole soul, to go for Refuge. You wish to practise the Dharma, to follow in the Buddha's footsteps, to be an effective member of the Sangha, to develop spiritually, even to gain Enlightenment. And you are determined, at least in your conscious mind, that you will do that. You commit yourself to the Three Jewels. You haven't as yet had any major spiritual experience, any transcendental breakthrough, but you're doing your best to be a real, authentic practising Buddhist of this tradition or that. This effective Going for Refuge is the level of Going for Refuge of the majority of sincere practising Buddhists.

Even in the Buddha's day there were many, many of his disciples who achieved only this level of Going for Refuge, and it is illustrated many times in the Pali scriptures. Someone hears the Buddha teach, they are greatly impressed, and they accept the teaching sincerely – but they do not actually see reality. Nonetheless, they go for Refuge, saying 'To the Buddha for Refuge I go; to the Dharma for Refuge I go; to the Sangha for Refuge I go.' And this is effective Going for Refuge. One has a theoretical understanding of the teaching; one tries to behave ethically; one practises meditation; and one does one's utmost to develop penetrative insight or clear vision. One does one's best to organize one's life in such a way as to make such things – especially meditation and the development of insight – possible. In short, one orients the whole of one's existence, as far as one possibly can, towards the Three Jewels. One gives Buddhism absolute priority in one's life. One is then effectively Going for Refuge.

And then there's what I've come to call real Going for Refuge, which is synonymous in traditional Buddhist terms with Stream-entry and also with what is called in the Buddhist texts the 'opening of the Dharma-eye' Real Going for Refuge means that your faith in the Three Jewels has become unshakeable. The traditional phrase is that no shramana, no brahmana, not even Brahma himself together with Mara the evil one, could shake your faith in the Buddha, the Dharma, and the Sangha.[119] It is absolutely unshakeable, like the Himalayas themselves. And your ethical practice is also firmly established. Moreover, in that real Going for Refuge, there is a distinct, unmistakable element of what is called *vipashyana*, or clear vision, which means a vision of the transcendental, not as something distant, but as something that is present, here and now, actually realized, at least to some extent. *Vipashyana* represents a sort of entry into, an approach to, the Unconditioned itself.

Again, there are a number of episodes in the Pali Buddhist scriptures that illustrate this level of Going for Refuge. The Buddha wandered around India for many years, going on foot from village to village, town to town, city to city, sometimes travelling through vast tracts of jungle. And in his wanderings he came across all sorts of people. He might meet a wandering ascetic, or a learned brahmin, or a poor outcast, or a prince. Whoever they were, more often than not he would get into conversation with them, and start telling them about the Dharma. Usually he took a gradual approach. He would start off by talking about the benefits of generosity, then about ethics, then about meditation. Only then, when the ground was thoroughly prepared, would he start speaking about his own specific teaching – conditionality – whether in the form of the Four Noble Truths or in some other form. The person – whether ascetic or brahmin or outcast or prince – listened, and sometimes it happened that he or she was absolutely overwhelmed. And this experience found expression in what became a sort of stock phrase, indeed, a phrase that has become common to the point of cliché in our own time. People said that they felt as though they had 'seen the light'. It was as though they had been living in darkness before, but now light had arisen, and was shining on them.[120] Another common way of putting it was that one felt as though one had been relieved of a great burden, a great weight – nowadays perhaps we'd describe this as the weight of anxiety, the anxiety that seems to pervade modern life.

This person's Dharma-eye would open. He or she would see reality, see the truth of conditionality, see that the whole of mundane existence is painful (at least potentially), transitory, and devoid of permanent unchanging selfhood. As a result of this insight the man or woman to whom the Buddha had spoken would be utterly transformed. And then, from the depth of their heart would come these words: *Buddham saranam gachchhami; Dhammam saranam gachchhami; Sangham saranam gachchhami* – 'To the Buddha for Refuge I go; to the Dharma for Refuge I go; to the Sangha for Refuge I go.' This is the *real* Going for Refuge, the Going for Refuge that is consequent upon the opening of the Dharma-eye. It's sometimes called 'transcendental Going for Refuge', because it's the Going for Refuge of Stream-entrants and others on the higher, purely transcendental, part of the spiral path. But it is certainly a level to which all Buddhists may realistically aspire.

Going for Refuge is the central and definitive act of the Buddhist life. It is often quite neglected in some Buddhist circles, but in more recent times there seems to have been a revival of interest in it, as serious practitioners have looked more deeply into the teachings of their traditions. Followers of the iconoclastic Zen tradition, for example, have discovered that the great Zen teacher Dogen's faith revolved around Going for Refuge, pure and simple. As he was dying, apparently the last practice Dogen did was to walk around a pillar upon which he had written 'Buddha, Dharma, Sangha'. And he said, 'In the beginning, in the middle, and in the end, in your life, as you approach death, always, through all births and deaths, always take refuge in Buddha, Dharma, Sangha.'

THE REFUGES AND PRECEPTS

Wherever you hear the Three Refuges chanted, they will always be followed by a recitation of the (usually) Five Precepts. One can say that if Going for Refuge, or commitment to the Three Jewels, is one's lifeblood as a Buddhist, observance of the Precepts represents the circulation of that blood through one's whole body. So the Precepts are the expression of one's Going for Refuge. Not only that: they also support it, because one cannot truly go for Refuge while leading a thoroughly unethical life.

Of course, the precepts are a basic Buddhist practice. Once one has been a Buddhist for some time it is perhaps easy to find oneself thinking that there is no need to spend much time considering them; one may perhaps think that one knows them pretty well already. If one does think this then one has probably not given them any serious thought at all, and it may well be time to start making a practice of them.

It is easy to be distracted by the showier aspects of the Buddhist tradition, to be fascinated by Buddhist art and the mystery and glamour of the Tantra, or to be drawn into trying to disentangle beautiful knotty conundrums of Buddhist philosophy. It is also easy to forget basic things like the ethical precepts – which we do at our peril.

When I received Tantric initiations myself, I was told that initiation is a very secret, very sacred thing – it's not to be talked about. In fact, one of my Tibetan lama teachers told me that I was permitted to speak about a particular initiation I had received only with one other person whom he named. That was how secret it was in those days. But nowadays, in the West, Tantric initiation, even Anuttara Yoga Tantra, the 'Highest Yoga Tantra', is being advertised. One enrols for a weekend course, one pays one's fee, and one gets initiated, perhaps along with several hundred other people. One doesn't have to prepare oneself, one doesn't even have to be a Buddhist.

This is certainly not in accordance with the Buddhist Vajrayana tradition. I remember one of my teachers telling me that if one wanted to practise Anuttara Yoga Tantra one first of all had to practise the Hinayana (this was the term he used; nowadays we usually say 'Theravada') – for twelve years; one then practised the Mahayana for six years; then one practised the Outer Tantra for six years; and only then would one be considered ready to receive Anuttara Yoga Tantra initiation. But nowadays it seems one can do it all in the course of a weekend. Of course, some teachers will justify this by saying that they are planting seeds that will mature in the future, but I must say that I personally reject this explanation as a shameful rationalization. If one really wants to plant seeds, one should teach Buddhist ethics.

11

THE THREEFOLD PATH: MEDITATION

THE NUCLEAR AGE ... the Space Age ... the Age of Information ... the Post-Christian Era.... Any attempt to characterize the presiding spirit of one's own times is bound to be a rash intellectual procedure. Particularly is this so today, when the sheer range and rapidity of cultural developments make it hard to foresee what will turn out to have been the most significant. But from the point of view of Buddhists in the West, the present age has perhaps most tellingly been described as the 'Age of Anxiety' or the 'Age of Psychology'. Whether it is called the Age of Psychology because it is called the Age of Anxiety or vice versa is hard to say, but the two terms reflect the fact that what we may call the mind, or consciousness, has been the subject of a great deal of investigation and reflection in the West during the twentieth century. In fact, simply from an empirical and mundane point of view, humanity at present probably knows more about the mind and its workings, its hidden recesses, than ever before in history.

Although poets and philosophers have long had some intimation of the existence of the subconscious mind, Freud succeeded in placing the whole concept on an irrefutably scientific basis, subsequently giving rise to a whole host of (often conflicting) psychological theories. As a result, a number of mental illnesses can be treated with some measure of success, and abnormal mental states generally are better understood. Furthermore, various hidden powers of the mind – clairvoyance, telepathy, and so on – have been given a scientific stamp of authenticity. Research into drug-induced mental states has also changed the way in which we view the mind. Even mystical experience is no longer regarded as an unfortunate result of neurosis, brain seizures, or vitamin deficiency.

Thus ever more fascinating vistas are gradually being revealed to us. We used to have in the West a very limited and superficial view of the human mind. We thought of it as something relatively static, we identified it with the conscious mind, with the individual consciousness, and with the physical body. But we are beginning to see that the range of the human mind, the possibilities open to the possessor of human consciousness, are far more extensive than we have previously imagined.

We are often told, with the help of an image beloved of depth psychology, that the mind is like an iceberg, of which we see only a small part – the conscious tip, as it were – protruding above the waves. Underneath, like the vast submerged mass of the iceberg, there are layers and layers, levels and levels, of which normally we are simply not aware. This image presents us with an important half of the picture. For the other half we need to call upon a different image, that of a mountain, particularly a mountain of the Himalayas, towering up for thousands upon thousands of feet. The lower slopes, the foothills, are always visible, but most of the time you don't see the summit at all: it is hidden by an impenetrable blanket of mist and cloud. The mind is also like this: not only does it have depths of which we are unaware; it has heights of which we are unaware, too.

This growing psychological awareness in the West puts us in a better position to be able to meet Buddhism and understand what it is about. If we have come lately to an awareness of, and interest in, the nature and workings of the mind, Buddhism specifically addresses itself to these questions. In fact, we may go as far as to say that Buddhism is concerned with little else other than the mind. For instance, Zen is famously (though anonymously) defined as 'a direct pointing to the mind'. This is all that Zen does, in a sense: it just says 'Look at your own mind.' And almost every school of Buddhism is saying in one way or another, the same thing: 'Look at your mind. Look at yourself. Be aware of the heights and the depths of your own consciousness.'

Inasmuch as the emphasis of Buddhism is always on the practical more than the theoretical, Buddhists are more concerned with the heights than with the depths of the mind. Buddhism envisages heights of mind beyond mind with a view to the scaling of those heights – that is, with the expansion of awareness beyond its present upper limits to ever higher spheres of consciousness. And the way this is achieved – according to all schools of Buddhism – is through the practice of meditation. In fact, meditation may be defined, for general purposes, as the systematic expansion of awareness or consciousness.

The first and last thing to know about meditation is that it is something to be practised, to be experienced, rather than something to be talked about or read about. At the same time, we need to have a general idea of what we are supposed to be doing when we meditate, where we are supposed to be going with it. Without any clear sense of direction in our practice, we may get a definite benefit from it, but we may just as definitely feel that we are groping in the dark. So the aim of the following introduction to meditation, to the systematic expansion of consciousness, is to offer some help to those who have begun actually to practise meditation, and to suggest how they may orient themselves more effectively in relation to their practice, as well as to give an idea of what meditation is to anyone new to the subject. We will approach meditation by way of a consideration of four principal themes: why we meditate; preparations for meditation; the five basic methods of meditation; and the three progressive stages of meditational experience.

WHY WE MEDITATE

A consideration of one's motivation for meditation is a good place to start, because motivation is an important and constant element in determining how effective one's meditation practice is, and even whether one continues to meditate at all. Having known a great many meditators, I would say that there are basically two types of motivation or approach. These may be provisionally designated as the 'psychological' approach and the 'spiritual' approach.

The basic psychological motivation for meditation is the search for peace of mind. People who are not particularly interested in Buddhism or philosophy or religion, or even in psychology, may still be looking for something that they call peace of mind. They find that the hurry and bustle, the wear and tear, of day-to-day living is a bit too much for them. The various strains and tensions to which they are subjected – financial pressures, personal difficulties, problems with relationships, even perhaps degrees of neurotic anxiety – all add up to a general feeling of unhappiness. They hear that meditation can give you peace of mind, and they have the impression that Buddhists are happy, tranquil people, so in this way they come to Buddhist meditation, looking for some inner tranquillity, for the peace which, it seems, the world cannot give.

As for the spiritual motivation for meditation, this is at root the desire or aspiration for Enlightenment. In wider terms, it encompasses the desire to understand the meaning of existence itself, the desire to come to some sort of intelligible terms with life, or even, more metaphysically, to know reality, to see the truth, to penetrate into the ultimate nature of things. In this way meditation may be approached as a stepping-stone to something higher – to an awareness, an understanding, an experience even, of ultimate reality itself.

These two approaches – the psychological and the spiritual – are not, of course, mutually exclusive. You can take up meditation with a psychological motivation, and then find that imperceptibly the sheer momentum of your practice carries you beyond the boundaries of the psychological into a world of spiritual experience. And on the other hand, even if your motivation is spiritual from the word go, you will still need to establish a healthy psychological foundation for your practice, which may well involve a purely psychological approach in the early stages.

Indeed, it is not easy to draw a hard and fast line between the realm of the psychological and the realm of the spiritual. They shade into each other in such a way that you cannot always be sure which realm your experience and approach falls into. There is an overlap, a sort of common ground, between them. In terms of expanding consciousness, we could say that the psychological approach represents a partial and temporary expansion of consciousness, whereas the spiritual approach stands for a total and permanent expansion of consciousness. There is a difference of degree (in a certain sense), rather than a difference of kind, between the two.

However, they are, in the end, quite distinct realms, quite distinct approaches or motivations, and they should not be confused with each other more than we can help. If we identify the spiritual with the psychological, then we will be setting unnecessary limits on our practice and what we are capable of achieving with it.

PREPARATIONS FOR MEDITATION

These are essential. If we find ourselves dissatisfied with our progress in meditation – if the milestones are not exactly flashing by – it is probably because we have plunged straight in without doing the necessary preparation first. If on the other hand we are really well prepared, we are virtually meditating already, whether we know it or not.

First – and most important – is ethics. Of course, all Buddhists try to observe five fundamental ethical precepts, i.e. to abstain from taking life, from taking what is not given, from sexual misconduct, from false speech, and from intoxication. But precisely how does ethics relate to one's practice of meditation?

Modern Indian meditation teachers usually speak of the ethical preparation for concentration and meditation in terms of bringing under control – of moderating – three things: food, sex, and sleep. As regards food, they say that you should never overload the stomach. At the same time you shouldn't, they say, ever leave it completely empty, unless you are deliberately undergoing a fast. The way they explain it, a quarter of your stomach should be for food, a quarter for water, and half of it should be empty. It is also said that you should avoid certain kinds of food – especially hot, spicy food, which is supposed to stimulate the passions (and of which Indian people are inordinately fond). However, one can probably take this idea of certain foods having particular psychological effects with a pinch of salt. Suffice it to say that heavy food, and food that is conducive to flatulence, should certainly be avoided. The borborygmi of a whole roomful of people who have dined 'not wisely but too well' on hot curry can produce a volume of noise that is seriously disruptive of any attempt to meditate.

Moving on to the question of sex, it is said, of course, that celibacy is best, but this is simply not a realistic aim for everyone. So, instead, we can say that moderation at least – some degree of restraint – should be observed. Meditation calls for a great deal of nervous energy, particularly as you go into deep concentration, and this nervous energy is dissipated in sexual release. However, it is up to the individual to work out exactly where the most effective balance in this respect may be struck, according to their own particular circumstances, and based on their own observation and reflection.

The third thing to be restrained is indulgence in sleep. This is not often mentioned in connection with meditation, but – again according to Indian meditation teachers – what we should find when we meditate is that we need to sleep a little less than before. If we sleep well as a general rule we probably tend to take it for granted, but of course sleep is a wonderful and mysterious thing indeed, as poets throughout the ages have testified. There is, for example, a particularly beautiful and striking passage in Cervantes' *Don Quixote*, in which Sancho Panza sings the praises of sleep. However, it is only recently that we have begun to understand the real purpose of sleep. It is not, as was formerly thought, just to rest the body. The generally accepted view nowadays is that you sleep in order also to be able to dream, to sort out all the vast mass of perceptions and impressions of the day and file them away neatly for future reference.

When you meditate deeply, you aren't aware of the body, and therefore you are no longer taking in impressions, no longer registering input. So you don't need to process so much data – there is much less sorting out and filing away to be done, and thus much less need to dream. In this way, deep meditation drastically reduces the number of hours you need for sleep.

This does not mean that one should necessarily sleep less in order to meditate more effectively. In fact, most people nowadays tend, if anything, to sleep rather less than they need to. It seems that since the widespread use of electric light at the beginning of the twentieth century, people sleep, on average, an hour less than they did before then. There is no need to deprive oneself of sleep – this will lead to alienation. But wallowing in bed after one has had enough sleep will obviously promote lethargy and mental lassitude.

So ethical preparation is, in the first place, control of food, of sex, and of sleep. On top of these, however, and equally important, is the need to curb aggressiveness. Not just overt physical aggression, but any rude, harsh, domineering speech or posture (one sees this especially in the way many parents behave towards their children) will impede the development of positive mental states. And a vegetarian diet should be adhered to – conditions permitting – as an expression of one's dedication to a harmless way of life.

In summary, ethical preparation for meditation consists in leading, as far as possible, a quiet life, a harmless life, and a simple life. What is required is a peaceful life without loud noise, hectic social activity, or violent physical exertion. All these things can leave one's whole system too 'tingling', 'raw', and altogether too grossly stimulated to transmit the refined impulses that are generated by meditation.

I should add, though, that while strenuous exercise is not to be recommended as preparation for meditation, some kind of gentle exercise or relaxation technique – like hatha yoga or t'ai chi ch'uan – together with careful attention to finding a meditation posture that enables one to stay relaxed, comfortable, and alert, is very beneficial. One need not feel obliged, by the way, to adopt the classical cross-legged meditation posture. Sitting astride meditation cushions, or sitting on a chair, does just as well. The important thing is to experiment until one finds a comfortable way of sitting. One of the advantages of attending a meditation class is that one can get some help with establishing an appropriate and supportive meditation posture.

The issue of work, of livelihood, is also an aspect of preparation for meditation. Working at a certain job for six, eight, even ten hours a day, five or six days of the week, year after year, inevitably has an enormous cumulative effect upon the mind. You are being psychologically conditioned all the while by your occupation. Choosing a means of livelihood that is peaceful and beneficial in one way or another is crucial, not only as preparation for meditation, but as a basis for one's whole development as a healthy human being.

Checking through all these factors might seem like more than enough preparation to deal with. But there is more. A most important part of the ethical preparation for meditation is to be mindful and self-possessed. One needs to be aware of the body and its movements, aware of emotions and emotional reactions, aware of thoughts, aware of what one is doing and why one is doing it. One needs constantly to cultivate calmness, collectedness, mindfulness, in everything that one does, whether speaking or remaining silent, working or resting, cooking or gardening or doing the accounts, walking or driving or sitting still. One must always remain watchful and aware. This is the best preparation for meditation. Maintaining a constant level of awareness in this way means that as soon as you sit down to meditate, as soon as you summon up an object of concentration, you slip into a meditative state without any difficulty at all.

There are just two further points of importance. Learning meditation solely from books isn't enough, unless one is exceptionally gifted. By its nature, meditation is a personal, individual thing, for which no amount of general guidance and instruction can be enough. Moreover, a personal teacher will bring to bear upon our difficulties a degree of objectivity that we are unlikely to be able to attain on our own. A teacher is needed at least until we have some advanced spiritual experience under our belt. Even then, there can arise all sorts of spiritual dangers that a teacher who knows us well can see us through.

Lastly, there is preparation by way of devotional exercises. These don't appeal to everybody, but for those who are devotionally – which can often mean emotionally – inclined, they may be very helpful indeed. They come in all sorts of different – and some very elaborate – forms, but at their simplest they involve making symbolic offerings to a rupa or image of the Buddha before starting to meditate. Lighting a candle symbolizes the light of vision that we are about to try to light in our own hearts; flowers symbolize the impermanence of all worldly things; and finally incense, permeating the air all around us, represents the fragrance of the good, the beautifully-lived life, which influences the world around us wherever we go in subtle, imperceptible ways.

We have examined in some detail – not to say laboured over – the subject of preparation for meditation for a very good reason. If you are prepared to pay attention to all these details, then there will be very little more to do. One might almost say that you won't then need to meditate at all; you will have only to remain still and close your eyes and you'll be there – concentrated.

THE FIVE BASIC METHODS OF MEDITATION

Here I want to focus on five methods of meditation which correspond to the five 'mental poisons' that stand between us and our own innate Buddhahood.[121] Enlightenment is within us all, but it is shrouded in spiritual ignorance or *avidya* – as the vast azure vault of the sky may be obscured from horizon to horizon by dark clouds. This obscuring factor of *avidya*, when it is analysed, is found to consist of the aforesaid five mental poisons.

The first poison is distractedness, inability to control wandering thoughts, mental confusion; and the meditation practice that acts as its antidote is the mindfulness of breathing. Then the second poison is anger, aversion, or hatred; and its antidote is the meditation practice called in Pali the *metta bhavana*, the cultivation of loving kindness. The third poison is craving or lust, and it is countered by the 'contemplation of decay'. Ignorance, in the sense of ignorance of our own conditionality, is the fourth poison; and it can be tackled by the contemplation of the twelve links of conditioned co-production. Finally, the fifth poison is conceit, pride, or ego-sense, whose antidote is the analysis of the six elements.

THE MINDFULNESS OF BREATHING

The mindfulness of breathing is the antidote to the mental poison of distractedness because it eliminates wandering thoughts. This is one of the reasons why it is generally the first practice to be learned; no other method can be practised until some degree of concentration has been mastered.

This practice is not about concentration in the sense of a narrow, willed application of the attention to an object. It involves gradually unifying the attention around one's own natural breathing process, integrating all one's mental, emotional, and physical faculties by means of gently but persistently bringing the attention back to the experience of the breath, again and again. The point is not to *think* about the breath, or do anything about it at all, but simply to be aware of it. There are four stages to the practice. For beginners, five minutes to each stage is about right.

Sitting still and relaxed, with the eyes closed, we begin by bringing our attention to the breathing. Then we start mentally to count off each breath to ourselves, after the out-breath, one to ten, over and over again. There is no particular significance to the counting. It is just to keep the attention occupied with the breathing during the early stages of the practice while the mind is still fairly scattered. The object of our developing concentration is still the breath (rather than the numbers).

In the second stage we continue to mark the breaths by counting them, but instead of counting after the out-breath we now count before the in-breath. Ostensibly there may not seem to be any great difference between these first two stages, but the idea of the second is that we are attentive right from the start of each breath, so that there is a quiet sharpening of the concentration taking place. There is a sense of anticipation; we are being aware before anything has happened, rather than being aware only afterwards.

In the third stage we drop the support of the counting and move to a general and continuous (at least, as continuous as we can manage) awareness of the whole process of the breathing, and all the sensations associated with it. Again, we are not investigating or analysing or doing anything special with the breath, but just gently nudging the attention to a closer engagement with it. As our concentration deepens, it becomes easier to maintain that engagement, and the whole experience of the breath becomes more and more pleasurable.

In the fourth and final stage we bring the attention to a sharper focus by applying it to a single point in our experience of the breath. The point we focus on is the subtle play of sensation where we feel the breath entering and leaving the body, somewhere round about the nostrils. The attention here needs to be refined and quiet, very smoothly and intensely concentrated in order to keep continuous contact with the ever-changing sensation of the breath at this point. The practice is brought to an end by broadening our awareness again to include the experience of the whole of the breath, and then the whole of the body. Then, slowly, we bring the meditation to a close and open our eyes.[122]

THE METTA BHAVANA

The cultivation of universal love, or *metta bhavana,* is the antidote to anger or hatred. Metta, *maitri* in Sanskrit, is a response of care and warmth and kindness and love to all that lives, a totally undiscriminating well-wishing that arises whenever and wherever we come into contact with, or even think about, another living being. The practice is divided into five stages.

In the first stage we develop love towards ourselves, something that many people find very difficult indeed. But if one can't love oneself one will find it very difficult to love other people; one will only project on to them one's dissatisfaction with – or even hatred of – oneself. So we try to appreciate or enjoy what we can about ourselves. We think of a time when we were happy and content, or we imagine being in a situation where we would feel quite deeply happy being ourselves, and then we try to tune into that feeling. We look for and bring awareness to elements in our experience of ourselves that are positive and enjoyable.

Then, in the second stage, we develop metta or love towards a near and dear friend. This should be someone of the same sex, to reduce the possibility of emotional projections – and it should be someone towards whom we have no erotic feelings, because the point of the practice is gradually to develop a focus on a very specific positive emotion that is closer to friendship than to erotic love. For the same sorts of reasons, this person should be still living and approximately the same age as oneself. So we visualize, or at least we get a sense of, this person, and we tune into the feeling they evoke in us, looking for the same response of benevolence that we have been developing towards ourselves. Usually this second stage is the easiest, for obvious reasons.

In the third stage, whilst maintaining the sense of an inner warmth, a sort of glow that we have generated towards ourselves and our good friend, we bring to mind in their stead a 'neutral' person. This is someone whose face we know well, whom we see quite often, but whom we neither particularly like nor dislike. It may well be someone who plays a more or less functional role in our life, like a postman, a shopkeeper, or a bank-clerk, or it may be someone we see regularly on the bus. We apply to this neutral person the same benevolence and care that we naturally feel for our friend. It must be emphasized that what we are trying to develop in this type of practice is not a thought – not an *idea* – about developing a feeling, but the actual feeling itself. Some people may find this quite difficult to achieve – they feel dry and numb when they try to be aware of their emotions. It is as if their emotional life is so unconscious that it is simply unavailable to them to begin with. However, with time and practice it all starts to flow more easily.

In the fourth stage, we think of someone we dislike, even someone we hate – an enemy – someone who has perhaps done us harm or an injury – though to begin with it may be best to think of someone with whom we just don't get on. At the same time we deliberately leave our heart open to them. We resist the urge to indulge in feelings of hatred or animosity or resentment. It is not that we necessarily condone their behaviour; we may well need to criticize and even condemn it; but we stay in touch with a fundamental care for their welfare. In this way, by continuing to experience our friendly attitude even in relation to an enemy, our emotion starts to develop from simple friendliness into real metta.

These first four stages are introductory. At the beginning of the fifth and last stage, we bring together in our mind all these four persons – self, friend, neutral person, enemy – and we cultivate the same love equally towards them all. Then we go a little further, we spread our vision a little wider, to direct this metta towards all beings everywhere, starting with those close to us, either emotionally or geographically, and then expanding outwards to include more and more people, and excluding no one at all. We think of all men, all women, all ages, nationalities, races, religions; even animals, even beings, maybe, who are higher than human beings – angels and gods – and even beings higher than that: Bodhisattvas and spiritual teachers, whether Buddhist or non-Buddhist; whoever is eminent in good qualities. We may also expand out beyond our own planet, sending metta to whatever beings may live in other parts of the universe, or in other universes. We develop the same love towards all living beings.[123]

In this way we feel as though we are being carried out of ourselves in ever expanding circles; we forget ourselves, sometimes quite literally, becoming enfolded in an ever-expanding circle of love. This can be a very tangible experience for those who practise the metta bhavana, even after a comparatively short time. Not for everyone, of course: it is very much a matter of temperament. Some people take to it like ducks to water and enjoy it immensely within a matter of minutes. For others it is a struggle to get a fitful spark of metta going, and the idea of radiating it seems a joke – they don't see how they are ever going to do it. But they can, and they do. In the end, with a bit of practice, a bit of perseverance, it happens, it arises. If the potential for Buddhahood is within all of us, then the potential for metta certainly is.

THE CONTEMPLATION OF DECAY

The contemplation of decay or impurity, which counteracts lust or craving or attachment, is not a practice that many people care to take up, though it is popular in some quarters in the East. There are three different forms of it. The first, and the most radical, is to go to a charnel ground and sit there among the corpses and charred remains. It may sound a drastic course of action, but it has to be so, in order to counteract the fierce power of craving. You look closely at what death does to the human body and you think, 'This is what will happen to me one day.'[124]

There is no special teaching here, nothing esoteric or difficult to understand. There is no big secret in this practice. You simply recognize that one day your own body will be swollen and stinking with putrefaction like this one, your own head will be hanging off, and your own arm lying there on its own, like that one, or that you too will be a heap of ashes in somebody's urn (cherished somewhere, we hope).

These are all clear models of our own end, so why not admit it? Why not face the fact? And why not change the direction of our life to take account of this fact? It is in order to bring out such a vein of self-questioning that monks in the East make their way – often quite light-heartedly – to the charnel ground and sit looking at one corpse after another: this one quite fresh, recently alive; that one a bit swollen; and that one over there – well, rather a mess. They go on until they get to a skeleton, and then a heap of bones, and finally a handful of dust. And all the time a single thought is being turned over in the mind: 'One day, I too shall be like this.' It is a very salutary practice which certainly succeeds in cutting down attachment to the body, to the objects of the senses, the pleasures of the flesh.

If this practice seems too drastic, or even just rather impractical, there is another way of doing it. Rather than literally going to the cremation ground, you can go there in your imagination and simply visualize the various stages of the decomposition of a corpse. Or even more simply, you can just remind yourself, you can just reflect on the fact, that one day you must die, one day your consciousness must be separated from this physical organism. One day you will no longer see, you will no longer hear, you will no longer taste, or feel. Your senses will not function because your body will not be there. You will be a consciousness on its own – you don't know where – spinning, perhaps bewildered, in a sort of void; you just don't know.

If even this sort of train of reflection seems a bit too harsh and raw, a bit too close to the bone, we can reflect on impermanence in general. Every season that passes carries its own intimations of impermanence. The sweetness of spring is all the more intense, all the more poignant, for its brevity, for no sooner are the blossoms on the trees in full bloom than they start to fade. And of course in autumn we can contemplate the decay and end of all things as we see the leaves turning yellow and falling, and our gardens dying back into the earth. This kind of gentle, melancholic contemplation, so often evoked in English poetry, particularly the odes of John Keats, and in the poetic tradition of Japan – this too can have a positive effect in freeing us to some extent from our unrealistic perception of the solidity and permanence of things.

But really there is no need to approach even the most drastic of these practices in a mournful or depressed spirit, because they are all about freeing ourselves from a delusion that just brings suffering in its wake. It should be exhilarating – if you take up this practice at the right time – to remind yourself that one day you will be free of the body.

I did the cremation ground practice myself once when I was a young monk in India. I went along to a cremation ground at night and sat there on the banks of the river Ganges. There was a great stretch of silver sand, and at intervals funeral pyres had been lit and bodies had been burned, and there was a skull here and a bone there and a heap of ashes somewhere else.... But it was very beautiful, all silvered over by a tropical moon, with the Ganges flowing gently by. The mood the whole scene evoked was not only one of serious contemplation, but also one of freedom and even exhilaration.

This sort of mood probably reflects the fact that the practice overcomes fear. It is said that the Buddha himself used it for this purpose. If you can stay alone in a graveyard full of corpses at night, you are unlikely ever to be afraid of anything again, because all fear, basically, is fear of losing the body, losing the self. If you can look death – your own death – in the eye, if you can absorb the full reality of it and go beyond it, then you'll never be afraid of anything again.

However, the more challenging forms of this practice are not for beginners. Even in the Buddha's day, we are told, some monks who practised it without proper preparation and supervision became so depressed by contemplating the impurity and decay of the human body that they committed suicide.[125] So normally one is advised to practise the mindfulness of breathing first, then the metta bhavana, and go on to contemplate corpses only on the basis of a strong experience of metta. But all of us can at least recall the impermanence of all things around us, and remember that one day we too will grow old and sicken, that we too must die, even as the flowers fade from the field and the birds of the air perish, to rot and return to the ground.

THE NIDANA CHAIN

The contemplation of the twelve links of conditioned co-production is the antidote to ignorance. We have already gone into the details of this chain of links – or nidanas – illustrating the principle of conditioned co-production in terms of human existence. In this meditation practice one consciously reflects on it, by means of the images that depict it in the outermost circle of the Tibetan Wheel of Life, as follows:

(1) Ignorance, *avidya*: represented by a blind man with a stick; (2) volitions or karma formations, *samskaras*: a potter with a wheel and pots; (3) consciousness, *vijnana*: a monkey climbing a flowering tree (we climb up into the branches of this world and reach out for its flowers and fruit); (4) mind and body, *nama-rupa* (i.e. name and form): a boat with four passengers, one of whom, representing consciousness, is steering; (5) the six sense-organs, *shadayatana*: a house with five windows and a door; (6) sense-contact, *sparsha*: a man and woman embracing; (7) feeling, *vedana*: a man with an arrow in his eye; (8) craving, *trishna*: a woman offering a drink to a seated man; (9) grasping, *upadana*: a man or woman gathering fruit from a tree; (10) becoming or coming-to-be, development, *bhava*: a man and a woman copulating; (11) birth, *jati*: a woman giving birth; (12) old age and death, *jara-marana*: a corpse being carried to the cremation ground.

Here is the whole process of birth, life, death, and rebirth according to the principle of conditioned co-production. As a result of our ignorance, and of the volitions based upon our ignorance in previous lives, we are precipitated again into this world with a consciousness endowed with a psychophysical organism, and thus six senses, which come into contact with the external universe and give rise to feelings – pleasant, painful, and neutral. We develop craving for the pleasant feelings, and thus condition ourselves in such a way that inevitably we have to be born again and die again.

These twelve links are distributed over three lives, but at the same time they are also all contained in one life – even in one moment. They illustrate – whether spread over three lives or a day or an hour or a minute – the whole way in which we condition ourselves; how we make ourselves what we are by our own reactions to what we experience.

When we look at the Wheel of Life we are looking in a mirror. In all its circles and all its details, we find ourselves. When I contemplate anger, in the image of a snake at the centre of the Wheel of Life, it is not anger in general I am concerned with. When I contemplate greed, in the likeness of a cock, I am not considering the universal psychological phenomenon of greed. When I contemplate ignorance, in the form of a pig, I am not studying some category of Buddhist thought. It is me there, just me: the anger, the greed, and the ignorance – they're all mine.

Seeing, next, a circle of people either going from a lower to a higher state or slipping from a higher to a lower state, I recognize myself in them. I am never standing apart from that wheel: at any one time I am going either one way or the other, up or down.

Looking beyond these figures I may imagine that at last I am examining a representation of six different and separate realms of existence – which in a sense they are. The human realm is clearly my own, where people are communicating, learning, creating. But when I look at the realm of the gods I find there my own moments and dreams of bliss and joy, and in the realm of the titans, my own ambition and competitiveness. Grazing and snuffling with the animals is my own lack of vision, my own consumerism, my own dullness. In the realm of the hungry ghosts is my own desolate yearning for some solid satisfaction from the objects of my craving. And in hell are my own nightmares, my own moments of burning anger and cool malice, my own brief seasons of hatred and revenge.

Finally, in contemplating the twelve nidanas of the outermost circle we get a picture of how the whole process goes on, the mechanism of the whole thing. We see ourselves as a piece of clockwork, as indeed we are most of the time. Much of the time we are really no more free, no more spontaneous, no more alive, than a well-programmed computer. Because we are unaware, we are conditioned and therefore fettered. So in this practice we become aware of our conditionality, the mechanical, programmed nature of our lives, our tendency to react, our self-imprisonment, our lack of spontaneity or creativity – our own death, our spiritual death. Almost everything we do is just tightening our bonds, chaining us more securely to the Wheel of Life. The contemplation of the twelve nidanas provides a traditional support for this kind of awareness.[126]

THE SIX ELEMENT PRACTICE

The analysis of the six elements is the antidote to conceit or pride or ego-sense: i.e. the antidote to the feeling that I am I, this is me, this is mine. In this method of practice we try to realize that nothing really belongs to us, that we are, in fact, spiritually (though not empirically) just nothing. We attempt to see for ourselves that what we think of as 'I' is ultimately (though not relatively) an illusion; it doesn't exist in absolute reality (even though clearly it does exist at its own level).

Before starting, we develop a degree of meditative concentration, and establish a healthy emotional basis for the practice to follow with perhaps a preliminary session of the metta bhavana. Then we contemplate the six elements in an ascending order of subtlety: earth, water, fire, air, ether or space, and consciousness.

So first of all, earth – the earth upon which we're standing or sitting, and the earth in the form of trees and houses and flowers and people, and our own physical body. In the first stage of the practice we consider this element of earth: 'My own physical body is made up of certain solid elements – bone, flesh, and so on – but where did these elements come from? Yes, they came from food – but where did the food come from? Basically, the food from which my body is substantially made came in the first place from the earth. I have incorporated a portion of the earth into my physical body. It doesn't belong to me. I have just borrowed it – or rather, it is temporarily appearing in this form of myself. To claim that it is mine is, in a sense, theft, because it does not belong to me at all. One day I have to give it back. This piece of earth that is my body is not me, not mine. All the time it is returning to the earth.' When we see this clearly enough we relinquish hold on the solid element in our physical body. In this way the sense of 'I' starts to lose its firm outlines.

Then we take the element of water, and we consider: 'So much of this world is water: great oceans and rivers, streams and lakes and rain. So much of my body, too, is water: blood, bile, spittle, and so on. This liquid element in me – where have I got it from? What I assume to be mine I have only taken on loan from the world's store of water. I will have to give it back one day. This too is not me, not mine.' In this way the 'I' dissolves further.

Now we come to a still subtler element: fire. In this stage we consider the one single source of light and heat for the whole solar system – the sun. We reflect that whatever warmth there is in our own physical body, whatever degree of temperature we can feel within us, all of it derives ultimately from the sun. When we die, when the body lies cold and still and rigid, all the warmth that we think of as our own will have gone from it. All the heat will have been given back, not to the sun of course, but to the universe. And as we do this the passion of being 'I' cools a little more.

Then, air: we reflect on the breath of life, on the fact that our life is dependent upon air. But when we breathe in, that breath in our lungs is not ours; it belongs to the atmosphere around us. It will sustain us for a while, but eventually the air we make use of so freely will no longer be available to us. When the last breath passes from the body we will give up our claim on the oxygen in the air, but in fact it was never ours to begin with. So we cease to identify ourselves with the air we are, even now, taking in; we cease to think, even tacitly: 'This is *my* breath.' And thus the 'I' gradually begins to evaporate.

The next element is called in Sanskrit *akasha*, a term translated either as 'space' or as 'ether'. It isn't space in the scientific sense, but rather the 'living space' within which everything lives and moves and has its being. We reflect that our physical body – made up of earth, water, fire, and air – occupies a certain space, and that when those constituent elements have gone their separate ways again, that space will be empty of the body that formerly occupied it. This empty space will merge back into universal space. In the end we see that there is literally no room for the sense of 'I'.

At this point we should, at least in principle, be dissociated altogether from the physical body. So sixthly and lastly we come to the element of consciousness. As we are at present, our consciousness is associated with the physical body through the five gross physical senses and through the mind. But when we die we are no longer conscious of the body; consciousness is no longer bound up with the material elements, or with physical existence at all. Then consciousness dissolves, or *re*solves itself, into a higher and a wider consciousness, a consciousness that is not identified with the physical body.

This higher and wider consciousness may be realized at many different levels. The individual consciousness, free from the body, may be expanded to a more universal, even collective, consciousness; from that to the *alaya-vijnana*, the repository or store-consciousness;[127] and from that we may even break through to the fringes of Absolute Mind. In this way our own petty individual mind is dissolved or resolved into the ocean of universal consciousness, so that we go completely beyond the sense of 'I', and become completely free from the sense of 'mine'.[128]

The five basic methods of meditation fall quite naturally into two important groupings (though there is some overlap between them). The mindfulness of breathing and the metta bhavana are primarily concerned with developing *shamatha*, that is, tranquillity, calm, and expansion of mind or consciousness. Any technique of concentration on a simple object or developing a fundamental basis of positive emotion will fall into this category. And it should be said that some effective acquaintance with such techniques is essential before one attempts any more complex or advanced ones.

The other three basic practices are *vipashyana* practices – that is, they are concerned primarily with the development of insight, a deep, suprarational understanding of reality. Any visualization or devotional practice or mantra recitation will also be concerned fundamentally with this goal.

The sheer wealth of different meditation techniques that one may attempt to master may seem bewildering – or enticing. But in a way one needs to be wary of the very idea of a meditation 'technique'. All the five basic methods of meditation involve following certain tried and trusted procedures, and we need to be thoroughly familiar with these if we are to make progress in meditation. But this is not to say that the practice of meditation consists simply in the application of particular techniques. Meditation is not so much a science as an art, and in this art, as in all others, it is the inner experience rather than the technique that is all-important. It is even possible to master the techniques of meditative concentration and yet realize nothing of the real spirit of meditation. Far better to master the spirit – as well as the technique – of just one practice, than manage the empty manipulation of a dozen of them.

THE THREE PROGRESSIVE STAGES OF MEDITATIONAL EXPERIENCE

These are, in Sanskrit, *shamatha, samapatti,* and *samadhi. Shamatha* means literally 'tranquillity', so it stands for peace and calm and equanimity of mind. It is a state of perfect inward concentration, perfect equilibrium, in which mental activity of any kind, especially discursive mental activity, is minimal, or entirely absent. It corresponds to the four levels of superconsciousness known in the scriptures as dhyanas (or *jhanas* in Pali).

However, *shamatha* may also be subdivided – according to a different principle from that which distinguishes the four dhyanas – into three levels or degrees. The first of these consists in concentration on a gross physical object, as when you have your eyes open and you are fully concentrated on some material object external to your own mind. The second is when you close your eyes and concentrate your mind on the subtle mental counterpart of that original gross material object. Here, the degree or level of concentration attained is much more refined, much more elevated. As for the third stage of *shamatha* – the highest of all – with this you are totally absorbed in the object. There is no difference now between the concentrating mind and the object on which you are concentrating; you have become one with it. These are the three levels of *shamatha*.

The second stage of meditational experience is *samapatti*, which literally means 'attainment'. *Samapatti* stands for those attainments we experience as a direct result of practising concentration. It may happen that you see an inner light or hear sounds – of mantras, divine voices, and so on – and you may even smell a sort of divine perfume pervading the room even though there is no physical cause for it. You may see beautiful landscapes – and skyscapes – unfolding themselves before your inner eye. This is *samapatti*.

You may see figures of Buddhas, Bodhisattvas, great teachers, mythological beings, and so on. You may experience changes in your bodily weight, or your temperature – and this last may be a change that is not just subjective; you may actually be particularly cool or warm to the touch. You may have an experience of telepathy (reading other people's thoughts) or of clairvoyance (seeing things at a distance) or of clairaudience (hearing things at a distance). All these things come under the heading of *samapatti*. More significantly, you may experience intense rapture and joy, or a surpassing peace and bliss. And even more significantly, you may have flashes of insight, flashes of intuitive understanding of the nature of things, when at least momentarily you realize and become one with the truth.

All these experiences, from the highest to the lowest level, are *samapatti*-type experiences. Inasmuch as people's temperaments and levels of development vary greatly, there is also a wide variety of experiences of this kind. This is an extraordinarily rich field indeed. Nobody, however gifted, experiences all these different *samapattis*, but everybody, in the course of their practice of meditation, will come across at least some of them.

The third and last stage of meditational experience is samadhi, which, as we know by now, is a more or less untranslatable term. In fact, it's difficult to say much about samadhi at all. The most you can say, really, is that it is a blissful state of transparent and luminous voidness, free from all thoughts, free from the dichotomy of subject and object. And the perfection of samadhi, samadhi in its fullness, samadhi at the highest possible level, is equivalent to Enlightenment, or, at least, one aspect of Enlightenment.

So when we develop samadhi, we have reached the fringes at least of Enlightenment; and there we come to the end of what we call meditation. Consciousness has been fully expanded. It has expanded from the individual to the universal, from the finite to the infinite, from the mundane to the transcendental, and from the consciousness of ordinary humanity to that even of supreme Buddhahood.

12

THE THREEFOLD PATH: WISDOM

IN THE LAST FEW months of his life, there was one theme that the Buddha returned to again and again. The Pali Canon describes him wandering from place to place with Ananda, his attendant, everywhere gathering his followers together and reminding them of the path to Enlightenment. And the theme he chose was the Threefold Path: ethics, meditation, wisdom. He would say, 'This is morality, this is concentration, this is wisdom. Concentration, when imbued with morality, brings great fruit and profit. Wisdom, when imbued with concentration, brings great fruit and profit. The mind imbued with wisdom becomes completely free from the corruptions, that is, from the corruption of sensuality, of becoming, of false views and of ignorance.'[129]

This way of putting it reminds us that the Threefold Path is progressive. There is no meditation, certainly not to any great extent, without ethics; and there is no true wisdom without meditation. This was very much stressed by the great leader of India's new Buddhists, Dr B.R. Ambedkar. In his book *The Buddha and His Dhamma* he says, 'Prajna (wisdom), without shila (ethics), is dangerous.'[130] Mere prajna, Dr Ambedkar says – that is, prajna in the sense of intellectual knowledge – is like a sword in the hand of an angry man. Someone who is merely learned, who is just well-read, can do a lot of harm. Shila and samadhi are also necessary.

Dr Ambedkar goes even further than this. He says that even prajna in the full sense – wisdom based on a foundation of ethics and meditation – is not enough. But what else, then, is necessary? What else *could* be necessary? What could one need beyond perfect wisdom? The answer is, of course, compassion. True wisdom, in fact, is always accompanied by compassion. The Mahayana says that, like a great bird, the Dharma needs both its wings – wisdom and compassion – if it is to fly.

THE DIFFERENCE BETWEEN VIJNANA AND JNANA

There are several Sanskrit words usually translated as 'wisdom' or 'knowledge', which can be rather confusing. To begin with, there are the words *vijnana* and *jnana*. Both these words come from the same verbal root: *jna*, to know. But although they have a shared derivation, there is a clear distinction between them, a distinction that is of absolutely fundamental importance: for Buddhism, for spiritual life, even, ultimately, for civilization and culture itself.

The two words both have several meanings, but here I want to use them in the sense they bear in the teaching of the four reliances, which occurs in a number of Mahayana texts.[131] The first of these reliances is that one should rely on the teaching, not on the person who teaches. Secondly, one should rely on the meaning, not on the expression. Don't be misled by the expression; try to find out what is really meant. And then, thirdly, one should rely on scriptures of definitive meaning, not on scriptures of interpretable meaning. Some passages in the Buddhist scriptures are obscure, even ambiguous, whereas others are clear and straightforward; so one interprets the obscure in the light of the clear and straightforward, the interpretable in terms of the definitive. And fourthly, one should rely on jnana, not on vijnana.

As this fourth reliance implies, although jnana and vijnana come from the same verbal root, there is a big difference between them; in fact, they are opposites. Jnana sees things as they really are; vijnana sees things only as they appear to be. Jnana is free from greed, hatred, and delusion; vijnana is completely ensnared in them. Jnana is transcendental; vijnana is mundane. Jnana is of the nature of nirvana; vijnana is of the nature of samsara.

The vast majority of people, of course, rely on vijnana. To put it in the terms used in the Yogachara tradition, their knowledge is determined by the physical senses, by the so-called rational mind, and by the ego mind or ego consciousness.[132] Very few people really rely on jnana, on transcendental wisdom. Stream-entrants do, and so perhaps do the very greatest of the great poets and thinkers, but nowadays we may in fact say that most people not only do not rely upon jnana, but even have no conception of jnana as distinct from vijnana. For them knowledge is essentially vijnana, something empirical and rational, something of a sophisticated scientific type. People simply have no conception of the possibility of another kind of knowledge, no conception of the possibility of jnana. One could therefore say that as a Buddhist one's greatest task in the West today is to explain, even insist upon, the difference between vijnana and jnana. Unless this difference is understood and acted upon, there can be no real spiritual life, no real Buddhism, no real – as distinct from effective – Going for Refuge.

So we must rely on jnana, not vijnana. But we cannot rely on jnana unless we have at least some experience of it. And we cannot experience it unless we develop it. But how are we to develop it? Well, we develop it through the whole momentum of our whole spiritual life. We develop it as a result of meditation, ethics, spiritual friendship, Dharma study, Right Livelihood, and so on. In short, we develop jnana and learn to rely upon it on the basis of effective Going for Refuge. One could say that our effective Going for Refuge is not really effective unless we're trying all the time to transform it into real Going for Refuge, unless we're trying to make the transition from vijnana to jnana, from the mundane to the transcendental.

PRAJNA

But when one comes across 'wisdom' in Buddhist literature, the word being translated is usually neither jnana nor vijnana, but prajna. Prajna is also from the verbal root *jna,* to know, and the prefix *pra* is simply an intensifier; so prajna may be said to be 'knowledge proper', or even knowledge *par excellence*. Like jnana, prajna sees things as they really are, sees them according to reality. Like jnana, prajna is free from greed, hatred, and delusion; it's transcendental and of the nature of nirvana. Nonetheless there is a great difference between the two, jnana representing a state that has been achieved, while prajna represents a function or faculty. Jnana, in a word, is static; prajna is dynamic.

The nature of prajna is illustrated by a passage in the *Platform Sutra,* which is the foundation text of Zen Buddhism. Hui Neng, the sixth patriarch, says 'Samadhi is the quintessence of prajna, while prajna is the activity of samadhi.'[133] (In the context of the *Platform Sutra* samadhi does not mean concentration and meditation, but corresponds to jnana.) At the same time we should not think that the two – that is to say, jnana and prajna – are really separate. As Hui Neng goes on to point out, they are like the lamp and its light. He says, 'With the lamp, there is light. Without it, it would be dark. The lamp is the quintessence of the light, and the light is the expression of the lamp. In name they are two things, but in substance they are one and the same. The same is the case with samadhi [i.e. jnana] and prajna.'

As we have already seen in considering wisdom as a spiritual faculty, according to Buddhism there are three progressive levels of prajna: wisdom derived from hearing; wisdom based on thinking; and wisdom based on meditation. The attainment of this third level of wisdom – *bhavana-mayi-prajna* – is the attainment of wisdom in the full sense.'[134] In other words, it's *bhavana-mayi-prajna* that makes a Buddha a Buddha.

WISDOM, COMPASSION, AND SKILFUL MEANS

And as a Buddha, of course, one's dearest wish is that others too should experience the freedom of heart and mind that comes with true wisdom. This does not mean, however, that one just goes around giving people little homilies on the true nature of existence – or not necessarily, anyway. A Buddha's wisdom is accompanied not only by compassion but also by what is known as 'skilful means' (the Sanskrit word is *upaya*). The historical Buddha, Shakyamuni, seems always to have been able to find the right way of putting things to people. There are many examples of this, but perhaps one of the most poignant is the story of his encounter with a young woman called Kisa Gotami.

Gotami was her clan name, and Kisa – which means 'thin' – was a sort of nickname. She had not been married long, and she was the mother of a small son. One day the boy was bitten by a snake and unfortunately he died. Kisa Gotami nearly went mad with grief. She refused to give up her son's body, but went from door to door asking people for medicine to bring him back to life. She wouldn't listen to reason, but eventually someone had the good sense to suggest to her that she should go to see the Buddha. He would surely be able to give her the medicine she wanted, they said. This was all Kisa Gotami needed to hear. She went straight to the Buddha, laid the body of her son at his feet, and said, 'Please give me the medicine. Please bring my son back to life.'

For a while the Buddha was silent, and then he said, 'All right, I'll give you the medicine. But first I want you to bring me something. I want you to go and get some mustard seeds.' Well, that sounded easy enough. Kisa Gotami leapt to her feet and was about to dash off, when the Buddha said – and we can imagine him saying this very kindly – 'There's just one more thing, just one condition. The seeds must come from a house where no one has died.'

We can imagine that Kisa Gotami scarcely heard this. As she hurried towards the village, one thought was uppermost in her mind: that if she could persuade someone to give her the mustard seeds, her son would live again. She stopped at the first house she came to, and explained what she wanted. Of course, when they heard her story, the people who lived there were ready to give her as many seeds as she wanted. But then she remembered the Buddha's one condition. 'Has anyone ever died in this house?' she asked. And the householders replied sadly, 'What is this that you are saying? The dead are many, the living are few.'

So she went to another house, and the same thing happened. Then to another; the same again. In the end, she understood. Death wasn't just something that had happened to her son. Death comes to all, to every man, to every woman. Everybody must die one day. She therefore left her son's body in the forest, came back to the Buddha, and knelt before him. Putting her hands together, she said, 'Lord, please give me a Refuge.' So the Buddha gave her a Refuge – in fact three Refuges: in the Buddha, the Dharma, and the Sangha. She left home, learned to meditate, and eventually that glimpse she had had of the true nature of existence flowered into Perfect Vision, wisdom in all its fullness.[135]

THE PERFECTION OF WISDOM

The importance that Buddhists have always attached to the attainment of wisdom is reflected in the fact that there is a whole school of Buddhist thought and practice devoted to the Prajnaparamita, the 'Perfection of Wisdom', which has been called a 'wisdom beyond words', or even a 'wisdom beyond wisdom'.

Of course, the Perfection of Wisdom tradition began with the Buddha; that's where the story starts. The Buddha attained Enlightenment under the bodhi tree at Buddha Gaya two thousand five hundred years ago. He 'saw things as they really are'. And at first, as we have seen, he doubted if it would be possible for him to communicate his vision to other people. It was so – well, out of this world. So he was inclined to remain silent.

But eventually, fortunately for us, he decided he would teach. Out of compassion he decided that he would teach the Dharma for the benefit of those whose eyes were covered with only a little dust.

So the Buddha taught; and what he taught was an expression in concepts, images, and words of his Enlightenment experience. Not that he gave a definitive description of that experience. He didn't say much about it, in fact; he only hinted at it, he only pointed in its direction, saying, so to speak, 'If you go in that direction you will see what I saw.' As we have seen, he said that his teaching was like a raft. Just as one uses a raft to cross the river and get to the opposite shore, so one uses his teaching to cross the flood of samsara and reach nirvana. His teaching, he insisted, was only a means to an end, only a finger pointing to the moon.

But, as time passed, as the Buddha himself passed away, as one generation of disciples was succeeded by another, some of the Buddha's later followers didn't do what he had asked them to do. They didn't look from the finger to the moon; instead, they fastened their attention on the finger, so to speak. Or, reverting to the earlier metaphor, they made themselves at home on the raft, forgetting to use it to cross the flood.

This was particularly the case with what – to stretch the metaphor a bit – one might describe as the more doctrinal part of the raft. The Buddha himself had given only hints, but in the course of centuries those hints hardened for some people into certainties, even into dogmas, elaborate doctrinal systems. This was especially the case with what is known as the Abhidharma, which was the preoccupation of Indian Buddhist scholars for centuries. It came to be regarded as literally embodying absolute truth, and is still so regarded in some Buddhist countries.'[36]

But not all Buddhists agreed that the Abhidharma literally embodied absolute truth. Not all Buddhists agreed that prajna and Abhidharma were identical. And some of these Buddhists produced a literature of their own, a literature that went beyond prajna in the Abhidharma sense – or, one could say, a literature that went beyond literalism, that in fact fought literalism tooth and nail. This was the literature of the Prajnaparamita tradition.

This literature was produced over a period of several hundred years, until it eventually comprised about thirty-five independent texts, some of them very extensive indeed. But large or small, they are all known as sutras; that is, they all purport to be discourses given by the Buddha himself, although one cannot take it that they were literally given by the historical Buddha and then written down exactly as he gave them. Their particular emphasis, however, especially their anti-literalism, does go back to the Buddha himself, and the Buddha's own teaching.

The main theme of all the Perfection of Wisdom sutras is, as we have seen, emptiness, shunyata. Perhaps the best known is the *Vajrachchhedika*, or 'Diamond-cutter Sutra', generally known simply as the *Diamond Sutra*. Then there is the *Heart Sutra*. There's a Prajnaparamita sutra in 8,000 lines, one in 25,000 lines, and one in 100,000 lines – that's the longest of them all. And this vast literature, consisting of many volumes, was translated in its entirety into English by Dr Edward Conze – a feat for which all Buddhists can be profoundly grateful.

Gratitude is very much a Buddhist virtue. In fact – this may come as a surprise – even the Buddhas feel gratitude. The Prajnaparamita sutra in 8,000 lines says that the Tathagatas or Buddhas

> *treat the Dharma with respect, revere, worship and adore it, for they know that this essential nature of dharmas is just the Perfection of Wisdom. For the all-knowledge of the Tathagatas has been brought about from this perfection of wisdom, and for that the Tathagatas are grateful and thankful to her. With justice can the Tathagata be called 'grateful and thankful'. In gratitude and thankfulness the Tathagata favours and cherishes the vehicle on which he has come, and the path by which he has won full enlightenment. That one should know as the gratitude and thankfulness of the Tathagata.*[137]

If the Buddha is grateful to the Perfection of Wisdom, how much more grateful we should be, not just to the Perfection of Wisdom, but to the Buddha himself. We should in fact be grateful to all our spiritual friends, grateful to all those who have brought us into contact with the Dharma, or helped us to deepen our contact with it or understanding of it – and grateful to the translators of Buddhist texts, including Dr Conze, the translator of the Perfection of Wisdom sutras. Gratitude, we may say, is one of the greatest of virtues.

Nowadays, sadly, it is a virtue that is rather neglected. Sometimes people are ashamed to feel or express gratitude. There's a sense perhaps that we've been given something we didn't deserve, or at least that we feel we didn't deserve. If we receive something from someone, this seems to put us in an inferior position, and we don't like to feel inferior. This would seem to be the sort of difficulty we have with the idea of gratitude.

When I first came into contact with Buddhism in 1942, Dr Conze had only just started translating the Perfection of Wisdom literature. There was, however, an English translation of a Chinese version of the *Diamond*

Sutra, and when I read this it made a tremendous impression on me, as did the *Platform Sutra*, the sutra of Wei Lang or Hui Neng, which I read at about the same time. Reading these two works – I was sixteen at the time – I realized I was a Buddhist and in fact had always been one. I have therefore always felt intensely grateful to the translators of these two books – to William Gemmell, the translator of the *Diamond Sutra*, and Wong Mow Lam, the translator of the *Platform Sutra*. This is why when I published my book on Buddhist canonical literature, *The Eternal Legacy*, I dedicated it to their memory.

The Prajnaparamita texts have been described as 'dangerously disorienting to the unwary student'. They're disorienting because they completely upset our ideas about reality. In particular, they challenge our literalistic thinking. This is something that I've been given reason to think a lot about over the years. We think so literalistically! I would say that at least half the questions I get asked in seminars, and even in people's letters, are based on literalism – that is, literalistic misunderstandings. If people could only realize that they were being literalistic, and quite how literalistic they were being, they wouldn't need to ask those particular questions. But the Prajnaparamita texts perform the very useful function of challenging our literalistic thinking, especially our literalistic thinking about Buddhism itself. They compel us, oblige us even, to realize that a raft, even the raft of the Dharma, is just that: a raft. They insist on our looking not just at the finger but at the moon to which the finger is pointing.

As well as challenging our thinking, the Perfection of Wisdom texts encourage us to feel devotion, to take our understanding beyond the intellectual to something that is 'felt in the blood, and felt along the heart', to borrow Wordsworth's phrase. In its opening lines, the *Ratnagunasamchayagatha* challenges us to 'call forth as much as you have of love, of respect, and of faith'. The Mahayana tradition that produced the Prajnaparamita literature eventually came to venerate Perfect Wisdom in the form of a goddess, also called Prajnaparamita, a development that simply expanded on the sense of gratitude the Buddha felt for the wisdom through which he had gained Enlightenment. The goddess Prajnaparamita is visualized as gold in colour, and she holds a Perfection of Wisdom text to her heart; she is sometimes called 'the mother of all the Buddhas'. Perhaps – to end this brief series of reflections on wisdom – this hymn to the Perfection of Wisdom, from the Prajnaparamita sutra in 8,000 lines, will give as good an idea of what is meant by 'wisdom' in

Buddhism as we are going to find. In the text, Shariputra addresses the Buddha, saying:

> *The perfection of wisdom gives light, O Lord. I pay homage to the perfection of wisdom! She is worthy of homage. She is unstained, the entire world cannot stain her. She is a source of light, and from everyone in the triple world she removes darkness, and she leads away from the blinding darkness caused by the defilements and by wrong views. In her we can find shelter. Most excellent are her works. She makes us seek the safety of the wings of Enlightenment. She brings light to the blind, she brings light so that all fear and distress may be forsaken. She has gained the five eyes, and she shows the path to all beings. She herself is an organ of vision. She disperses the gloom and darkness of delusion. She does nothing about all dharmas. She guides to the path those who have strayed on to a bad road. She is identical with all-knowledge. She never produces any dharma, because she has forsaken the residues relating to both kinds of coverings, those produced by defilement and those produced by the cognizable. She does not stop any dharma. Herself unstopped and unproduced is the perfection of wisdom. She is the mother of the Bodhisattvas, on account of the emptiness of own marks. As the donor of the jewel of all the Buddha-dharmas she brings about the ten powers (of a Buddha). She cannot be crushed. She protects the unprotected, with the help of the four grounds of self-confidence. She is the antidote to birth and death. She has a clear knowledge of the own-being of all dharmas, for she does not stray away from it. The perfection of wisdom of the Buddhas, the Lords, sets in motion the wheel of the Dharma.*[138]

13

THE COSMIC SIGNIFICANCE OF THE BODHISATTVA IDEAL

WHAT IS THE DHARMA? This is the question we have been pursuing, now from this angle, now from that. And the same question, of course, has exercised the Buddha's followers ever since the Buddha himself was alive. The Buddha, we know, lived and taught for some forty-five years before his final passing away, which is traditionally known as the *parinirvana*, the attainment of supreme nirvana, the ultimate peace, beyond conditioned things, eternal and complete and self-illuminating. And after the Buddha's *parinirvana*, there arose among his disciples two groups, or two parties if you like.

One party was on the whole quite satisfied with the Buddha's verbal teaching. They were deeply interested in the different doctrinal formulations of the teaching: the Four Noble Truths, the Eightfold Path, the seven stages of purification, the five skandhas, the twelve nidanas, and so on. In fact they concentrated on the verbal teaching so much that they came to regard it as being Buddhism, the whole of Buddhism. For them this *was* the Dharma.

But the other party was not quite satisfied with this. Yes, they accepted the Buddha's verbal teaching and all the doctrinal formulations, but they felt that this was not the whole story. Above and beyond – or if you like behind – the verbal teaching, the actual life and personality (to use a much abused term) of the Buddha had also to be taken into consideration. What the Buddha himself was as a man, an Enlightened man, an Enlightened being, and what he did, was at least as important as what he said. The verbal, doctrinal teaching gave expression to the Buddha's wisdom, but his life, his person, his activity, gave expression to his compassion.

In maintaining this, this group of Buddhists would have been able to cite many examples of the Buddha's generosity and kindness towards all those with whom he came into contact. The Buddha's lifetime was still within living memory, and the Buddhist community was taking great care to preserve all the many teachings, as well as all the anecdotes and stories about the Buddha, memorizing them and passing them on orally – for it would be several hundred years before any of it would be written down. But perhaps the most telling account of what the Buddha was really like is to be found in the records of his relationship with the man with whose name, as it happens, that oral tradition is most closely associated: Ananda.

Ananda was one of the Buddha's cousins, and his attendant for the last twenty years of his life. He is credited with having had perfect recall, so that when it came to recording – or rather memorizing – the Buddha's many teachings for posterity, Ananda was the main source of information. After all, he was with the Buddha all the time; he heard whatever he said and remembered it word for word. If he happened to miss a teaching, the Buddha would repeat it to him later. So Ananda, perhaps more than anyone, is intimately associated with the Buddha's doctrinal teachings.

But as far as Ananda himself was concerned, there was something else that was even more important to him. When the Buddha was close to death, Ananda was found weeping, saying to himself again and again, 'The Master is about to pass away from me: he who is so kind.'[139] These words of Ananda's, as he stood there by the door of the hut where the Buddha was lying ill, are of the very greatest significance. Ananda had been with the Buddha for twenty years. He had heard the Buddha deliver hundreds of discourses, abstruse, philosophical, deeply mystical discourses. He had heard him answer thousands of questions. He must have admired his brilliance, his affability, the ease with which he handled difficult questions. And no doubt he had also witnessed all sorts of odd things about the Buddha, all sorts of strange, supernormal happenings.

But what was the overall impression of the Buddha's character upon Ananda after all those years, all those teachings? It is expressed in those few words that Ananda uttered as he wept: 'he who is so kind'. This is very significant. Ananda was not grieving for him 'who is so wise', or him 'who is so Enlightened', or him 'who has such a deep philosophical understanding', or him 'who is such a brilliant debater', or him 'who has worked so many miracles', or him 'who is so brave', or him 'who is so tireless'; but for him 'who is so kind'.

Hence the Buddha's compassionate heart had to be taken into account as much as his wise mind – this is what the second party of his followers maintained. Buddhism comprises not just wisdom but also compassion, they said, and both of them together form the spiritual ideal. Yes, Buddhists should seek to gain Enlightenment – this gives expression to the wisdom aspect of the Dharma. But they should seek to gain Enlightenment for the sake of all sentient beings. It is this that gives expression to the Dharma's compassionate aspect.

From this instinct on the part of these early Buddhists eventually emerged what became known as the Mahayana school of Buddhism. It was the Mahayanists who came up with the image we have already encountered: the bird of Enlightenment held aloft by the two wings of compassion and wisdom. And among the many teachings of the Mahayana, towering above them like a mountain peak above so many foothills, was its central conception: the Bodhisattva Ideal. For in the Bodhisattva wisdom and compassion are perfectly combined.

THE BODHISATTVA AND THE WILL TO ENLIGHTENMENT

But what is a Bodhisattva? A Bodhisattva is a being (*sattva*) who lives for the sake of Enlightenment (*bodhi*). Thus the Bodhisattva Ideal is nothing other than a statement of the Buddhist ideal itself, the ideal of the attainment of Enlightenment, the ideal of evolution from a state of unenlightened to a state of Enlightened humanity. But it is even more than that. The Bodhisattva is further defined as one who seeks to gain Enlightenment not just for the sake of his or her own emancipation from suffering and ignorance, but in order that all sentient beings may also gain Enlightenment. This was the Mahayana's way of drawing in the compassionate aspect, the altruistic dimension, of the desire to gain Enlightenment.[140]

So the next question is: how does one become a Bodhisattva? How does one embark on the actual realization of this ideal? The general Mahayana answer to this question is that one becomes a Bodhisattva by the arising of what is called the *bodhichitta*. Some scholars translate *bodhichitta* as 'thought of Enlightenment', but this is exactly what it is not. It is not a thought about Enlightenment but an urge in the direction of Enlightenment, an urge of one's whole being. In fact, going even further than this, the great Mahayana teachers say that the bodhichitta is not a conditioned mental state or function at all. In traditional terms it is not included in the five aggregates (*skandhas*) that between them make up the whole of conditioned existence. The bodhichitta is something transcendental, something belonging to the Beyond, a reflection of the Unconditioned in the midst of the conditioned. It is perhaps best to translate it as the 'will to Enlightenment'.

But we must not think that this will to Enlightenment is anybody's individual will. The bodhichitta is not individual. It arises in different Bodhisattvas, but there are not as many bodhichittas as there are Bodhisattvas. There's only one supreme, transcendental bodhichitta, in which individuals participate, or which individuals manifest, in varying degrees. It is a sort of cosmic will, a universal will to universal redemption. And those of whom it takes possession, in whom it arises or manifests, become – or are – Bodhisattvas.

This is the metaphysical answer to the question of how one becomes a Bodhisattva. But if one is going to take this ideal seriously, if one is going to regard following the path of the Bodhisattva as a practical proposition, one is naturally going to need some idea of how to go about it. Strictly speaking, the Bodhisattva's career begins with the taking of a vow. The bodhichitta is universal, but the Bodhisattva is an individual, and the bodhichitta therefore expresses itself in his or her life and work in an individual manner. This individual expression, in and through the Bodhisattva, of the cosmic, transcendental bodhichitta is known as the Bodhisattva Vow. This vow, though, is not just a verbal expression, not just a statement of intent that one hopes will galvanize one into action. By the time you take it, the whole momentum of your being will be behind your intention; it represents a reorientation of your entire being.

THE BODHISATTVA VOW

The Bodhisattva Vow is traditionally spoken of in the singular but it is really plural. There are quite a number of sets of vows, but the best known is that of the Four Great Vows, which are still repeated, especially in Mahayana monasteries, all over the Buddhist world: 'May I deliver all beings from difficulties; may I eradicate all passions; may I master all dharmas; may I lead all beings to Buddhahood.'

But this is still not practical enough as far as we are concerned. Clearly to take these vows in full confidence that one could fulfil them, one would need already to have done a good deal of spiritual practice. The situation is analogous, in a way, to the relationship between the mundane Eightfold Path and the transcendental Eightfold Path. Once Perfect Vision in the full sense has arisen, one can perfect each of the remaining seven stages of the path. But one can work towards the arising of that Perfect Vision through following the path on a mundane level.

THE SIX PERFECTIONS

Similarly, once the bodhichitta has arisen in the Bodhisattva, he or she can take the Bodhisattva Vow in full confidence that that vow will be fulfilled. Then, as the 'establishment aspect' – as it is called – of the arising of the bodhichitta, the Bodhisattva practises six *paramitas*, six perfections or transcendental virtues: giving, uprightness or ethics, patience, vigour, meditation, and wisdom.[141] But before the arising of the bodhichitta, when one is still aspiring to become a Bodhisattva, one can undertake to develop these virtues as best one can, so that the practice of these six perfections may in fact be regarded as another formulation of the path to Enlightenment.

GIVING

The first of the perfections is *dana*: giving or generosity – essentially a positive, outward-going attitude, an urge to give and to share. One can enumerate all the different kinds of things that can be given away – there are all sorts of lists and classifications in Buddhist literature – but potentially one can give away anything that can be possessed. One traditional list enumerates six kinds of giving that the would-be Bodhisattva can practise.

There is, to begin with, the obvious kind – obvious but very important: the giving of material things like food, clothing, and so on. Then there's a less obvious gift, the giving of fearlessness. Great importance is attached to this in Buddhist circles. The Bodhisattva, by his very presence, creates in other people a positive attitude, an attitude of fearlessness, of freedom from fear. Anxiety, as we have already noted, is one of the great problems of today. You see it writ large on most people's faces, because most people's way of life conduces to anxiety and fear. This fear is often repressed; because it is repressed it becomes unconscious; and when one has unconscious fears one tends to project them so that they spread over the whole of one's life, and one feels threatened on all sides. But if you are a Bodhisattva, by your presence, by your example, you counteract all this. Through your positivity you create confidence and freedom from anxiety wherever you go, and through your wisdom you help people to see that it isn't worth being attached to or bound down by conditioned things. You give them a new, larger perspective, indeed a cosmic perspective, and in this way you emancipate them from conditioned things and create in them an attitude of fearlessness.

Thirdly, the Bodhisattva gives education and culture. These are considered to be very important in all Buddhist countries because it is understood that unless there is a certain level of education in the true sense, not just book learning, but culture in the sense of a refinement of spirit, no spiritual life is really possible. In practical terms this is expressed in a general encouragement of the arts and sciences.

Fourthly, the Bodhisattva is quite ready to sacrifice, if necessary, life and limb. This is something that surpasses the scope of most of us nowadays; few people are called upon actually to sacrifice their life or even their limbs for the sake of what they believe. But there have been times in the past when people have died for their beliefs, and there are areas of the world, even at present, where if you have spiritual principles and stand up for them in public, you may be risking your life. We shouldn't forget how fortunate we are in being able to profess publicly and follow those spiritual principles in which we believe. Under less favourable circumstances we might have to pay for our belief, or at least our profession of it, with our lives.

Then again, the Bodhisattva is also prepared to give away his or her merits. In the Buddhist way of thinking, merits are something you acquire as the result of good deeds and generous actions; but we're told that the Bodhisattva is quite ready to give away whatever merits he or she has acquired. If you're a Bodhisattva you don't want to mark yourself off from other beings as being more meritorious or virtuous than they are. This is why, at the conclusion of a meditation or devotional ritual, Buddhists often recite verses 'transferring merit'. The verses generally say something to the effect that you don't wish to keep the merits accruing from this spiritual practice to yourself; you wish to share them with all living beings whatsoever.

The sixth gift is the gift of the Dharma, the Truth, the Teaching. This is the greatest of all gifts. You can give people food and clothing but they may not lead a very noble life. You can give them fearlessness but even that may not carry them very far. Even if you give them education, culture, and so on, even if you share your merits with them, they still may not be leading a truly human life. But once you give the gift of the Dharma, once you open their spiritual eyes, once they can see things in a more universal perspective, once they can begin to see the pattern of it all and accord their lives with that pattern, once they are oriented in the direction of Enlightenment, then they truly begin to live, rather than merely existing. So the gift of the Dharma is the best gift of all.

At least, it is the best gift in a sense, according to the traditional sixfold classification. But there is another form of giving that is even higher or at least more comprehensive, a gift that includes all the others. This is the gift of oneself. In 'Song of Myself', Walt Whitman says, 'When I give, I give myself.' It is easy to give material things but not give yourself with them. You can make other people fearless, you can free them from anxiety, and still not give yourself. It is even possible to give the gift of the Dharma but not give yourself. So to give oneself is the greatest of all gifts, the supreme gift that includes all others. And this gift too the Bodhisattva makes. If you are a Bodhisattva, you give yourself, you radiate yourself out towards all other living beings, not holding anything back. This is the ultimate form of giving – and certainly not one to be undertaken prematurely, before one has developed the inner resources to be able to give so unstintingly. But, of course, everyone can start to practise generosity in some way; it is the most basic of virtues. Indeed, it is often said in Buddhist countries that without a spirit of giving – which finds expression in practice – there is no spiritual life.

MORALITY

The second perfection practised by the Bodhisattva, or aspiring Bodhisattva, is the transcendental virtue of shila. As we have already seen, shila is sometimes translated as 'morality', but perhaps it is better to avoid this term with its unhelpful connotations. Morality in the Buddhist sense is 'skilful action' – action expressive of skilful mental states, states that are free from craving, aversion, and ignorance. There are various traditional patterns of skilful behaviour – for instance, the Five Precepts, the Ten Precepts, and the Sixty-four Precepts undertaken by Bodhisattvas. As we have seen, these sets of precepts are not just lists of rules, but training principles to be applied with intelligence and awareness to all the different spheres of human life and activity. In this context – to add to the aspects of ethical behaviour that have already been discussed – I want to consider three very basic areas of life: food, work, and marriage.

First, a word about food. According to the Mahayana sutras, if you are a Bodhisattva you should eat – since even a Bodhisattva has to eat – just for the sake of health and vigour, not to satisfy neurotic cravings. You should also eat without causing harm to other living beings, which means in practice being vegetarian, as far as possible.

The Buddhist tradition frequently oscillates between discussion of abstruse philosophy and consideration of much more homely matters such as diet. Some scholars of Buddhism tend to smile at such apparent lurches from the sublime to the ridiculous, and are surprised, for example, that in the *Lankavatara Sutra*, in the midst of profound metaphysical and epistemological speculation, you suddenly find a chapter on the unskilfulness of eating meat.[142] And of course the scholars say, 'It must have been interpolated. The Buddha couldn't possibly have spoken on a subject like this. Someone must have added it later on.'

But not so. This sort of attitude simply betrays the lack of a sense of proportion. After all, we eat food every day, and it has a constant effect on our bodies and our minds, so it is much more important than we generally think. One might even go so far as to say that there is little point in calling oneself a Buddhist if one is going to continue having the same old roast beef and two veg for dinner. One of the things we have to appreciate, as we have seen again and again, is that taking up the Buddhist path isn't just about learning the philosophy. We have to start changing each and every aspect of our lives. And diet, after all, is one of those really basic things; you can hardly have anything more basic than food. So certainly when one starts following the spiritual path, an important and radical change has to be made here.

As far as work is concerned, whether one is simply working to earn money or whether one's work is vocational, the important thing is that the work should be in accordance with what is traditionally called Right Livelihood: that is, it shouldn't harm or exploit others, and it shouldn't degrade oneself, or narrow or mechanicalize the mind. I used to rather shock people when I was asked about work – as I often am – by saying 'Do as little as possible.' And I would still say this if by work is meant work done simply for the sake of earning money. If one's work is also one's vocation, of course, there need be no limitation whatever – but to have a vocation is rare under modern conditions. Perhaps the best solution is to arrange to work part-time, if that is possible. Then one's free time can be used for creative activities, meditation, study, and the cultivation and development of friendship.

But these days I wouldn't necessarily stick to my old dictum that one should work as little as possible. In recent years a number of Western Buddhists have been experimenting successfully with the establishing of 'team-based Right Livelihood' businesses, creating a context in which Buddhists can work together, so that one's work is very much part of one's spiritual practice, and one's need to spend time meditating and studying the Dharma is recognized and taken into account as a matter of course. If one is able to find or create such a situation, one need place no limits on one's involvement in the work situation. Indeed, to be a little provocative, one might even say that in such circumstances one should work *as much* as possible.

The third area of ethical practice I want to mention here is the question of marriage – although 'marriage' is another of those words I prefer to avoid, because it raises all sorts of misconceptions, and indeed it is somewhat outmoded these days. The Buddhist conception of marriage, so far as it has a conception at all, is entirely different from the Western Christian conception. To begin with, in Buddhism marriage is not regarded as a religious sacrament, or as legally binding and enforceable in a court of law; it is seen simply as a relationship between two people, a relationship that is known to and accepted by the family, friends, and social circle – and which can be ended, if appropriate, without any fuss and bother, as long as the welfare of all those concerned – especially children – is taken into account. In Buddhist countries there has never been any rigid or universal pattern of marriage relationship: monogamy, polygamy, and polyandry are all permitted. And, as we have seen, homosexuality and heterosexuality are viewed in the same light; the only criterion is the quality of the human relationship involved.

PATIENCE

The third of the perfections the Bodhisattva practises is *kshanti*. *Kshanti* is often translated as 'patience', but it covers a number of virtues – not just patience and forbearance, but also such things as gentleness, docility, even humility, as well as love, tolerance, and receptivity. Or, to put it another way, *kshanti* consists in the absence of anger, and of all desire for retaliation and revenge. This is *kshanti*, and it is one of the most beautiful of all the Buddhist virtues.

ENERGY IN PURSUIT OF THE GOOD

Fourthly, the Bodhisattva, or aspiring Bodhisattva, practises *virya* or vigour, which is usually defined as 'energy in pursuit of the good' – 'the good' here meaning Enlightenment for the sake of all sentient beings. We have, of course, already come across *virya* as one of the five spiritual faculties and one of the seven factors of Enlightenment – and there is good reason for this, because without energy no spiritual life is possible. One might even say that the central problem of the spiritual life is therefore finding enough energy – especially emotional energy – for it. It isn't something you can do without really trying, or if you're half-asleep.

But many people haven't got much energy. Exhausted or overwhelmed, dull or sluggish, they seem not to have any energy available to them. But why not? Where has the energy gone? What's happened to it? Well, the chances are – apart from the possibility that one is suffering from one of the debilitating illnesses that are becoming increasingly common – that one's energy isn't available either because it's blocked, or because it's wasted, or because it's too coarse. So, obviously, we have to learn to unblock our blocked energy, conserve our wasted energy, and refine our coarse energy. There are various ways of doing this: through awareness, through engaging in creative work, through communication, meditation, enjoyment of the fine arts, faith and devotion, and so on. In this way energy can be freed, released, made available for the spiritual life.

I need hardly say that according to the Mahayana tradition the Bodhisattva himself or herself is the embodiment of energy. If you are a Bodhisattva, your emotional energy – your energy in general – is wholly and totally available to you for the purposes of your spiritual career; there is a smooth, uninterrupted, harmonious flow of energy – indeed, you yourself are that flow of energy – in the direction of Enlightenment. This free flow of energy means that the Bodhisattva does many things and accomplishes a great deal, but there is no question of haste, strain, or tension.

MEDITATION

The fifth perfection of the Bodhisattva is meditation. As we have already seen, there are three levels of meditation: the concentration and unification of one's energies; ascent into higher stages of consciousness – we could call this 'meditation proper'; and the turning of the mind to the contemplation of reality.

WISDOM

The sixth and last of the Perfections of the Bodhisattva is wisdom. As we already know, in the Buddhist context wisdom means intuition, transcendental intuition if you like, of the Unconditioned. It means seeing reality face to face – not thinking about it, not entertaining ideas about it, but seeing it directly and experiencing it for oneself. There are many ways of describing it, but a very popular way – and one we haven't come across so far – is in terms of what are called the five knowledges. These are the five principal aspects or modes of wisdom, just like five facets of a jewel. They are symbolized in Tibetan iconography by the Mandala of the Five Buddhas, each Buddha of the mandala being associated with a particular facet of knowledge or wisdom.

First of all, there is what is known as the knowledge of the Dharmadhatu. This is the basic knowledge, of which the other four are only partial, limited aspects. The Dharmadhatu, as we know, is the universe as the sphere of manifestation of reality, the gravitational field of reality – the whole universe being pervaded by reality just as space is pervaded by the sun's rays. So 'knowledge of the Dharmadhatu' is knowledge of the whole cosmos as being pervaded by – indeed as being ultimately non-different from – Unconditioned reality itself. In the Mahayana, this knowledge is symbolized by the figure of Vairochana, the Illuminator, the white Buddha, the Buddha of the centre of the mandala.

Next we have the mirror-like knowledge, so called because the Enlightened mind sees everything. It pierces through all veils. It understands the true nature of everything, seeing it in its ultimate depth, its ultimate reality. And it sees with complete objectivity and impartiality. Just as a mirror reflects without distortion whatever is placed in front of it and remains untouched, untainted, by the objects it reflects, so the mirror-like wisdom reflects all things, sees all things, knows all things, understands all things, pierces and penetrates all things, but it is not touched, not affected, by things – they don't stick to it. It's perfectly free, perfectly independent; there's no subjective reaction, but complete, pure, perfect objectivity. The mirror-like wisdom just reflects the whole of existence. It is symbolized by Akshobhya, the imperturbable one, the one who cannot be moved, the dark-blue Buddha of the eastern quarter.

The third of these five knowledges is the knowledge of equality or sameness. Because the Enlightened mind sees everything with complete objectivity, without reacting, seeing the same reality in everything, on this account it has the same attitude towards all, is even-minded towards all, has the same love and compassion towards all. Just like the sun's rays, it shines impartially without any differentiation or distinction. And this knowledge, the knowledge of equality, sameness, oneness, is symbolized by Ratnasambhava, the jewel-born Buddha, the yellow Buddha of the southern quarter.

After this comes the all-distinguishing knowledge. The mirror reflects everything equally, but it does not confuse or blur the distinctive features of things. It reflects a rose as a rose, a tree as a tree, a man as a man, a mountain as a mountain. It doesn't merge and blur them all together. This is very important. It means that the Enlightened mind sees things not only in their unity, but also in their diversity, and it sees them in both these ways together. It sees their unity, their common essence, but also sees them in all their unique, unrepeatable, ineffable individuality. For this reason, philosophically speaking, Buddhism is neither monistic nor pluralistic, but both and more than both. Unity does not obliterate difference, and difference does not obscure unity. Both are there together – unity in difference, difference in unity. This all-distinguishing knowledge is symbolized by Amitabha, the Buddha of infinite light, the red Buddha of the western quarter.

The fifth knowledge is the all-performing knowledge. The Enlightened mind devotes itself to the welfare of all living beings. It helps living beings in whatsoever way it can. It devises various 'skilful means' – ways of helping, methods of working – but it does all this naturally and spontaneously. It doesn't have to think things out. It just functions purely, simply, freely, spontaneously, and everything gets done. In a sense, it does nothing. In another sense, it does everything. This all-performing knowledge is symbolized by Amoghasiddhi, the infallible success, the green Buddha of the northern quarter.'[143]

BALANCING THE PERFECTIONS

In this context wisdom can be seen as the sixth of the six perfections practised by the Bodhisattva. Just as the five spiritual faculties can be considered to consist of two pairs, with a balancing fifth factor, the six perfections can be thought of in three pairs. Giving and uprightness represent between them the altruistic and the individualistic aspects of the spiritual life. Then the second pair, patience and vigour, represent – metaphorically speaking – the 'feminine' and the 'masculine' approaches to the spiritual life. And lastly, meditation and wisdom represent the internal and external dimensions, as it were, of the Enlightened mind. The Bodhisattva synthesizes and balances all these pairs of opposites – individualistic and altruistic, 'feminine' and 'masculine', internal and external – in his or her own Enlightened or well-nigh Enlightened mind. In the Bodhisattva's spiritual life there is no one-sidedness.

THE BODHISATTVA'S CAREER – TRANSCENDING TIME AND SPACE

In the course of his or her spiritual career, the Bodhisattva passes through ten stages of spiritual progress. In the first stage the bodhichitta, the will to Enlightenment, arises, and manifests in or through you. In the eighth stage, you become 'irreversible': that is, you cannot fall back from the attainment of Supreme Enlightenment for all; there is no danger of your ever regressing to the comparatively lower ideal of Enlightenment for yourself alone. And in the tenth and last stage you attain Supreme Enlightenment itself, for the sake of all sentient beings.

Now all this – the practice of the six perfections, the arising of the bodhichitta, the passage through all ten stages of spiritual progress – takes an immensely long period of time. Indeed, according to the tradition, the length of time it takes is absolutely unthinkable and awe-inspiring. We're told that it takes not less than three kalpas, or three aeons, and although there is no precise figure given, a kalpa is very lengthy indeed, a period of millions of years. During this period the Bodhisattva, passing through the stages of spiritual progress, also passes through many different lives in many different spheres, many different worlds, many different planes. But all the time he or she holds fast, as though to a golden thread, to the will to Enlightenment.

The Bodhisattva Ideal is of the very essence of the Mahayana form of Buddhism, and could well be called the finest flower of Buddhist spirituality. Its significance is not just individual or personal, but cosmic in the true sense of that much misused word. 'Cosmic' really means universal, pertaining to the cosmos or the universe as a whole, not limited to any one period of history, not even limited to this earth. And we find that the Bodhisattva Ideal, according to the Mahayana sutras, is unlimited in time and unlimited in space.

Similarly, when the Bodhisattva dedicates himself to the attainment of Enlightenment for the sake of all sentient beings, this expression is meant quite literally. By 'all sentient beings' – these words that reverberate through the entire Mahayana tradition, re-echoing like a great chorus throughout all the Mahayana sutras – one means not just beings living on this earth, on this particular plane of conditioned existence, but the beings of all worlds, all planes, all spheres whatsoever.

We find a hint of this in the meditation practice called the development of universal loving kindness, the metta bhavana – which, incidentally, is often practised to help induce the arising of the will to Enlightenment. As we saw in the chapter on meditation, one starts this practice by developing love towards oneself, then towards a near and dear friend, then towards a neutral person, then an enemy. Then, in the final stage of the practice, one's metta goes out in ever-widening circles. First of all you direct metta to all the people in the room where you are meditating (if you are meditating with others), then to all the people in the locality, in the city, the country, all the continents one by one, then the beings of the whole earth, all human beings, animals, and so on, and then finally all living beings whatsoever in all the directions of space. Thus one develops metta not just for the beings of this earth but for beings inhabiting other planets, other worlds, even other galactic systems. It goes as far, as wide, as universal, as this.

The expression 'all sentient beings', which occurs so often in the context not only of the Bodhisattva Ideal but of the Mahayana generally, as well as in the context of the loving kindness practice, suggests three interrelated things. First of all, it makes it clear that according to Buddhism there is not just one world but a plurality, even an infinity, of worlds. Secondly, it leaves room for the possibility that some of these worlds, at least, are inhabited by other intelligent beings. And thirdly it suggests that these worlds and these other intelligent beings are not outside the scope of Buddhism, of the way to Enlightenment, either in theory or in practice.

Some years ago there arose a dispute among some German Catholic theologians – German Catholic theologians generally being in the forefront of Catholic theological thinking. The question that arose was this. Suppose, as a result of the discoveries of modern science, we find that other worlds are inhabited. Suppose we find intelligent beings on Mars or Venus or even the Moon. Would the Christian scheme of redemption apply to those beings? Did Christ die for them? Or did he die only for the inhabitants of this earth? This question was much discussed and, predictably, opinion was divided. Some held that Christ's salvation was for the benefit of the beings of this earth only, while others believed that it was for the benefit of all sentient beings – to use the Buddhist expression – whatsoever.

But so far as Buddhism is concerned, the question of its scope was settled long ago, in fact from the very beginning. Buddhism can be described as a universal teaching in the fullest sense, a teaching applicable to all intelligent beings at any time, whether now, ten million years ago or ten million years hence, in any part of the universe, whether in this galactic system or any other. It is, as the 'Ti Ratana Vandana' says, *akaliko* – it is applicable at all times and in all places.

THE LOTUS SUTRA

This is brought out strongly in some of the Mahayana sutras, especially the *Saddharma-pundarika Sutra*, the 'White Lotus of the True Teaching', often called simply the *Lotus Sutra*. The *Lotus Sutra* is the grandest of all the Mahayana sutras. Others may be more profound in their teaching, or more subtle, but the *Lotus Sutra* is the most awe-inspiring, the most colourful, the most impressive, the most dramatic. One might even go so far as to say that it is perhaps the grandest of all the spiritual documents of mankind. Of it, W.E. Soothill, who was a Christian missionary in China, and one of the first translators of the sutra into English, says:

> *From the first chapter we find the Lotus Sutra to be unique in the world of religious literature. A magnificent apocalyptic, it presents a spiritual drama of the highest order, with the universe as its stage, eternity as its period, and Buddhas, gods, men, devils, as the dramatis personae. From the most distant worlds and from past aeons, the eternal Buddhas throng the stage to hear the mighty Buddha proclaim his ancient and eternal Truth. Bodhisattvas flock to his feet, gods from the heavens, men from all quarters of the earth, the tortured from the deepest hells, the demons themselves crowd to hear the tones of the Glorious One.*[144]

The scene of the sutra is the Vulture's Peak, that great rocky crag overlooking Rajagriha in northern India. You can still go there today; I've stood there myself in the evening, looking out over the valley, and certainly a very peaceful and very solitary, very sublime spot it still is. It was the scene of many discourses given by the historical Buddha to his more intimate disciples. But in the *Lotus Sutra* it isn't just an earthly mountain, it isn't just a rocky crag. It symbolizes the very summit of conditioned existence.

As the sutra opens, we see the Buddha surrounded by twelve thousand arhants – that is, twelve thousand 'saints' who, according to the traditional definition, have realized nirvana for their own sake alone, as well as by eighty thousand Bodhisattvas, and tens of thousands of gods and other non-human beings with their followers. And on this occasion, seated on the Vulture's Peak, surrounded by this great congregation, the Buddha, Shakyamuni Buddha, delivers a discourse, at the conclusion of which, as so often happens in a Mahayana sutra, we're told that flowers rain down from the heavens and the whole universe shakes. Then the Buddha closes his eyes, the smile almost fades from his lips, and for a long, long time he remains immersed in meditation. And as he is in that state of profound meditation, a ray of white light issues from between his eyebrows and lights up the entire universe, revealing in the infinitude of space innumerable world systems in all directions. And in each of these world systems revealed by this white light is seen a Buddha teaching the Dharma to his disciples, and a Bodhisattva sacrificing life and limbs for the sake of Supreme Enlightenment.

This great marvel, this apocalyptic vision, having taken place, the Buddha then reveals to the great assembly a higher, more esoteric, more profound teaching than has ever been given before. Some of the disciples are able to accept this teaching immediately, but others are not. Indeed, they react against it so strongly that they simply walk out – a very significant episode. But to the others, those who have been able to receive the teaching, the Buddha gives a prediction, a prediction of a particular kind typical of Mahayana sutras.

This kind of prediction usually follows upon a Bodhisattva's making his vow, whether in the form of the Four Great Vows or any other form, in the presence of a living Buddha. The Buddha in whose presence the Bodhisattva has made his vow then tells that particular Bodhisattva what his name will be when he too becomes a Buddha, what the name of his Buddha-field will be, and what his aeon or kalpa will be called. On this particular occasion, Shariputra, for example (who, of course, is in fact an arhant rather than a Bodhisattva) is told that he will become a Buddha known as Lotus Radiance, that his Buddha-field will be called the Pure, and that his aeon will be called the Great Jewel-adorned Aeon.

There are still greater revelations to come. A third of the way through the sutra there occurs the most impressively dramatic scene of the whole pageant. Suddenly there appears a great stupa (a stupa being a sort of reliquary in which the relics of a Buddha are kept), springing up out of the earth and towering way up into the sky, like a huge mountain. It is made, we are told, of the seven precious things: gold, silver, lapis lazuli, crystal, and so on. Not only that; it is magnificently adorned, and from it come light, fragrance, and music, which fill the entire earth. While the disciples are still marvelling at this incredible sight, from the stupa there comes forth a mighty voice, praising Shakyamuni Buddha for preaching the *Lotus Sutra*, and bearing witness to the truth of what he has said.

You can imagine the astonishment, even the consternation, of the disciples, advanced though they are, when all this happens. But after they've got over their surprise, one of them has the presence of mind to ask what it all means, and Shakyamuni Buddha explains that the stupa contains the intact body of an ancient Buddha called Abundant Treasures. Furthermore, he says that this Abundant Treasures lived millions of years ago, and made a great vow that after his *parinirvana* he would appear whenever and wherever the *Lotus Sutra* was taught and would bear witness to the truth of its teaching.

The disciples are very interested to hear this and they naturally wish to see the Buddha Abundant Treasures. But it seems that Abundant Treasures has made another vow, to the effect that if a Buddha in whose presence his stupa appears wishes to show Abundant Treasures to his disciples, a certain condition must first be fulfilled: the Buddha who wishes to open the stupa must cause all the Buddhas who have emanated from him and who are preaching the Dharma throughout the universe to return and assemble in one place.

This condition Shakyamuni Buddha, 'our' Buddha, fulfils. He emits another ray of light from his forehead that illuminates innumerable pure Buddha-fields in the ten directions of space, revealing all the Buddhas there. And all these Buddhas, in all the directions of space, realize the significance of the message. They all tell their own Bodhisattvas that they must go now to the Saha-world. (*Saha* means 'endurance' or 'suffering', and our world is given this name because amongst all the worlds, according to the Mahayana sutras, it is a particularly unpleasant one, and one is not at all fortunate to be born here.)

Our world is then purified, we are told, for the reception of those Bodhisattvas. The earth is transformed into a pure blue radiance like that of lapis lazuli, marked off neatly in squares with beautiful golden cords, and it is adorned not just with ordinary trees but with trees made entirely of jewels, all bright and shining. Gods and men, we are told, other than those of the congregation, are transferred elsewhere, whatever that may mean. Villages, towns, mountains, rivers, and forests just disappear; and the earth smokes with incense, and is strewn with heavenly flowers.

When this process of purification has taken place, five hundred Buddhas arrive from these distant worlds or Buddha-fields, each attended by a great Bodhisattva, and take their seats on magnificent lion thrones under jewel trees. But once these five hundred are seated the available space has been used up, and the Buddhas have hardly begun to arrive. What is Shakyamuni Buddha to do?

Well, we are told that he therefore purifies and transforms untold millions of worlds in the eight directions of space, to accommodate all the incoming Buddhas. And when this has been done, when they've all assembled, all the hundreds of thousands of them, Shakyamuni Buddha ascends into the sky as high as the door of the stupa, and draws the bolt of the door, with a sound like ten thousand thunders. The door opens, and inside is seen the intact body of the ancient Buddha Abundant Treasures. Shakyamuni takes his seat beside Abundant Treasures, and the whole congregation then scatters flowers on the two Buddhas.

So there's this great stupa, towering in the sky, with the Buddha Abundant Treasures seated in it and Shakyamuni Buddha seated beside him. But the congregation is still right down on the ground, and they all wish, we are told, to be raised to the level of those two Buddhas. Exerting his supra-normal power, Shakyamuni Buddha therefore raises the whole assembly into the sky, at the same time asking them, in a loud voice, a very important question.

I'm afraid we'll have to leave them there. I've already told more of the story than our present purpose really requires. But perhaps enough has been said to make it clear that in the Buddhist vision the activities of the Bodhisattvas, like those of the Buddhas, are not confined to this world. Many people find episodes like these from the *Lotus Sutra* rather surprising when they first come across them. Somehow they are not quite what one imagines that a Buddhist scripture will be like. Perhaps Buddhist literature is generally expected to be rather abstruse and philosophical and conceptual, not to say analytical and academic. But the *Lotus Sutra* seems to read more like science fiction – transcendental science fiction of course.[145]

This reminds me of a time when I was staying in Bombay with a Polish friend of mine. One day he gave me a book called *Star Maker* by Olaf Stapledon – a comparatively early but good example of science fiction. And my friend said 'You'll like this. It's just like a Mahayana sutra.' And indeed when I read it I found that the comparison was a fair one. Of course, there is a great deal of difference between the Mahayana sutras and even the best science fiction because the former have a definite spiritual, not to say transcendental, content. But there are a number of important resemblances too. Both the Mahayana sutras and science fiction go beyond this particular planet; and both of them tend to show humanity as ranging backwards and forwards in time, and throughout space, from one side, as it were, to the other, which can be a very liberating experience even if only imaginatively realized.

Every so often these days there's a flurry of interest in unidentified flying objects. Some people believe that they originate from Venus or even more distant parts of the universe, and that they are sent or occupied by beings more highly evolved than ourselves. Many films and television programmes reflect the general interest in time and space travel. But one could say that all these modern myths have the same general significance: the extrapolation of consciousness beyond the usual frontiers into the universe at large.

THE COSMIC SIGNIFICANCE OF THE BODHISATTVA IDEAL

The Bodhisattva ranges not only from world to world, from one universe to another, but from one plane of existence to another. This is depicted in one particular version of the Tibetan Wheel of Life. Some paintings of the Wheel show the Bodhisattva Avalokiteshvara appearing in each of the realms: the realm of the gods, the titans, the animals, the hell-beings, the hungry ghosts, and the human realm. Avalokiteshvara's name means 'the lord who looks down in compassion', 'the hearer of the cries of the world'; he is the embodiment of compassion; and he appears amongst the beings of each plane, each realm, in a Buddha-form appropriate to their particular needs.

Among the gods he appears as a white Buddha playing a stringed instrument – a lute or a sort of guitar, to judge from the illustrations. And the music he plays is the melody of impermanence. The gods are very long-lived, and they have a happy life, so they tend to forget that one day it will come to an end and they will die. They have to be reminded of the impermanence of things, so that they'll start thinking about and practising the Dharma. Hence amongst the gods Avalokiteshvara, the Bodhisattva of Compassion, appears as a white Buddha playing on a guitar – a rather unconventional image for a Buddha, it has to be said.

Then amongst the titans, those great war-like beings who are perpetually fighting with the gods for the possession of the wish-fulfilling tree, Avalokiteshvara appears as a green Buddha brandishing a flaming sword – the sword of knowledge. He is, as it were, saying to the asuras, the titans,

'All right, you are trying to defeat the gods, you are very warlike. Well, you don't have to give up fighting, but why don't you try to gain true victory? – the true victory that is gained only through knowledge.'[146] So he brandishes among them the flaming sword of spiritual knowledge that wins true spiritual victory, as it were saying to all these warring multitudes, these giants, even perhaps to the great nations of today, that one doesn't gain victory by conquering others. One gains victory by conquering oneself – that is the true spiritual victory.

Then, among animals Avalokiteshvara appears as a blue Buddha, and he shows the animals a book. The book of course represents knowledge, understanding, culture, everything that distinguishes the human from the animal, and the animal from the human; and Avalokiteshvara shows it, as it were, not only to animals but to animal-like human beings, indicating the next stage, the next level of evolution, which will lead them on to the spiritual path.

Fourthly, Avalokiteshvara appears among the beings in states of suffering, states of torment, as a smoke-coloured Buddha, and he showers upon them ambrosia, which cools and alleviates their suffering. When people are suffering and tormented, there is no use in preaching to them. What you must do, the only thing you can do, is to try to alleviate their suffering.

Similarly, when Avalokiteshvara appears among the hungry ghosts as a red Buddha, he regales them with food and drink that they can actually consume. (Hungry ghosts are said to be in the very unpleasant predicament of being perpetually starving, but having mouths no bigger than pinheads. Any food or drink they manage to swallow turns to sharp daggers in their stomachs.) Swami Vivekananda once said, 'It's a sin to preach religion to a starving man.' Give him something to eat and drink first, and then give him the gift of the Dharma.

Lastly, Avalokiteshvara appears among human beings as a yellow Buddha, carrying the staff and begging-bowl of a religious mendicant. This symbolizes the spiritual life, the path to Enlightenment which only human beings are capable of following in its entirety. (To make spiritual progress, the beings of other realms or planes of existence must be reborn as human beings.)

Avalokiteshvara is not the only archetypal Bodhisattva who symbolizes compassion. There is also, for example, the Bodhisattva Kshitigarbha, who is one of the most popular Bodhisattvas in the Far East. His name means 'earth-womb', and he is connected with the depths, in fact with hell. Kshitigarbha's concern is to rescue those who appear to be irrecoverably lost. He descends into the depths, the dregs of sentient existence, goes right down into the depths of insanity, despair, and torment, in order to remedy, even transform, conditions there. The figure of Kshitigarbha, this great Bodhisattva who descends into the depths of hell, represents the transforming power of the Buddha's influence, the Bodhisattva's influence, even under the most difficult and unfavourable circumstances.[147]

Thus the Bodhisattva Ideal, as depicted in the Mahayana scriptures, is not limited by time or space. The Bodhisattva traverses all time, all space, even all worlds, ascending into the highest heights and plumbing the lowest depths. The Bodhisattva Ideal exemplifies, more perhaps than any other spiritual ideal, the potential for Enlightenment of humanity, and it exemplifies it in the clearest, the most unmistakable, the most glorious manner possible. And even more than that. The Bodhisattva Ideal is not just a human ideal, not just an ideal for human life and conduct, though it includes that. The figure of the Bodhisattva is a sort of force, the activity of which is not limited to this world or this plane, but which is at work throughout space, in all worlds. One can call it the bodhichitta, the will to Enlightenment; one can call it what one likes. One can, indeed, call it the Dharma, for that is what it is. But whatever one calls it, one may be sure that it works from eternity to eternity, leading not only this world, not only the human race, but the whole of existence, to higher and ever higher levels of being. It is the Unconditioned at work in the midst of the conditioned; it is light at work in the heart of darkness.

NOTES AND REFERENCES

1 *Dhammapada* i.5, trans. Sangharakshita (unpublished).

2 *Dhammapada* xx.279, trans. Sangharakshita (unpublished).

3 The *Mahamangala Sutta* (the fourth sutta of the Minor Chapter in the *Sutta Nipata*) doesn't mention the eight worldly dhammas specifically. The eleventh verse of the sutta refers to 'worldly vicissitudes' in one translation, 'all terrestrial happenings' in another; this is understood to refer in particular to the eight worldly dhammas enumerated here. The scriptural *locus classicus* is *Anguttara-Nikaya* viii.5, and they are also enumerated by Buddhaghosa in the *Visuddhimagga* xxii.51.

4 *Anguttara-Nikaya* ii.54–57.

5 The full canon has been translated into English and published by the Pali Text Society; other translations, such as that of the *Digha-Nikaya* by Maurice Walshe and of the *Majjhima-Nikaya* by Bhikkhu Bodhi have become available in recent years – see further reading list. Where possible, references to the Pali Canon in these notes will be given to Nanamoli's *The Life of the Buddha* (Buddhist Publication Society, Kandy 1992), a short work in which many of the key teachings have been collected.

6 *Majjhima-Nikaya* 72.

7 Plato, *Phaedrus and the Seventh and Eighth Letters*, translated with an introduction by Walter Hamilton, Harmondsworth 1975, p.136.

8 *Alagaddupama Sutta* (*Majjhima-Nikaya* 22).

9 Nanamoli pp.107–8; Vinaya Pitaka, Cullavagga x.5.

10 This is the Buddhist school called the Jodo Shin Shu, founded by the Japanese monk Shinran in the 13th century CE, and today the largest of the Japanese branches of the Mahayana.

11 Bhabra Rock Edict, *The Edicts of Ashoka*, trans. N.A. Nikam and R. McKeon, Asia Publishing House, Bombay 1959, p.61.

12 *Adhyasayasasamcodana Sutra.* Quoted by Shantideva. See *Compendium of Teachings (Siksa-samuccaya)*, trans. Cecil Bendall and W.H.D. Rouse, Motilal Banarsidass, Delhi 1971, p.17.

13 Nanamoli p.52; Vinaya Pitaka, Mahavagga i; *Anguttara-Nikaya* viii.53.

14 Nanamoli pp.70–1; Vinaya Pitaka, Mahavagga i.

15 Nanamoli p.37; Vinaya Pitaka, Mahavagga i.

16 A *sutra* (Sanskrit) or *sutta* (Pali) is a 'discourse', and is the most characteristic of the literary forms found in the Buddhist scriptural canons. They vary in length from a few lines to several volumes. Most sutras purport to be records of the Buddha's own teaching, and some are teachings given by the Buddha's leading disciples and later ratified by him.

17 See note 15.

18 See for example the *Threefold Lotus Sutra*, trans. Bunno Kato et al., Kosei Publishing Co., Tokyo 1995, pp.129–134.

19 *Anguttara-Nikaya* i.94.

20 The story of Angulimala – his name means 'necklace of fingers' – is told in Nanamoli pp.134ff; *Angulimala Sutta* (*Majjhima-Nikaya* 86).

21 Milarepa's extraordinary life story is told in L. Lhalungpa's *The Life of Milarepa*, London 1987.

22 See J.S. Strong, *The Legend of King Asoka: A Study and Translation of the Asokavadana*, Delhi 1989.

23 For more information on these myths, see Vessantara, *Meeting the Buddhas*, Windhorse, Birmingham 1994, pp.198–210 and p.146.

24 Nanamoli p.226; *Mahatanhasankhaya Sutta* (*Majjhima-Nikaya* 38).

25 Nanamoli pp.42ff; Vinaya Pitaka, Mahavagga i.6; *Samyutta-Nikaya* lvi.11.

26 Nanamoli p.269; Vinaya Pitaka, Cullavagga vii.4.

27 The originators of what has become known as the Tibetan Wheel of Life were followers of the Sarvastivada school of Indian Buddhism, which formed around the 3rd century BCE; its adherents used to paint images of the Wheel of Life inside the gateways to their monasteries. For a fuller description of the *bhavachakra*, the 'Wheel of Becoming', see pages 40–8.

28 There are many references to the twelve cyclical nidanas in the Pali Canon; see especially the *Mahanidana Sutta* (*Digha-Nikaya* 15). The positive nidanas are

less frequently enumerated, but are to be found in the *Samyutta-Nikaya*: C.A.F. Rhys Davids, *Book of the Kindred Sayings*, vol.ii, p.27, quoted in Sangharakshita, *A Survey of Buddhism*, 9th edition (forthcoming), Windhorse, Birmingham pp.139–40.

29 The pioneer of translations of Buddhist works into Western languages was Eugene Burnouf, the French philologist whose work suddenly drew Buddhism to the attention of the Western world (his French translation of the *Lotus Sutra* was published in 1852). In 1879 Sir Edwin Arnold published his epic poem *The Light of Asia*; it was this work which formed the popular view of the Buddha's life and personality. See Stephen Batchelor, *The Awakening of the West*, Parallax, Berkeley 1994, chapter 14.

30 Nanamoli p.197; *Samyutta-Nikaya* xxii.87.

31 For more on why there are these different sets of nidanas, see Sangharakshita, *A Survey of Buddhism*, op. cit., p.128.

32 *Skandha* literally means 'heap' or 'aggregate'. The Buddha taught that what we think of as the self or personality is made up of five 'heaps': *rupa* (form); *vedana* (feeling); *samjna* (perception); *samskaras* (volitions); and *vijnana*. There is no aspect of 'self' that does not fall into one of these categories, and all of them are characterized by the three *lakshanas*: impermanence, unsatisfactoriness, and insubstantiality. It is our clinging to the notion of a self which is somehow exempt from these characteristics which is the cause of our suffering. This is what is being referred to at the beginning of the *Heart Sutra*: 'The Bodhisattva of Compassion, when he meditated deeply, saw the emptiness of all five skandhas, and sundered the bonds that caused him suffering.' For references to the *skandhas* in the Pali Canon, see Nanamoli pp.28 & 46.

33 The Tibetan name for the work usually known as the *Tibetan Book of the Dead* is *Bardo Thodol*, which literally means 'The liberation through hearing in the in-between state'. The text, said to have been composed by the 8th-century guru of Tibet, Padmasambhava, is traditionally spoken to a corpse, guiding the consciousness of the deceased person through the experience of the bardo. See *The Tibetan Book of the Dead*, trans. Francesca Fremantle and Chogyam Trungpa, Shambhala, Boston and London 1987.

34 The *satkaryavada* line of reasoning was 'held at the time of Nagarjuna by the [Hindu] Samkhya School ... it may be regarded as the representative Brahminical view of causation'; the *asatkaryavada* 'was upheld by the Sarvastivadins and Sautrantikas, and is the representative Hinayana view.' Sangharakshita, *A Survey of Buddhism*, op. cit., p.352.

35 See note 32.

36 Reference to these four kinds of attachment is made in *Samyutta-Nikaya* xii.2; see Nanamoli p.220.

37 See note 28.

38 Nanamoli p.10 (*Majjhima-Nikaya* 26).

39 See *Mahagovinda Sutta* (*Majjhima-Nikaya* 19), verse 45.

40 The three lakshanas are enumerated in many places in the Pali Canon – see, for example, *Samyutta-Nikaya* xxxv.1; xxii.46; Udana iii.10; *Anguttara-Nikaya* iii.47. The *locus classicus* is *Dhammapada* 277–9.

41 See Nanamoli p.43 for a brief reference. Of the many canonical references, perhaps the reflections of the Buddha in section 18 of the *Mahasatipatthana Sutta* (*Digha-Nikaya* 22) are especially worth consulting.

42 Shakespeare, *Measure for Measure*, III.i.128–31.

43 *Majjhima-Nikaya*, i.135.

44 See, for example, *Itivuttaka* section 100.

45 See Edward Conze, *Buddhism*, Cassirer, Oxford 1957, pp.46–48.

46 See Vinaya Pitaka, Culavagga i.

47 Nanamoli p.230; *Samyutta-Nikaya* xii.61.

48 Of the many texts which bear the name Upanishad, there are thirteen principal ones. They originate from the period 8th to 4th century BCE, and form the basis of the school of Hindu philosophy known as the Vedanta. The *atman* is one of their main themes.

49 The Tantra in particular sees things in this way, with its teaching of the *sahaja* or innate nature of reality; see page 54.

50 These three liberations are referred to in one of the texts of the Abhidhamma Pitaka of the Pali Canon, the *Patisambhidhamagga* ii.58. Buddhaghosa goes into them in some detail in his *Visuddhimagga* xxi.66–71.

51 Nanamoli p.224; *Samyutta-Nikaya* xxxviii.1; *Anguttara-Nikaya* iii.53.

52 *Dhammapada* 204: *nibbanam paramam sukham*, 'Nirvana is the highest bliss.'

53 *Klesha nirvana* is synonymous with the attainment of arhantship; *skandha nirvana* is synonymous with *parinirvana* ('full' nirvana), a term which is usually used to refer to the death of the Buddha but in fact is applicable to the death of any arhant.

54 This is from Blake's poem 'London', in *Songs of Innocence and Experience*.

55 In Zen Buddhism the 'Great Death' is synonymous with absolute samadhi. See, for example, Mumonkan, 'The Gateless Gate', in *Two Zen Classics*, trans. K. Sekida, Weatherhill, New York 1996, p.129.

56 The Perfection of Wisdom sutras are all available in English translation. For an introduction, see Sangharakshita, *Wisdom Beyond Words*, Windhorse, Glasgow 1993.

57 See the 'Large Sutra on Perfect Wisdom with the Divisions of the Abhisamayalankara, Part I', trans. Edward Conze, pp.129–30, Oriental Studies Foundation Inc, London 1961.

58 The followers of the Tathagatagarbha doctrine, whose ideas are outlined in the Mahayana text called the *Mahaparinirvana Sutra*, especially adhered to the idea of the true, real, or great self. See Paul Williams, *Mahayana Buddhism*, Routledge, London and New York 1989, pp.98–100.

59 See note 52.

60 *Mahaparinirvana Sutra*, trans. Kosho Yamamoto, Karinbunko, Japan 1974, vol ii, p.565.

61 In Chandrakirti's commentary on Nagarjuna's (*Mula-*)*Madhyamakakarika*, xiii.8.

62 *Dhammapada* xiv.183.

63 See Sangharakshita, *Vision and Transformation*, Windhorse, Birmingham 1999, p.30.

64 For a brief introduction to the Five Buddhas of the mandala, see pages 221–2.

65 This is the threefold division of the Noble Eightfold Path; it is sometimes called the threefold training. See, for example, the *Mahaparinibbana Sutta* (*Digha-Nikaya* 16: ii.81).

66 This goes back to the Pali Canon, which distinguishes 'genuine or natural morality' (*pakati-sila*), by which was meant right speech, right action, and right livelihood, from 'prescribed morality' (*pannati-sila*), which meant the external rules observed by monks or laymen.

67 Nanamoli p.236; *Majjhima-Nikaya* 118.

68 Nanamoli p.324; *Digha-Nikaya* 16: ii.156 (*Mahaparinibbana Sutta*); *Anguttara-Nikaya* iv.76.

69 For a canonical reference, see *Samyutta-Nikaya* lv.

70 Nanamoli pp.235–6; *Majjhima-Nikaya* 64: i.432–435; *Digha-Nikaya* 33: iii.234 (*Sangiti Sutta*).

71 Hebrews 13:14.

72 There are many traditional accounts of the life of the Buddha. For an introduction see Sangharakshita, *Who is the Buddha?* Windhorse, Glasgow 1994.

73 The Buddha, the Dharma, and the Sangha have been known as the Three Jewels since the earliest years of Buddhism. They are also known as the Three Refuges. Again, this dates from the first days of Buddhism; when people encountered the Buddha and were convinced by his teaching, they would exclaim, 'To the Buddha for refuge I go! To the Dharma for refuge I go! To the Sangha for refuge I go!'

74 The precepts are enumerated many times in the Pali Canon; see, for instance, Nanamoli pp.238–9; *Anguttara-Nikaya* v.172–3. Also see page 166.

75 For more about confession in the Buddhist tradition (which is very different in conception from the Christian practice of confession), see, for example, Sangharakshita, *Transforming Self and World*, Windhorse, Birmingham 1995, chapter 2.

76 Buddhaghosa lists these five kinds of *priti* (Pali *piti*) in the *Visuddhimagga*, iv.94–8.
77 *Majjhima-Nikaya* i.95: *The Collection of Middle Length Sayings*, trans. I.B. Horner, Pali Text Society, London 1967, pp.123–124.
78 This is a reference to the Mahayana *trikaya* (literally 'three bodies') doctrine, according to which a Buddha appears on the material plane as the *nirmanakaya*, the 'body of form', on the archetypal plane as the *sambhogakaya*, the 'glorious body', and as an unconditioned consciousness beyond space and time as the *dharmakaya*, the 'body of truth'. For a straightforward account of this rather abstruse teaching, see Vessantara, *Meeting the Buddhas*, Windhorse, Birmingham 1994, pp.27–30.
79 For more about the 'turning about', the *paravritti*, see Sangharakshita, *The Meaning of Conversion in Buddhism*, Windhorse, Birmingham 1994, chapter 4.
80 It is the Mahayana accounts of the Buddha's life which recount the mythical attack of 'Mara's hordes' on the Buddha-to-be as he was nearing Enlightenment. See, for example, Ashvaghosha's *Buddhacharita*, chapter 13, and the *Lalitavistara Sutra*, published as *The Voice of the Buddha*, trans. Gwendolyn Bays, Dharma Publishing, Berkeley 1983, volume ii, p.480.
81 In his *Buddhist Dictionary* (Buddhist Publication Society, Kandy 1980), Nyanatiloka translates *ceto-vimutti* (Pali) as 'deliverance of mind' and *panna-vimutti* as 'deliverance through wisdom', saying that 'deliverance of mind', in the highest sense, is that kind of concentration (*samadhi*) which is bound up with the path of arhantship; 'deliverance through wisdom' is the knowledge (*nana*) bound up with the fruition of Arahatship.' Nyanatiloka gives the Pali Canon reference as *Anguttara-Nikaya* v.142.
82 e.g. Nanamoli p.162; Udana v.5; *Anguttara-Nikaya* viii.20.
83 The three *ashravas* (Pali *asava*) are listed in many places in the Pali Canon. See, for example, Nanamoli p.236; *Sangiti Sutta* (*DighaNikaya* 33: iii.216). Some sources lists a fourth *asava, ditthasava*, the mental poison of wrong views.
84 The *viparyasas* (Pali *vipallasa*) are listed in *Anguttara-Nikaya* iv.49.
85 See note 25.
86 'When practised by the holy ones, technically known as Aryans, of whom there are four kinds, it is known as the transmundane (*lokottara*) or transcendental Eightfold Way; when practised by non-Aryans, that is to say by *prthagjanas* (Pali *puthujjanas*) or worldlings, it is known as the mundane (*laukika*) Eightfold Way. The point of this distinction is the difference between a virtue consciously and deliberately practised, with more or less success, as a discipline, and a virtue that is the natural expression, the spontaneous overflow, of an inner realization.' Sangharakshita, *A Survey of Buddhism*, op. cit., p.161.

87 *Dhammapada* viii.100, trans. Sangharakshita.

88 Nanamoli p.239; *Anguttara-Nikaya* v.177.

89 These four levels of awareness are not to be confused with the 'four foundations of mindfulness' – awareness of the body, feelings, consciousness, and mental objects – outlined in, for example, the *Mahasatipatthana Sutta*, (*Digha-Nikaya* 22); and *Samyutta-Nikaya* v.139–156. For more on the four levels of awareness, see Sangharakshita, *Vision and Transformation*, op. cit., chapter 7.

90 The Dharma-eye or 'eye of truth' is one of five 'eyes' enumerated by Buddhist tradition, together with the 'eye of flesh', the 'divine eye', the 'eye of wisdom', and the 'universal eye'. The opening of the Dharma-eye is a metaphor for the attainment of insight. See Sangharakshita, *Going for Refuge*, Windhorse, Birmingham 1997, pp.18–19.

91 The seven *bodhyangas* are enumerated, for example, in Nanamoli p.245; *Mahasatipatthana Sutta* (*Digha-Nikaya* 22: ii.303).

92 The Abhidharma (the word simply means 'about Dharma', though its adherents came to think of it as 'the higher Dharma') began as an attempt to systematize the Buddha's teachings, and became a scholastic enterprise which lasted several hundred years and involved an exhaustive analysis of mind and mental events. See Sangharakshita, *The Eternal Legacy*, Tharpa, London 1985, chapter 7, 'The Fundamental Abhidharma'.

93 'What is vigour? The endeavour to do what is skilful.' Shantideva, *The Bodhicharyavatara*, 'The Perfection of Vigour' verse 2.

94 *Visuddhimagga* iv.98.

95 This story appears to be told not about the Buddha but about the Buddha's first teacher, Alara Kalama. See *Digha-Nikaya* 16: ii.130–131 (*Mahaparinibbana Sutta*).

96 Buddhaghosa, *The Path of Purification (Visuddhimagga)*, trans. Nanamoli, Buddhist Publication Society, Kandy 1991.

97 *Majjhima-Nikaya* 24.

98 See note 74.

99 For a list of the sixty-two wrong views, see the *Brahmajala Sutta* (*Digha-Nikaya* 1).

100 See note 9.

101 *Dhammapada* 103, trans. Sangharakshita.

102 The Middle Way was part of the Buddha's first teaching: 'Bhikkhus, there are these two extremes that ought not to be cultivated by one who has gone forth. What two? There is devotion to pursuit of pleasure in sensual desires, which is low, coarse, vulgar, ignoble, and harmful; and there is devotion to self-mortification, which is painful, ignoble, and harmful. The middle way discovered by a Perfect One avoids both these extremes; it gives vision, gives

knowledge, and leads to peace, to direct knowledge, to enlightenment, to nibbana.' Nanamoli p.42 (*Mahavagga* i.6).

103 For thousands of years the 'Untouchables' have suffered untold misery at the bottom of the Hindu caste system. Many of them have converted to Buddhism over the last forty years, inspired not only by the Buddha's rejection of caste, but also by the example of Dr B.R. Ambedkar. Dr Ambedkar was an Untouchable who, through talent, luck, and force of character, became independent India's first Law Minister, and drew up the Indian Constitution, in which Untouchability was declared illegal. Despite this, ex-Untouchables are still subject to crippling social restrictions. When in 1956 Dr Ambedkar converted to Buddhism, 380,000 of his followers did too. Ambedkar's death just weeks after his conversion left the new Buddhists without a leader. Sangharakshita rallied Ambedkar's followers, forging a link which led to the establishment of the TBMSG (Trailokya Bauddha Mahasangha Sahayak Gana), as the FWBO is known in India. Today the new Buddhist community numbers about 9,000,000 people.

104 For a canonical reference see, for example, *Samyutta-Nikaya* v.199–200 (quoted in *Buddhist Texts through the Ages*, trans. E. Conze, Oneworld Publications, Oxford 1995, p.51.)

105 For a detailed look at the place of devotion in Buddhism see Sangharakshita, *Ritual and Devotion in Buddhism: An Introduction*, Windhorse, Birmingham 1995.

106 See note 93.

107 For a canonical reference, see Nanamoli p.239; *Mahasatipatthana Sutta* (*Digha-Nikaya* 22). For more on the four right efforts, see Sangharakshita, *Vision and Transformation*, op. cit., pp.113–26.

108 These images for the dhyanas are given at *Majjhima-Nikaya* i.276–8 (see Nanamoli pp.247–8).

109 See note 28.

110 The word 'mantra' means, according to one etymology at least, 'that which protects the mind'. A mantra is said to be the sound symbol which expresses the Enlightened qualities of a Buddha or Bodhisattva in sonic form. Reciting a mantra, therefore, as well as being a means of concentration, helps one to sustain a connection with the transcendental.

111 The word 'sangha', strictly speaking, refers to the 'arya-sangha' – the community of those men and women – past, present, and future – who have gained insight into the transcendental. The term is also used much more broadly to refer to the greater (maha) sangha, which can be said to consist of all those who follow the path taught by the Buddha.

112 Some Buddhists are happy to take it that the heavens and hells of

Buddhist tradition literally exist, while others prefer to take the teaching more symbolically, seeing that even within the sphere of human life it is possible to lead a heavenly, a hellish, an animal-like existence, and so on.

113 See Sangharakshita, *Transforming Self and World*, op.cit, pp. 204–5. Also Buddhaghosa, Commentary on the 'Dhammasangani' – the first book of the Abhidhamma Pitaka, vol ii. *The Expositor*, chapter X, ed. C.A.F. Rhys Davids. Pali Text Society, 1921. p.360.

114 See Francis H. Cook, *Hua-yen Buddhism: The Jewel Net of Indra*, Pennsylvania State University Press, 1977.

115 *Dhammapada* 1–2, trans. Sangharakshita.

116 See note 74.

117 Sangharakshita, *Complete Poems 1941–1994*, Windhorse, Birmingham 1995, pp.475–6.

118 Nanamoli p.238; *Majjhima-Nikaya* 41.

119 See *Samyutta-Nikaya* lv.1.

120 The Pali Canon uses stock phrases to express people's response to the Buddha's teaching. The response (here as translated by Maurice Walshe in *The Long Discourses of the Buddha*, Wisdom, Boston 1995, p.195) is: 'Excellent, Reverend Gotama, excellent! It is as if someone were to set up what had been knocked down, or to point out the way to one who had got lost, or to bring an oil-lamp into a dark place, so that those with eyes could see what was there. Just so the Reverend Gotama has expounded the Dhamma in various ways.'

121 Nanamoli p.131; Udana iv.1; *Anguttara-Nikaya* ix.3.

122 Nanamoli pp.122–3; *Majjhima-Nikaya* 62.

123 This meditation is described by Buddhaghosa in the *Visuddhimagga*, trans. Pe Maung Tin, Pali Text Society, London 1975. pp.342–3.

124 Nanamoli p.242; *Mahasatipatthana Sutta* (*Digha-Nikaya* 22), vv.6–10.

125 This is related in the 'Parajika': trans. I.B. Horner, *Book of the Discipline*, part I, Pali Text Society, London 1949, p.117.

126 This meditation practice is a recapitulation of the process the Buddha describes himself as having undergone just before his Enlightenment. 'I thought: What is there when ageing and death come to be? What is their necessary condition? Then with ordered attention I came to understand: Birth is there when ageing and death come to be; birth is a necessary condition for them.' In this way he traced back each of the links of conditioned co-production. See Nanamoli pp.25–7; *Samyutta-Nikaya* xii.65.

127 For an explanation of the *alaya-vijnana*, see Sangharakshita, *The Meaning of Conversion in Buddhism*, Windhorse, Birmingham 1994, chapter 4.

128 A canonical reference to the 'six element practice' is to be found in Nanamoli pp.214–5; *Majjhima-Nikaya* 62.

129 *Digha-Nikaya* 16: ii.81 (*Mahaparinibbana Sutta*), *The Long Discourses of the Buddha*, trans. Maurice Walshe, Wisdom, Boston 1995, p.234.

130 'Prajna is like a sword in the hand of a man. In the hand of a man with shila it may be used for saving a man in danger. But in the hand of a man without shila it may be used for murder.' B.R. Ambedkar, *The Buddha and his Dhamma*, Siddharth Publications, Bombay 1991, p.210.

131 See, for example, the *Vimalakirti-nirdesa* in *The Holy Teaching of Vimalakirti*, trans. Robert A.F. Thurman, Pennsylvania State University, 1983, p.99.

132 For more on *vijnana* see Sangharakshita, *The Meaning of Conversion in Buddhism*, op.cit., chapter 4.

133 See *The Diamond Sutra and the Sutra of Hui-neng*, trans. A.F. Price and Wong Mou-lam, Shambhala, Boston 1990, p.94.

134 The three levels of wisdom are enumerated in, for example, *Digha-Nikaya* 16: iii.219.

135 See *Poems of Early Buddhist Nuns (Therigatha)*, trans. Mrs C.A.F. Rhys Davids and K.R. Norman, Pali Text Society, Oxford 1997, pp.88–9.

136 See note 92.

137 Trans. Edward Conze, *The Perfection of Wisdom in Eight Thousand Lines and its Verse Summary*, Four Seasons Foundation, San Francisco 1995, p.178.

138 *op.cit.* p.135.

139 Nanamoli p.318; *Mahaparinibbana Sutta, Digha-Nikaya* 16.

140 A distinction is made between 'historical' Bodhisattvas, living men and women who have undertaken the commitment to gain Enlightenment, and 'archetypal' Bodhisattvas, archetypal figures who embody Enlightened qualities.

141 These are enumerated many times in the traditional literature. See for example the *Pancavimsatisahasrika* 194–5, quoted in Edward Conze, *Buddhist Texts Through the Ages*, Oneworld Publications, Oxford 1995, p.135

142 Trans. D.T. Suzuki, *Lankavatara Sutra*, chapter 8 'On Meat Eating', Motilal Banarsidass, Delhi 1999, pp.368–71.

143 For more about the five Buddhas of the Mandala, see Vessantara, *Meeting the Buddhas*, Windhorse, Birmingham 1994.

144 See *The Lotus of the Wonderful Law*, trans. W.E. Soothill, Curzon Press, London 1987, p.13.

145 For more about the *White Lotus Sutra*, see Sangharakshita, *The Drama of Cosmic Enlightenment*, Windhorse, Glasgow 1993.

146 See note 101.

147 For more about Kshitigarbha, see Vessantara, *Meeting the Buddhas*, Windhorse, Birmingham 1994, pp.199–201.

FURTHER READING

GENERAL

Kalyanavaca (editor), *The Moon and Flowers*, Windhorse, 1997
Kulananda, *Western Buddhism*, Thorsons, 1997
Sangharakshita, *A Survey of Buddhism*, Windhorse
Sangharakshita, *The Three Jewels*, Windhorse, 1998
Alex Kennedy, *The Buddhist Vision*, Rider, 1985

ON THE BUDDHIST PATH

Sangharakshita, *Vision and Transformation*, Windhorse, 1999
Sangharakshita, *A Guide to the Buddhist Path*, Windhorse, 1996

ON ETHICS

Sangharakshita, *The Ten Pillars of Buddhism*, Windhorse, 1996

ON MEDITATION

Kamalashila, *Meditation*, Windhorse, 1996
Paramananda, *Change Your Mind*, Windhorse, 1996

ON WISDOM

Sangharakshita, *Wisdom Beyond Words*, Windhorse, 1993

ON THE WHITE LOTUS SUTRA

Sangharakshita, *The Drama of Cosmic Enlightenment*, Windhorse, 1993

INDEX

BOOKS OF RELATED INTEREST FROM NAB

THE HEALING POWER OF COMPASSION

The Essence of Buddhist Acts

—*Pamela Bloom*

This book is a collection of remarkable true fables. These, fables have the power to transform painful experience into blessings. Each story is inspiring and illustrates how to heal the heart with peace and joy. It's a must read for all the people seeking the healing experience of Universal Oneness.

ISBN: 81-7822-227-2

THE FIRST AND BEST BUDDHIST TEACHINGS

Sutta Nipata Selections and Inspired Essays

—*Susunaga Weeraperuma*

Sutta Nipata is the oldest sacred book in Buddhist literature and is considered an authentic version of the Buddha's discourse. Susunaga Weeraperuma interprets the teachings of *Sutta Nipata* in this book. He lucidly expresses his understanding of this ancient wisdom in the idiom of our time. Great philosophical and psychological insights abound in the collection of essays. There are additional essays that address various issues like depression, facing death, growing old etc.

ISBN: 81-7822-257-4

KALACHAKRA MEDITATIONS

Based on the Discussion Between J. Krishnamurti and David Bohm in The Ending of Time

—*Ramesh Grover*

This book is based upon an actual meditative processing of the author's memory recall, and will be of use to others in keeping a watch, attending to what their mind preceives and reaching out to an understanding of the mischief of thought in perpetuating the delusion of 'I'. The author shares not only his joys and sorrows, as he moves within the movement of the time and thought, but also his feel of freedom in the 'ending of psychological time'. There is thus, a perception of the truth of freedom.

ISBN: 81-7822-279-5